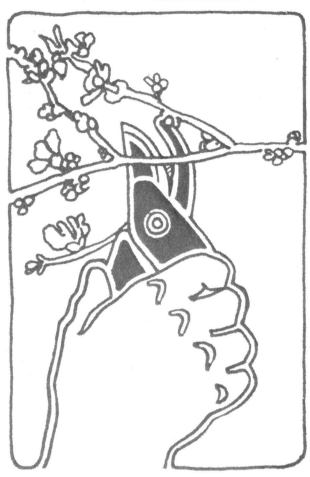

Pruning
Handbook

By the Editors of Sunset Books and Sunset Magazine

Lane Publishing Co. • Menlo Park, California

ACKNOWLEDGMENTS

In the many months of research which resulted in this new book, the editors utilized the accumulated knowledge and practical pruning experience of many interested individuals—from home gardeners to professionals. We are extremely grateful to them and to the many business firms and private and public agencies whose representatives also contributed so generously. We would like especially to thank the following:

Wilbur L. Bluhm, County Agricultural Agent, Salem, Oregon.

John E. Bryan, Director, Strybing Arboretum, San Francisco, Calif.

California State Department of Highways, Sacramento, Calif.

Francis Ching, Director, Los Angeles State and County Arboretum, Arcadia, Calif.

Ken Doty, Berkeley Horticultural Nursery, Berkeley, Calif.

John R. Dunmire, Assistant Editor, Sunset Magazine, Menlo Park, Calif.

Philip Edinger, Special Editor, Sunset Books, Menlo Park, Calif.

Dr. James R. Feucht, Extension Associate Professor, Colorado State University, Fort Collins, Colorado.

Brian Gage, Ornamental Horticulture Instructor, San Jose Regional Vocational Center, San Jose, Calif.

Bert Googins, Berkeley Horticultural Nursery, Berkeley, Calif.

W. Richard Hildreth, Director, Saratoga Horticultural Foundation, Saratoga, Calif.

Dr. Z. Horvath, President, Bay Area Lily Society, San Francisco, Calif.

Frederick M. Lang, Landscape Architect, South Laguna, Calif.

Walter Lawrence, Superintendent, S. P. McClenahan Co., Portola Valley, Calif.

Henry McClenahan, S. P. McClenahan Co., Portola Valley, Calif.

Arthur Menzies, Assistant Director, Strybing Arboretum, San Francisco, Calif.

Art Modin, Head Gardener, Sunset Magazine, Menlo Park, Calif.

Mrs. Karl Mueller, San Francisco Fuchsia Society, San Francisco, Calif.

Sciaini Hardware, Cloverdale, Calif.

Lee Sharfman, Armstrong & Sharfman, Land Design Associates, Los Angeles, Calif.

L. K. Smith, Landscape Architect, Thousand Oaks, Calif.

U. S. Dept. of Agriculture; University of California, Berkeley, Calif.

Walter Vodden, Superintendent, Blake Garden, Berkeley, Calif.

Wayne C. Whitney, Extension Horticulturist, University of Nebraska, Lincoln, Nebraska.

Supervising Editor: Joseph F. Williamson, Garden Editor, Sunset Magazine

Research and Text: Lee Klein

Coordinating Editor: Sherry Gellner

Illustrations: E. D. Bills
Design: Joe Seney
Cover Photograph: Ells Marugg
Cover Design: John Flack

Editor, Sunset Books: David E. Clark

Fourteenth Printing July 1981

CONTENTS

An Introduction to Pruning Fundamentals

You may think of pruning as simply keeping a plant in bounds or making it smaller. Actually, your aptitude with pruning shears can improve the condition and appearance of the plants in your garden in many different situations.

Prune to thin dense growth. A common reason for pruning is to thin out dense growth to let in the air and light that are necessary for leaves on the inside and lower portions of the plant to function. Pruning to thin out crowded conditions can also pay dividends by providing more room, light, moisture, and air to adjacent plants. If you live in a harsh-winter area, you'll also want to thin to reduce the danger of breakage caused by heavy snow loads. Where brush and forest fires are a hazard, good garden housekeeping can reduce fire risk. Deadwood and withered leaves should be trimmed off plants as part of such housekeeping.

Prune to correct or repair damage. If a storm breaks a limb, cut off the stub back to another branch or to the trunk. As soon as you see a branch that has died, remove it. Because such a branch may be diseased, removal can prevent the infection from spreading to healthy wood. (Make such cuts back into live wood, dipping the shears in a disinfectant after each cut.) To prune plants damaged by a freeze, see page 19.

Prune to encourage flower and fruit production. Plant growth in nature is cyclical: a plant forms flowers, the flowers become fruits, and seeds in the fruits become new plants. The quality of flowers and fruits is not an integral part of this natural cycle. However, when man takes these plants into his garden, both the quantity and quality of flowers and fruits become important. For information about pruning for flower production, see page 18. If pruning to encourage fruit production is your objective, see pages 17–18.

Prune to direct or control growth. Every time you make a pruning cut (or a pinch with your thumb and forefinger), you stop plant growth in one direction and encourage it in another. Effective use of this knowledge of plant behavior not only will shape the plant in the form you want but also will keep it the size you want.

Light pruning   **Heavy pruning**

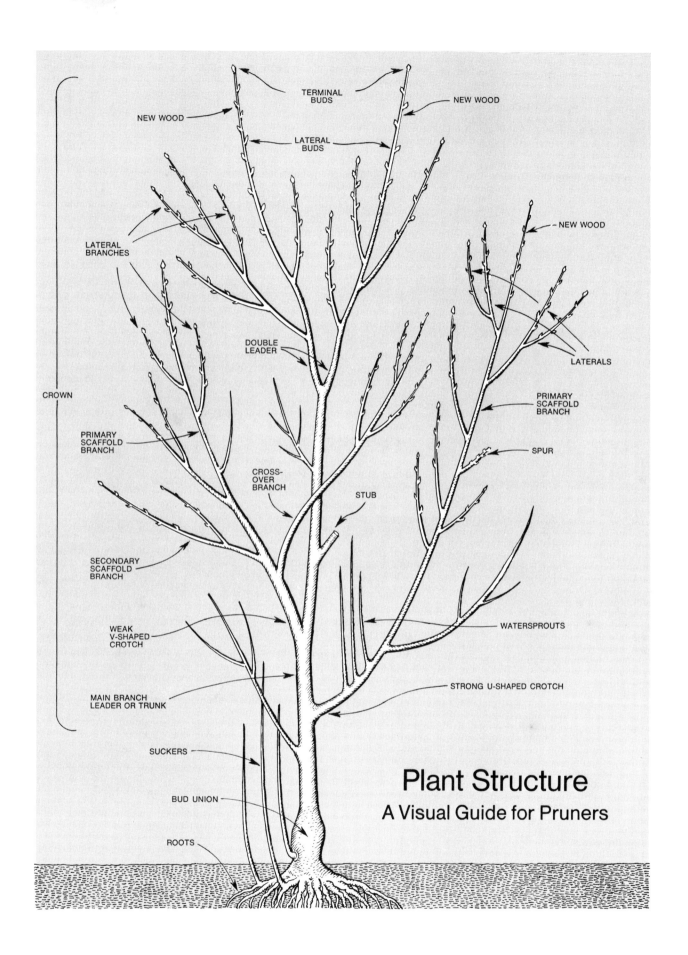

TERMINAL BUDS

NEW WOOD

NEW WOOD

LATERAL BUDS

LATERAL BRANCHES

NEW WOOD

DOUBLE LEADER

LATERALS

CROWN

PRIMARY SCAFFOLD BRANCH

PRIMARY SCAFFOLD BRANCH

SPUR

CROSS-OVER BRANCH

STUB

SECONDARY SCAFFOLD BRANCH

WATERSPROUTS

WEAK V-SHAPED CROTCH

STRONG U-SHAPED CROTCH

MAIN BRANCH LEADER OR TRUNK

SUCKERS

Plant Structure

A Visual Guide for Pruners

BUD UNION

ROOTS

Prune to thin dense growth

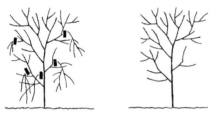

Prune to repair storm damage

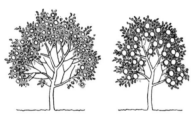

Prune to encourage fruit production

SINGLE
STEM
INTO
A SHRUB

Prune for special effect

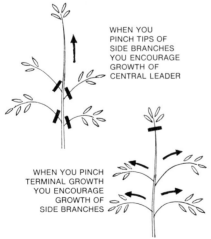

WHEN YOU
PINCH TIPS OF
SIDE BRANCHES
YOU ENCOURAGE
GROWTH OF
CENTRAL LEADER

WHEN YOU PINCH
TERMINAL GROWTH
YOU ENCOURAGE
GROWTH OF
SIDE BRANCHES

Prune to direct growth

Prune to achieve a special effect or an artificial form. These situations can include everything from pruning to reveal the branches of normally leafy plants to pruning to transform trees into shrubs. Decorative pruning techniques (such as espalier and topiary) are discussed on pages 21–23.

Prune to compensate for transplanting. At most times a healthy plant has its root mass and leaf mass in a state of equilibrium. There are just enough leaves to manufacture food and just enough roots to take in water and minerals. The two parts supply and depend on each other. When a plant is dug up for transplanting, many roots are usually severed. To compensate for the resulting imbalance between leaf and root mass, you should prune the top of the tree (see page 17).

How plants respond. In order to prune effectively, it's not necessary to understand the complexities of plant structure and the processes of photosynthesis and plant nourishment. It *is* important, though, to have a fundamental understanding of how plants develop, grow, and respond to pruning cuts. The diagram of an imaginary plant on the preceding page illustrates and identifies those parts of the plant structure that are important to a pruner. Familiarize yourself with these names because they form the basic vocabulary used throughout this book.

As a wielder of a pruning tool, you will work more effectively if you think of each stem (you may call it a stem, twig, branch, or trunk) as a live conveying tube — a pipe carrying water and nutrients for growth. By diverting nutrients you can shape and train your plants, stopping growth in one direction and encouraging it in another.

Buds are important. Perhaps the most important of all plant parts to a pruner are the buds. You can manipulate and direct plant growth by removing selected buds. There are three general classifications of buds: terminal, lateral, and latent.

The bud at the end of a stem or branch is called a terminal bud; it carries the plant growth upward. If you remove terminal buds, you cause increased growth in side buds, making denser, bushier plants.

Buds on the sides of stems and branches are lateral buds; they develop into leaves or, as the plant becomes larger, into branches. If you remove lateral buds, you channel energy into terminal growth.

In some plants, buds may lie dormant in the stem or bark for many years. These are latent buds, starting growth only after pruning or injury removes growth above them. Latent buds account for the sprouting of shrubs and trees from stumps.

REMOVING terminal shoot activates buds in immediate area of cut into growth.

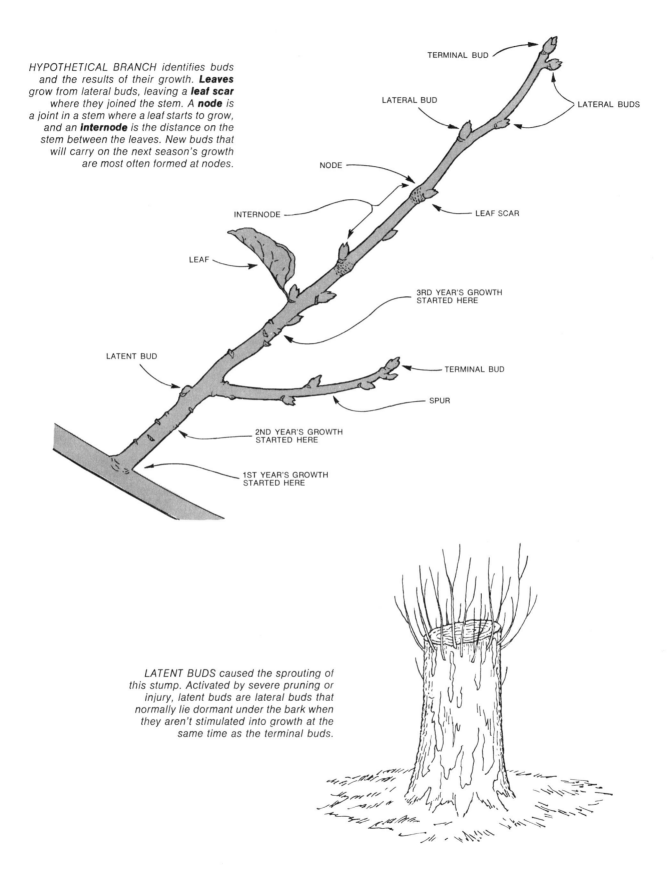

HYPOTHETICAL BRANCH identifies buds and the results of their growth. **Leaves** *grow from lateral buds, leaving a* **leaf scar** *where they joined the stem. A* **node** *is a joint in a stem where a leaf starts to grow, and an* **internode** *is the distance on the stem between the leaves. New buds that will carry on the next season's growth are most often formed at nodes.*

TERMINAL BUD

LATERAL BUD

LATERAL BUDS

NODE

LEAF SCAR

INTERNODE

3RD YEAR'S GROWTH STARTED HERE

LEAF

TERMINAL BUD

LATENT BUD

SPUR

2ND YEAR'S GROWTH STARTED HERE

1ST YEAR'S GROWTH STARTED HERE

LATENT BUDS caused the sprouting of this stump. Activated by severe pruning or injury, latent buds are lateral buds that normally lie dormant under the bark when they aren't stimulated into growth at the same time as the terminal buds.

Pruning Tools

Many home gardeners are bewildered by the number of tools available for pruning. Both the great variety of implements and their wide range in quality can be overwhelming to a beginning gardener. Your work habits and the kind and number of plants you are growing determine what tools are best for you. A small garden with only a few trees, shrubs, or vines calls for few tools, whereas a garden with a larger landscaping plan requires a greater and more specialized supply of pruning tools.

When considering your tool needs, don't forget about your thumb and forefinger; they are your least expensive — and most invaluable — tool. Most home gardeners can manage with only three additional basic implements: hand pruning shears, pruning saw, and hand loppers. For more extensive pruning, you might consider adding hedge shears, pole saw and pruners, a power saw, and sealing compound to your collection of equipment.

Look for good quality and workmanship when purchasing tools. A good pair of shears, for instance, can last a lifetime when used properly and given reasonable care. An equally important part of equipment selection is getting the right tool for the right job. Many different kinds of cuts are made during pruning, each requiring a specific implement to produce the best results (a sharp, clean cut with minimum bruising of the plant). Using the wrong tool not only can produce a bad cut but also can damage both the plant and the misused pruning tool.

Know your tools

To help select the right blade for the job, let's examine various groups of pruning tools, beginning with the handiest of all — one-hand pruning shears.

One-hand pruning shears. You'll find two basic designs: the anvil, which cuts by the action of a straight blade against an anvil, and the hook and curved blade type. Many gardeners who use both find it hard to see any difference in the kinds of cuts made. But each type also has its followers who prefer one or the other exclusively. Whichever type you buy, get shears of good quality. Skimpily made models prove to

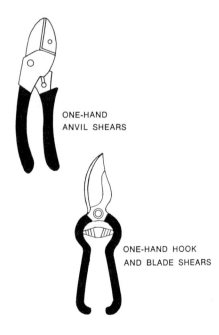

ONE-HAND
ANVIL SHEARS

ONE-HAND HOOK
AND BLADE SHEARS

be bad investments because they make inferior cuts and probably will have to be replaced in a very short time.

Besides these two basic designs, you'll find many other kinds of hand pruners, each designed for a specific job, such as cutting flowers (some are designed to cut and hold the flower stems). There are fruit shears for lemons, grapes, and other plants whose stems don't break off readily. A Japanese-designed shear, favored by many bonsai growers, makes a concave cut.

Various manufacturers offer such refinements as Teflon-coated blades, as well as the usual stainless steel replaceable blades (on the anvil types), self-lubricating bearings which need no oil, sap grooves (said to keep the blades cleaner), various types of handles and grips, and one-hand-operable catches. One model has a ratchet that adjusts the cutting power of the blade: when you meet resistance, a slight release of pressure on the grip shifts it into another notch, giving you more leverage for the cut.

Lopping shears (two-hand pruners). The added leverage of their long handles will give you more cutting strength than you get from one-hand shears, and the handles will also help you reach farther. As with one-hand pruners, you can choose between two basic styles: hook and blade, and anvil. With the hook and blade style, the hook holds the branch while the blade slices through it. The anvil style has a draw-in slicing action as the sharp blade cuts against the anvil.

Variations on these two styles of loppers include wood or tubular steel handles (vinyl or rubber covered), adjustable anvil (so you can resharpen the blade many times before it has to be replaced), adjustable cutting action, and handle lengths varying from 15 to 35 inches.

Hedge shears. This is the tool for shaping hedges and shrubs and for cutting back or shearing perennials and ground covers. Depending on your particular needs, you can choose between electric (see *Power tools,* page 11) or hand-operated hedge shears.

Most models of manual hedge shears have one serrated blade to keep your work from sliding away from you. In addition, many models have a limb notch to aid in cutting an occasional big stem. The better models have neoprene, rubber, or spring shock absorbers between the handles. Blade lengths average 8 inches, and handles — available in several different materials and coatings — are normally about 10 to 12 inches long. Most manufacturers offer a model with extra-long handles (20 to 22 inches) for trimming tall hedges.

Pruning saws. Use these for cutting a branch or stem thicker than 1 inch. To use any other tool — shears or loppers — for a branch that size will strain both the tool and you. When overtaxed, shears and loppers tend to crush as they cut, producing ragged, mashed edges that invite disease to develop.

Nor should you try to cut a branch with a carpenter's saw fetched from the garage. Unlike ordinary saws, pruning saws are designed to cut quickly through fresh, green, wet wood. Pruning saws have the additional advantage over ordinary saws of being designed to cut on the pull stroke — and pulling is the most natural motion for cutting overhead branches. You can hook a limb with a pull saw, bringing it toward you, and control it while you saw; but a push saw of the ordinary variety tends to shove the limb out of reach.

Some gardeners prefer to prune with a saw even when shears might do. A saw often cuts old, hard wood easier and more cleanly. Or gardeners use both tools to prune the same plant: shears for the small young wood of a rose, a small saw for old canes. Choose the pruning saw that best suits your needs.

(Continued on next page)

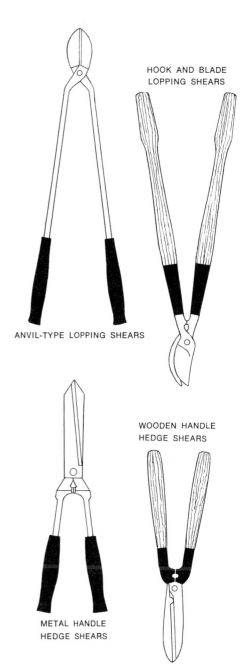

HOOK AND BLADE
LOPPING SHEARS

ANVIL-TYPE LOPPING SHEARS

WOODEN HANDLE
HEDGE SHEARS

METAL HANDLE
HEDGE SHEARS

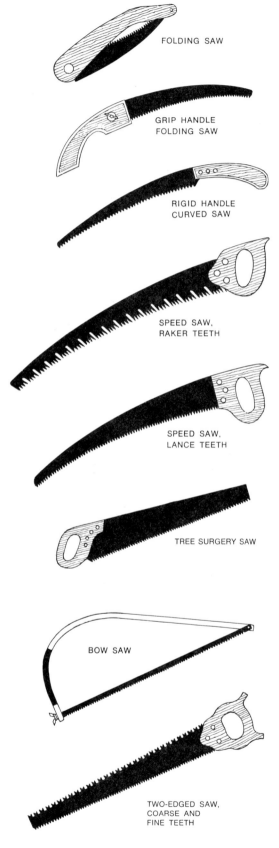

FOLDING SAW

GRIP HANDLE
FOLDING SAW

RIGID HANDLE
CURVED SAW

SPEED SAW,
RAKER TEETH

SPEED SAW,
LANCE TEETH

TREE SURGERY SAW

BOW SAW

TWO-EDGED SAW,
COARSE AND
FINE TEETH

When evaluating a saw, first lift it to test its weight and balance. Then look at the size of the teeth. Big teeth (5 or 6 per inch) go along with a big blade and make a saw suitable only for heavy work. Smaller teeth (up to 10 per inch) are for smaller branches, deadwood, or hardwood, such as citrus.

Look straight down the blade and see how the teeth are set. For the best cut, you should see a V of teeth alternately bent to either side along the full length of the blade.

Here are the more familiar types of pruning saws, starting with the kind most gardeners like best: saws that cut when you pull.

Folding saw. The most popular available one has blades 7 to 16 inches long. Small ones with fine teeth (8 or 10 per inch) fit into your back pocket and are good for roses and shrubs. Large ones (6 teeth per inch) can handle fruit trees and most dormant pruning.

Folding saw with grip handle. Basically the same as the folding saw, this one has a handle that offers an easier grip and doesn't shield all of the blade when folded.

Curved saw with rigid handle. Knowing this one won't unexpectedly fold during action (as is the case with the two curved saws with folding handles) is comforting, but this saw is more trouble to store and carry. Blade lengths vary from 12 to 16 inches.

Speed saw with raker teeth. The fastest cutter of 3-inch and larger limbs, it is good for green wood because rakers (slots in place of every fifth tooth) pull sawdust out, keeping the blade from jamming. Anything a small chain saw can cut, a speed saw can also cut — though it requires more effort.

Speed saw with lance teeth. This cuts deadwood better than the speed saw with raker teeth.

Tree surgery saw. With teeth angled forward on a heavy 2-foot blade, this one looks and works much like a carpenter's handsaw because it cuts on the push stroke. Although many gardeners favor it for use on big limbs, it can make overhead sawing and undercutting difficult chores.

Bow saw. Better suited for cutting firewood, this inexpensive saw can be used for pruning. Its major disadvantage is that it is hard to maneuver among crowded branches. A bow saw cuts on both the push and pull strokes; it is available in many sizes from 15-inch blades on up.

Two-edged saw. One side of this saw has small teeth that cut on the push; it's intended for small limbs and deadwood. The other side has coarse teeth that cut on both strokes; it's for larger branches and green wood. The versatility this saw promises sounds better than it really is. Because it represents a compromise, the two-edged saw doesn't do either job too well.

Pole pruner and pole saw. These tools give you the extra reach you need to cut or saw branches high overhead. The poles may be wood, aluminum, or fiberglass. Some poles telescope and lock into the required position; others come with extensions and quick-connecting devices. (Choose wood or fiberglass poles if there is any chance at all of contacting electric wires in your pruning.)

You can buy a pole pruner and pole saw separately, with interchangeable pruning and saw attachments for the same pole, or in combination. A popular type is a combination pruning saw and cord or chain-operated cutting shears. The shears are inside a beaklike hook that you place over the branch you want to cut; then you pull a cord to draw the blade through the branch. Most shears of this type will handle limbs up to 1 inch. (Good tip: wrap the cord a turn or two around the pole so it won't bow out when you pull the cord.) Saws on most pole tools are similar to the curved saws described previously in that they cut on the pull stroke.

Power tools. You might find an electric (or gasoline powered) hedge trimmer and a lightweight power saw useful. Electric hedge trimmers, which come both cordless and with a long cord, are helpful when your pruning chores require a lot of shearing. Many gardeners use both electric and manual shears for hedge maintenance — the electric for one-plane surfaces (sides and top), the manual for sharp corners.

The lighter, smaller models of chain saws are practical for the home gardener confronted with heavy branch work and clearing.

Rasp. An unusual pruning implement is this surface-forming tool widely used by carpenters for smoothing rough edges of boards. A rasp finishes pruning cuts to perfection, leaving a well-smoothed cut. You can buy one at most hardware stores.

Sharpening pruning shears and saws

As important as proper tool selection is conscientious tool maintenance. Even with normal use, there comes a time when your pruning tools don't work as efficiently as they did when new. Plant sap and dust accumulate on blades, rust forms, and cutting edges get nicked and become dull. Pruning shears in this state can be restored to good condition by cleaning, sharpening, and oiling as illustrated below. But if your shears are in worse shape — having large notches in the blade or a gap at the point where blades should touch — take them to a professional with the tools and experience to do a thorough job.

Shears with special nuts, bolts, or complicated mechanisms requiring precise adjustments with specific tools should be taken to an expert or sent to the manufacturer (many offer to repair or sharpen their own products for a nominal charge).

Since some very special tools and skills are needed to sharpen the teeth on a pruning saw, don't try to sharpen them yourself. Take the saw to a commercial saw sharpener.

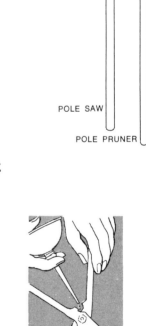

POLE SAW WITH HANGING HOOK

POLE SAW AND PRUNER

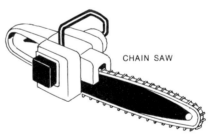

RASP

POLE SAW

POLE PRUNER

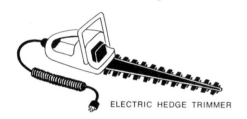

ELECTRIC HEDGE TRIMMER

CHAIN SAW

1   **2**   **3**   **4**

RESTORING PRUNING SHEARS. **1)** *Rub rust and grime from disassembled shears with medium grade emery cloth. Don't sand sharp part of cutting edge.* **2)** *Sharpen cutting edge by moving mill file at slight angle across blade; go from back toward cutting edge.* **3)** *Square edge and remove nicks from hook with round file. If hook has square edge and is not nicked, leave alone.* **4)** *Oil joint after assembling shears. Wash and dry sharpened shears after each use; wipe with oiled rag before storing.*

Pruning Techniques

The majority of your plants should be pruned one cut at a time. Before you make the first cut, study the plant carefully, trying to imagine what it will look like after pruning.

How do you determine which parts to remove and which to keep? This choice can be puzzling, even to professionals. Here is the only honest answer to this question: learn to understand the growth habits of the plants in your garden and then apply some common sense.

Contrary to what you might think, it's neither desirable nor necessary to prune every woody plant in your garden on a regular basis. If planted in the proper place, most trees and shrubs require only minimum corrective pruning for plant maintenance.

Some plants, of course, do require a regular pruning program for optimum performance. Many flowering shrubs, fruit trees, and fruiting vines (such as grape) are typical examples. Specific pruning requirements and directions for the individual plants are listed in the Pruning Encyclopedia, pages 24–95.

Here are some general guidelines that apply to most of the plants in your garden: 1) Before you make a cut, study the plant from all angles. 2) Estimate what is required. 3) Begin by taking out any undesirable growth. Most cuts are obvious — dead or diseased wood, crossing or crowded branches, growth that is unattractive or that detracts from the shape you want (see illustration). As you gain pruning confidence, most corrective pruning will become second nature. You'll find yourself doing a bit of it almost every time you walk through your garden.

This type of garden housekeeping normally can be done at any time of year. But you should avoid pruning so late in the growing season that an unexpected frost might damage the new growth stimulated by pruning cuts. In the coldest-winter regions, midsummer is the latest time you can prune with safety.

Basic Pruning Techniques

To prune is to remove plant parts for a purpose. Removal of plant parts involves everything from pinching off new growth with the fingers to removing large, heavy limbs. All of these pruning cuts have one thing in common: all should be made back to or just above some

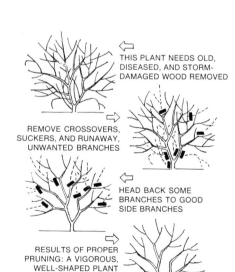

THIS PLANT NEEDS OLD, DISEASED, AND STORM-DAMAGED WOOD REMOVED

REMOVE CROSSOVERS, SUCKERS, AND RUNAWAY, UNWANTED BRANCHES

HEAD BACK SOME BRANCHES TO GOOD SIDE BRANCHES

RESULTS OF PROPER PRUNING: A VIGOROUS, WELL-SHAPED PLANT

growth. If you remember to make all pruning cuts above such a growing point (see illustration), you cannot go too far wrong, even if you know little else about pruning.

On pages 4–7 are the fundamentals of how plants grow and how they respond to pruning cuts. Keep these facts in mind as you read below about the various pruning techniques, and you'll understand more clearly how pruning affects a plant's ultimate size, shape, and appearance.

Most pruning methods can be grouped into just four basic techniques: *pinching, thinning, heading back,* and *shearing.* By following these techniques and applying them sensibly to your garden, you can do the work with maximum efficiency.

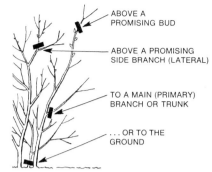

ABOVE A PROMISING BUD

ABOVE A PROMISING SIDE BRANCH (LATERAL)

TO A MAIN (PRIMARY) BRANCH OR TRUNK

. . . OR TO THE GROUND

Where to make pruning cuts

Pinching

The most basic of all pruning techniques is to use the thumb and forefinger to remove the stem tips of new growth (see illustration). Conscientious pinching, when a plant is young and developing, can control growth and eliminate the need for a lot of pruning later on. As long as a tip of a stem remains on a healthy, young plant, growth energy flows to it. If you pinch out the stem tip, most of its share of energy then becomes available to other growing tips and buds. For example, when you pinch the tips of side branches, you speed up and encourage growth of the central leader (main trunk). Or when you pinch out the tips of the leader and main branches, you speed up and encourage growth of the side branches.

Thinning

Although thinning also stimulates growth of remaining parts, it involves the removal of an entire branch back to a main branch, back to the trunk, or back to the ground (see illustration).

Heading back

Instead of removing an entire branch, you can shorten it by heading back (cutting back) to a promising bud or a promising lateral branch (see illustration). Remember always to cut back to a growing point, such as a bud or another branch. The growth will then continue along established channels. Indiscriminate heading back may stimulate a rash of unwanted growth, resulting in small branches growing randomly.

Shearing

Shearing is the only one of the four basic pruning techniques in which you seemingly disregard the rule of cutting just above a growing point. With this technique you simply clip the surface of densely foliaged plants, using hand or electric shears. Shearing is normally used only for hedges and decorative pruning, such as topiary (see pages 19 and 23). Customarily, plants used for these situations have buds and branches so close together that, wherever you shear, you are cutting fairly close to a growing point.

(*A word of caution:* just because shearing is a good pruning technique for hedges, don't make the mistake of assuming that shearing must also be good for other plants. Shearing shrubs and trees as if they were hedges will usually prompt a flush of new growth, resulting in unnaturally shaped plants.)

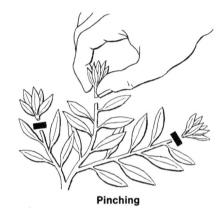

Pinching

Thinning

Heading back

REPEATED
HEADING BACK
WITH NO THINNING

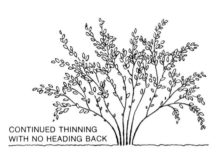

CONTINUED THINNING
WITH NO HEADING BACK

Don't leave a stub

Too much of one kind of pruning makes all plants look alike, masking their distinctive characteristics. As you become more adept at all of the previously described pruning techniques, you'll find that, for most plants in your garden, you'll use not just one technique but a combination — pinching, thinning, and heading back.

For example, continued heading back, without some thinning, results in unattractive stunted plants (see illustration). Dense top growth resulting from severe heading back reduces light penetration inside the plant, causing a loss of leaves there. Flowers and fruit are usually reduced or completely eliminated by repeated heading back because this cuts off the potential flowering wood. The technique of heading back, though, can be put to good use in the training of hedges and compact, decorative plants if your goal is a formal or unusual shape.

A pruning program that stresses thinning would probably be preferable to one that emphasizes heading back. But continual thinning without some heading back or pinching may very well lead to branches becoming long and willowy, upright branches becoming top-heavy, and the entire plant taking on a scraggly appearance (see illustration). Long and pendulous branches can easily split or be snapped off by winds, sometimes merely because of their own weight.

How to Make Pruning Cuts

Remember two important things when making pruning cuts: avoid leaving too much cut surface exposed; don't cut so far from the bud that you leave a stub (see illustration) but don't cut so close that you injure or undercut the bud you're trying to encourage. Not only does a properly made cut look better but also, more importantly, smooth wounds heal more rapidly and are not as likely to become infected as jagged, torn cuts.

Handling a pair of pruning shears may seem elementary, but a novice can easily misuse them. For the best clean cut, be sure that the blade side of the shears or loppers is positioned closest to the portion of wood that is to remain on the plant (see illustration and cover photograph). If you reverse the shears with the hook in that position, it is impossible to make a clean cut. The resulting stubs are untidy and will

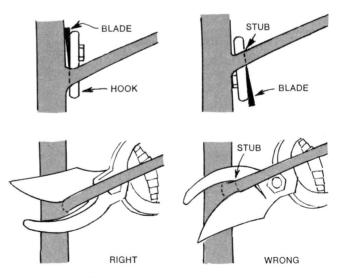

How to position pruning shears

die back to the growing point, leaving dead stubs through which decay and insects can enter the plant.

The correct way to make the cut itself (one generally accepted by experienced pruners) is to moderately slant the cutting blade in the direction the bud is pointed, keeping the lowest point of the cut even with the bud (see illustration). Practice will help you come close to this ideal cut most of the time.

Cuts too large to be made with hand or lopping shears require the use of a pruning saw. When a branch to be cut is too heavy to be comfortably supported with the free hand while you're using a saw, remove it this way: make a cut from underneath, halfway through the limb; stub it off about 6 inches from the finished cut, sawing from the top of the limb; then resaw it at the proper place (see illustration). This three-cut process prevents splitting and bark stripping, both of which could damage a tree.

On cuts larger than 1 inch in diameter, it's wise to apply a wound dressing or sealing compound. Such preparations made especially for pruning protect the plant until the cambium layer can grow over the cut surface and seal it. Inspect large cuts regularly, applying additional coats of protective material as needed until the wound is entirely healed.

CORRECT TOO CLOSE TOO SLANTED TOO LONG
Correct and incorrect pruning cuts

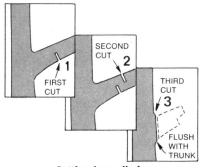

Cutting large limbs

Training Young Trees

From the moment you place a young tree in the soil, pruning is extremely important to its proper growth and development.

Young trees can be purchased in three kinds of packages: bare root, balled and burlapped, and in containers. Initially you prune each kind in a different way. The amount and type of early training and pruning required will depend upon the tree's growth habit and your objectives.

Bare root trees. Most deciduous trees can be dug up, sold with their roots exposed, and replanted during the dormant season — from December into, or through, March. Because a bare root tree is sold with many of its roots removed, its top should be pruned back to compensate for this loss. Normally your nurseryman will do this for you. This pruning involves selecting and heading back the best scaffold branches and removing the others. If the tree has no branches at the time of purchase, it should be allowed to grow just above the height where branches are desired and then be pinched back a couple of inches. This will stimulate the lower buds into growth.

Balled and burlapped. Because many conifers, broad-leafed evergreens, and a few deciduous trees have sensitive root systems, they are sold with their roots protected by a ball of earth and a covering of burlap. Although these will not normally require much top pruning, the plants may also have lost some roots and would benefit from some top pruning to compensate. Heading back lightly to promising buds is all that is normally required.

Trees in containers. Container trees should have been protected from any root damage and can be planted directly from the container with little or no top pruning (unless, of course, you damage the root ball when removing it from the container).

Getting your tree off to a good start. No matter how a tree is packaged, once you've planted it, pruned the top as necessary, and given it proper watering, you can relax and watch it grow. Don't be in a hurry to establish the ultimate shape of the tree at this point except to correct faults, such as a potential double leader.

(Continued on next page)

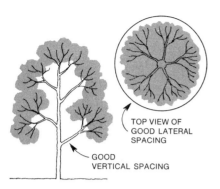

Branch spacing

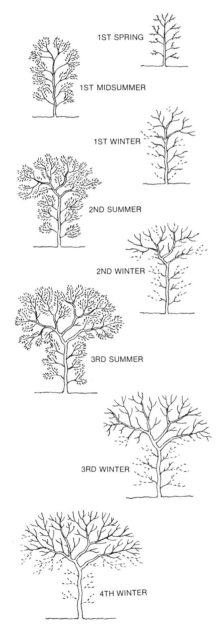

How to develop umbrella-shaped tree

If you want the tree to grow rapidly, don't remove leaf shoots or unwanted laterals along the trunk. A young tree needs all the leaves it can produce to manufacture food for growth. Its trunk diameter will increase much more rapidly, making the tree self-supporting at an earlier age, when you leave side branches along the trunk. Keep them 1 to 1½ feet long, and they'll do the job.

Another good reason for leaving surplus leaves and branches on a young tree is that strong sunlight sometimes injures exposed trunks of newly planted trees. Citrus and walnut, for example, are particularly susceptible to sunburn.

After the second or third year, you can begin to think of the tree's ultimate form. Your best guide in selecting the permanent framework will be the inherent form of the tree. (See the *Sunset* book *Garden Trees.*) Remembering that branches always remain the same distance above the ground and won't get higher as the tree grows, remove branches on the trunk below those you have selected as the lowest scaffold branches. (Remove scaffold branches that come off the trunk at a sharp angle and form a narrow crotch.) Aim for good branch spacing, radially as well as vertically, on the trunk (see illustration).

If you want a tree with a strong central leader, select and encourage the most upright stem, cutting competing branches. You can train the developing tree into the shape you want if you cut and pinch when you see it straying out of line.

Guiding your tree's development. Let's say you want an umbrella-shaped tree for the patio — a tree that you can walk under. You can choose a shade tree that's a fast grower or one with a slow to moderate rate of growth. The fast growers — such as willow, poplar, Chinese elm, mulberry, and fig — are exceptions to the usual training rules since they are so vigorous they will often reach the height which provides horizontal branches before you expect them to. With the slow to moderate growers, you develop the umbrella shape most efficiently this way:

1) Choose a type of tree that naturally has a good number of horizontal branches — flowering dogwood, Washington thorn, silk tree, apple tree, almond, and others.

2) First spring (and subsequent springs): allow the tree to grow.

3) First midsummer: select the upright shoot that is to be the leader and pinch out any shoots that would compete with its upward dominance. Repeat pinching wherever strong new growth diverts energy from upward progress.

4) First winter: if the tree has formed strong, overly developed side branches, cut them back to small side shoots. Don't remove any summer-pinched branches along the trunk.

5) Second summer: if the main stem is 8 feet or more, pinch out the tip. The tree should be tipped 1 to 1½ feet above the height you want branches. Continue to pinch back tips of branches along the trunk.

6) Second winter: select a well balanced, evenly distributed framework of branches to form the tree's crown and remove any additional nonframework branches and twigs in the crown area. Shorten, but do not remove, side branches along the trunk.

7) Third summer: keep branches along the trunk tipped; allow crown framework branches to develop.

8) Third winter: thin out badly placed branches in the crown; shorten side branches along the trunk up to where the crown limbs begin.

9) Fourth winter: remove side branches along the trunk.

Now sit back and enjoy your tree, keeping an eye out for new growth that departs from the pattern you've established.

Fruit Tree Training

If fruit production is not a major consideration, you can train a young fruit tree much like an ornamental, reaching a compromise between an attractive tree and the efficient, but not necessarily attractive, fruit-producing structures seen in commercial orchards.

As with ornamental trees, there are two reasons to prune a bare root fruit tree before planting it. One reason is to keep a balance between the top of the tree and the roots (which were pruned when the tree was dug from the grower's field); the other is to start the tree off with a sturdy framework. Most nurserymen will do this necessary pruning, but in case you buy a tree that hasn't been pruned, here are some general rules.

If fruit production is important:
1) Cut back the trunk of the tree to within 2 or 3 feet of the ground.
2) Cut off all side branches; don't injure the buds remaining on the pruned tree (some of them will form the new side branches).

If a garden tree with higher branches is your goal:
1) Cut off at least the top third of the trunk.
2) Cut off all side branches except for the top three or four. Shorten these to 3 to 5 inches, making each cut to a good outside-facing bud.

Commercial training systems for fruit trees

Commercial growers have developed the following three training systems for orchard efficiency:

Central leader system. Leave the central leader intact, allowing the scaffold branches to grow out from it (a fruit tree version of a Christmas tree). Such a tree is strong, but the excessive shadiness of the center tends to discourage good fruit production.

Open center system. Remove the top of the central leader, forcing large side branches to grow out and become the basic framework of the tree. This results in a tree that is not as strong as a central leader tree but one that admits more light for good fruit production.

Modified leader system. Cut back the central leader — but not as low as in the open center method. This results in a tree with both a central leader and strong scaffold branches.

Central leader

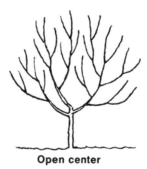

Open center

Modified leader

Fruit thinning

Most fruit crops should be thinned in order to give remaining fruit enough space and nutrition to mature fully. Leave spaces of about 6 to 8 inches between apples, about 4 inches between peaches, and about

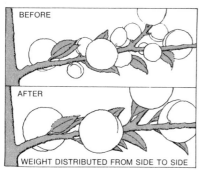

Fruit thinning

4 inches between nectarines. After keeping an eager eye on your bearing fruit trees, especially during the weeks when the crops begin to develop, you will probably be reluctant to do a thorough job of thinning. But remember that thinning does produce better quality fruit (see illustration). If you want proof, you can leave one branch unthinned and compare the difference between it and its neighboring branches at harvest time.

Special Kinds of Pruning

Sometimes it's necessary to prune to make plants perform in special ways. Such pruning can include everything from carefully timed pruning for flower production to altering the natural form of a plant to make it suitable for a hedge, an espalier, or a topiary. Below are discussed some special kinds of pruning.

Pruning to encourage flower production

Pruning some flowering shrubs at the wrong time will reduce — or perhaps even eliminate — one season's bloom. How do you determine when to prune? As in many pruning situations, the plant itself provides the clue to what is required.

Most flowering shrubs fall into one of two broad classes: those that bloom in spring on last season's wood and those that bloom in summer and fall on new wood formed during the current spring. Exceptions are shrubs that bloom twice, first on year-old wood in spring and again on new wood later (some types of *Clematis* bloom twice) and shrubs that bloom on wood that is one or more years old (*Chaenomeles*, pictured on the cover, is an example of such an exception).

Specific pruning instructions for flowering plants are given under each plant listed in the Pruning Encyclopedia, pages 24–95. Here, though, are some general rules to guide you:

Spring flowering shrubs. These bloom on wood formed the previous season. Plants in this group, such as *Syringa,* should be pruned while in bloom or immediately afterward so that the plant can have a maximum amount of time before winter to develop the wood for next season's show of flowers. If you delay pruning these plants until winter or early spring, you will be cutting off wood that is about to bloom.

Summer and fall blooming shrubs. These bloom on wood formed during the current spring. Such shrubs (fuchsias are good examples), unlike spring flowering ones, allow you a choice of when to prune. You can prune while they are in bloom (or immediately afterward) or you can wait until next spring — after danger of frost is past but before new growth begins.

Transforming shrubs into trees

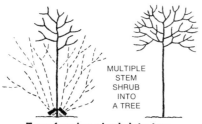

MULTIPLE STEM SHRUB INTO A TREE

Transforming shrub into tree

Many shrubs can be transformed into small, single-trunked trees by removal of all but one superior vertical stem and then removal of side branches between ground level and shoulder height (see illustration). Pruned this way, old oleanders, pittosporums, and other shrubs take on new structural interest as small trees.

Some shrubs, such as an old cotoneaster, may have several strong potential trunks. Exposing these trunks by removing side branches and any other branches coming from the ground level creates a handsome, multi-trunked tree.

Pruning shrubs this way can give a fresh, airy look to old gardens. In addition, the area under the shrubs, formerly smothered and useless, will be opened up for new plantings.

REMOVING *side branches opens up shrubs and provides new planting areas.*

Pruning hedges

Hedges can take two shapes — informal and formal. An informal hedge can be simply a row of one kind of plant. It should be allowed to grow naturally, with only an occasional shaping by cutting back or pinching back to keep the plants bushy and in bounds.

Formal hedges are another matter. Their training begins the day they are planted, and they must be pruned regularly all of their lives. It's a mistake to allow a formal hedge to reach the size you want before pruning it.

Begin training of a formal hedge by planting gallon-can-size plants 18 inches apart in a row. Force bushy and compact growth by shearing off 2-6 inches of plant tops several times each year. Do shearing between February and October, being careful not to do the last trimming too late in heavy-freeze areas because new growth that is stimulated may be damaged by early frost. Don't try to establish the desired height of the hedge during the first season. Begin shearing the sides when necessary.

All of this early shearing causes side branches to develop, forming a dense and low-branched framework. Such growth is possible only when plants are young and are being severely headed back.

If young plants are already nicely branched at planting time, you don't have to shear them back so severely. Head back the tops and sides as necessary to induce branching. Continue this procedure over several seasons until you have the desired shape and size. Subsequent shearings should remove as much of the new growth as possible to keep the hedge from growing too big.

At all stages of growth, hedges should be sheared so that their sides slope in somewhat at the top (see illustration). If a hedge flares out on top, the lower leaves won't get enough light. This will cause them to drop off, leaving a hedge that is open, twiggy, and leggy at the bottom.

Pruning to minimize freeze damage

To decide whether or not a plant will recover from a bad freeze, examine it for live leaf buds. Buds that are withered and brown are dead. The location of the first live bud indicates how far back from the tip the plant has been damaged.

If you can't find any live buds, examine the cambium layer between the bark and the heartwood. To diagnose, make a small scrape through the bark with your fingernail or a dull knife: brown tissue is dead; green tissue is still alive.

(Continued on next page)

Hedges . . .

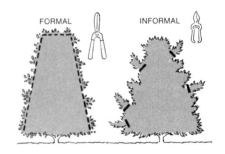

FORMAL   INFORMAL

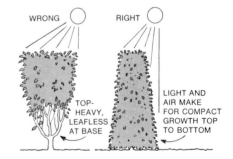

WRONG   RIGHT

TOP-HEAVY, LEAFLESS AT BASE

LIGHT AND AIR MAKE FOR COMPACT GROWTH TOP TO BOTTOM

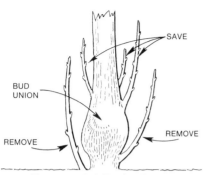

New growth following freeze damage to grafted plant

Many plants killed to the ground have growth buds just below the surface. Since these buds will frequently grow, don't discard the plant; wait for a year, giving it a chance to activate the buds. To maintain the original variety of plant, make sure the growing buds are from above the bud union and not the understock if your plant was budded or grafted (see illustration).

If a conifer shows bare twigs or brown needles in spring, a possible cause is a damaging freeze the previous winter. The tree is probably unharmed and will recover fast if ⅓ or fewer needles dropped and the buds aren't destroyed. After new growth starts, cut into the twigs that have dropped their needles. If the inside of a twig is green, it is alive and will grow; if the inside is brown, the twig is dead.

The tree is extremely weakened if ⅔ of the needles dropped. If more than ⅔ of them dropped, it will take much care to bring the tree back.

New leaders will develop from dormant side buds in cases where terminal buds were killed. You'll need to prune selectively for a year or two to reshape the tree.

Pruning conifers

These "evergreens" fall into two broad classes: those with branches radiating out from the trunk in whorls and those that sprout branches in a haphazard, random fashion. Spruce, fir, and most pines are examples of the whorl type; arborvitae, hemlock, juniper, and taxus (yew) are examples of random-branching conifers. Conifers normally don't require pruning. But if a conifer must be pruned, it will respond well if you abide by a few rules. You should selectively prune back to another branch or bud on the whorl-branching types, but generally, you can shear the random-branching types.

On the whorl-branching types, you can induce branching and thicken the tip growth by pinching back the candles of new growth about halfway.

Avoid damaging the central leader on conifers unless you want to limit the height. If the central leader is damaged, you can stake one of the next lower branches vertically and train it as a new leader (see illustrations).

Another guideline to shaping conifers is to prune according to how the trees or shrubs are to be used in the landscape. When they are planted as a screen, low divider, or ground cover, trimming is usually all that is necessary to keep them attractive, neat, and in scale with their surroundings.

You can either slightly shorten a branch or take it off altogether. When shortening, don't cut beyond the last green growth; if you do, you'll probably limit the branch to that length. Most species won't develop a new shoot if cut back farther.

When some conifers reach to within a foot or so of the size at which you want to limit them, cut back the new growth so that about 1 inch of it remains. This will produce enough small side branchlets to make full, dense foliage. Once this bushy growth has been established at the ends of the branches, you can hold the plant to the same size year after year by cutting off all new growth that develops beyond the lines you want to maintain.

Another way to slow growth is to prune some roots before the early spring growth begins. Do this by thrusting a sharp spade down through some roots or by digging a trench and severing some roots with an ax.

You'll need to prune some conifers — *Cedrus deodara,* for instance — in other specific ways to control their size. Look for these instructions under the plant names in the Pruning Encyclopedia, pages 24–95.

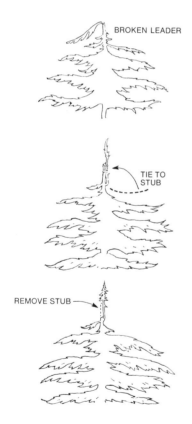

Replacing damaged central leader

When a conifer has been damaged by cold or breakage, you may have to remove entire limbs. If this happens, it's almost impossible to restore its natural shape. But you can often make the most of this situation by trimming or training the damaged plant into an unusual sculptural form.

Decorative pruning

Plants trained for decorative purposes require a greater amount of pruning than is necessary for ordinary garden maintenance.

Espalier. Espaliering — the practice of training a tree or shrub to grow flat — is an exacting but rewarding art. You can espalier either in formal, rigid patterns or in a more informal way, letting the plant's natural growth habits guide you. Almost any tree or shrub that isn't too rigidly upright or formal in growth can be trained to grow flat against a wall or along a fence, wire, or trellis. Continually removing growing points that go in an unwanted direction and allowing the rest of the growing points to develop in their own way is all that's necessary to establish an informal espalier.

Fruit trees make especially good subjects because espaliering exposes a maximum of branch surface to the sun, stimulating heavier flower and fruit production. The following points about espaliering fruit trees also apply to ornamental trees.

- In cool summer areas, give an espalier as much sun as possible by planting against a south wall or fence. Reflected heat will stimulate flower production and help ripen fruit. (Many ornamentals, of course, can be espaliered on north-facing walls or even on shaded east, west, or south-facing walls not suitable for fruit trees.)
- Where summer temperatures consistently hit the high 90s or higher, reflected heat is likely to damage the plant or sunburn the fruit, so espalier on a free-standing trellis.
- Espaliered fruit trees should have supports sturdy enough to hold the heavy fruit load. Use galvanized pipe or 4 by 4 wood posts and string the supports with 14-gauge galvanized wire. Leave 4 to 12 inches between the trellis and wall or fence for air circulation and for working room. Train the lowest horizontal branches on wires about 14 inches above the ground, spacing upper horizontals about a foot apart.

Below, two training methods for espaliering an apple tree are described. The major difference between the two training methods is that you start one by planting a bare root whip and the other by planting a little tree with branches.

With both methods you can have as many horizontal tiers as you want. Both methods require four prunings each summer to head back side branches that grow off the main horizontals. Such regular pruning of side branches forces growth into short, stubby, fruiting spurs.

If you start with a bare root whip:
1) After planting the bare root whip, head it back at (or just below) the first wire to stimulate the three uppermost buds below the cut into growth.

2) For the first summer or two, let the lower two buds develop into branches forming a V, and let the top bud form the trunk extension. Keep the trunk extension cut back so its tip is lower than the tips of the V.

3) When the V tips reach the desired length, tie them to the first horizontal wire, keeping the tips lower than the rest of the branch. For tying, use a material that won't cut the branch — soft cord, plastic ties, or strips of fabric are possibilities. Remove all growth from the trunk

Espaliering step by step . . .
Starting with a bare root whip

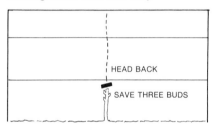

HEAD BACK
SAVE THREE BUDS

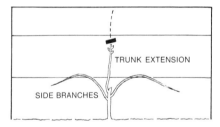

TRUNK EXTENSION
SIDE BRANCHES

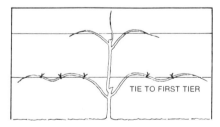

TIE TO FIRST TIER

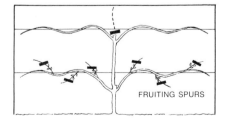

FRUITING SPURS

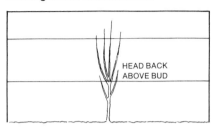

HEAD BACK
ABOVE BUD

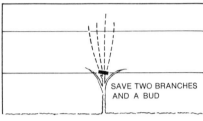

SAVE TWO BRANCHES
AND A BUD

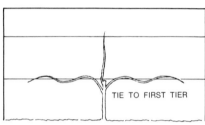

TIE TO FIRST TIER

below the first-tier branches and pinch off tips of the laterals above them.

4) Cut back the trunk extension several inches below the second wire. This will force several buds to grow there. Keep three — the uppermost to make a new trunk extension and the other two to make side branches. Let each side branch grow to form another V. Cut back laterals on the first tier to three buds; these will become fruiting spurs.

5) When V branches reach the desired length, tie them to the second horizontal wire as in step 3. Don't pinch back laterals on the second tier at this time.

6) Repeat this training procedure in subsequent seasons until your espaliered tree has reached the height and number of tiers you want.

If your tree already has branches:

1) At planting time select the best two branches below the first wire to form the first horizontal tier. Top (head back) the main leader to a bud just above them. Cut off all other branches.

2) During the first growing season, gradually bring the first tier of branches to a horizontal position. Proceed as described in the preceding steps 3 through 6.

Cordon. This space-saving system of growing fruit trees originated in Europe, where it's still in use. The name, meaning "rope" or "cord," refers to the tree's appearance. The cordon differs from the espalier in that the tree is trained to a single main stem, with laterals carefully controlled. A cordon may be trained vertically, horizontally, or obliquely.

To develop a dwarf fruit tree as a cordon, buy 1-year-old whips and cut them back to 18 inches at planting time to force side shoots to develop. Use the uppermost shoot as a leader and tie it to the supporting structure.

In June or July, pinch back all fully developed side shoots to 4 leaves. Repeat in September, shortening those that weren't fully developed earlier and any late-growing shoots.

In winter curtail the previous year's growth. Remove all wood beyond the fat fruit buds on each spur. Where there are no fruit buds, keep laterals shortened to 3 or 4 leaves until buds form; then cut back. Thin fruit bud clusters when they are too crowded.

By mid-July of the second year, cut back all mature laterals. Lop off laterals from side shoots to 1 leaf, leaving the immature shoots to be pruned in September. In early autumn or winter, cut secondary growth from summer-pruned shoots to 1 leaf.

Pleaching. Pleaching is a system of interweaving and plaiting branches of trees together to form a hedge or arbor. You can pleach any tree that has branches and branchlets tough and supple enough to be bent and interwoven without breaking.

To get an arbor of pleached trees, build a sturdy framework of wood, angle iron, or galvanized pipe on which to train the trees. You will need a vertical support for each tree, as well as sufficient material to build a pergola-type trellis between the tops of the uprights.

Plant a tree next to each vertical support (supports should be 9 to 15 feet high) and tie the tree to the support. Remove side branches that develop along the trunk. When foliage is abundant and reaches well into the overhead framework, you are ready to start training.

Remove all upright growth, being sure not to leave any stubs. Lead all side branches to those of neighboring trees, bending them down to the framework and tying as necessary. You can also weave them under and over the wires or lace them with other branches. Where branches cross, intertwine them; they'll form natural grafts. Each year, bend, tie, or weave the new growth to keep a flat, level canopy.

Pollarding. When you shear off the top of a tree so that it puts out a dense head of slender shoots, you are pollarding. The results of pollarding can be unsightly; on the other hand, they can be attractive and beneficial. It all depends on the tree you choose to pollard and how you do it.

More popular in Europe than here, pollarding is more a practical sort of pruning than a decorative one. Unless you have to keep a tree a certain size, there's little reason to pollard.

Here's how to proceed: when young trees produce trunks about 8 feet high with branches about the thickness of a man's wrist and high enough to walk under, cut the branches down to 2 to 5 feet long and let them callus over.

Each spring the trees will produce more slender, long branches. Each winter cut these branches back to the same place and let the cuts callus over. Eventually, knobs at the ends of the short branches will become very large.

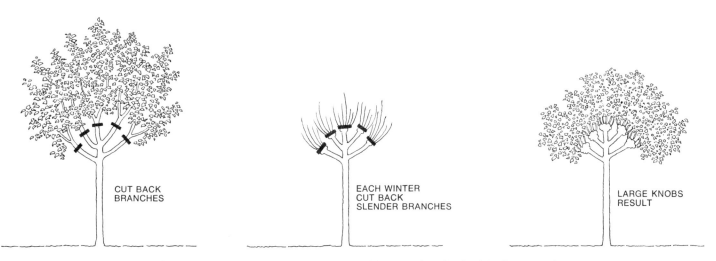

CUT BACK
BRANCHES

EACH WINTER
CUT BACK
SLENDER BRANCHES

LARGE KNOBS
RESULT

LARGE, CALLUSED KNOBS characteristic of pollarding are formed by annual cutting back to the same place.

Topiary. The sculptural shearing techniques of topiary produce trees and shrubs in bird and animal forms and in such geometric shapes as pyramids, spheres, and cones. Plants normally used as hedge material lend themselves well to topiary because they hold a sheared shape well. Choose from such plants as boxwood, chamaecyparis, cotoneaster, juniper, privet, olive, podocarpus, pittosporum, pyracantha, and yew.

Examine plants carefully, parting the foliage to find a basic branch form you can work with. Cut off all nonessential limbs, leaving just the trunk and branches that you want to keep. Wherever you want to form a clump along the middle part of a trunk or branch, leave some side branches, shearing them to approximately the outline of the clump you desire. Of course, there must be a clump at the end of each branch that you keep, so shear the terminal branchlets there to clumps of the shape you want. Remove all little twigs and leaves along the branches between the clumps.

Typically, clumps won't be full at first — they may look quite rangy and sparse. But if you keep the tree or shrub growing strongly, new branches and leaves will fill out the clumps in a season or more.

Watch for new branches that may arise from hidden buds along the parts of the branches that are supposed to remain bare. Snip or rub them off whenever they form.

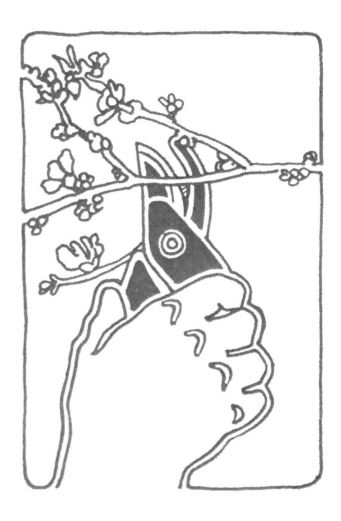

Encyclopedia

You'll find on the next 71 pages instructions for pruning each of the most popular vines, shrubs, and trees. All plants except fruits are listed alphabetically by botanical names. If you have to look up a plant using its common name ("Oak," for example), a cross-reference will lead you to the full description found under its botanical name *(Quercus)*. In contrast, fruits — apple, blackberry, cherry, and so forth — are listed only under their common names. Where drawings are used as part of the pruning instructions, a thin black rectangle across a stem or branch represents a pruning cut.

Instructions given in this guide assume that your plants are healthy and properly located. The ultimate timing of pruning will depend on climate factors and the plant's condition, not the calendar alone.

AARON'S BEARD.
See Hypericum calycinum.

ABELIA. Evergreen, partially evergreen, or deciduous shrubs. Will withstand heavy pruning but need only light and selective pruning to maintain size and graceful arching form. In spring shape lightly by removing unwanted branches. Cut ⅓ of old, grayish-colored stems back to ground each fall or winter to maintain attractive, arching, open branch pattern. New shoots that develop in spring will produce best flowers.

CUT BACK ⅓ OF OLD STEMS TO GROUND IN LATE FALL OR WINTER TO HELP RETAIN OPEN, ARCHING SHAPE

NEW SHOOTS THAT DEVELOP IN SPRING WILL PRODUCE BEST FLOWERS

GRACEFUL, ARCHING FORM of abelia results from selective pruning.

To control height, pinch out growing tips. With shearing, can be easily trained as a hedge, but you'll lose some of its graceful beauty. In coldest areas, cut back to ground and protect with straw or mulch. Warm weather will bring new growth. Makes attractive, informal flowering hedge if controlled by selectively thinning out some branches.

ABELIOPHYLLUM distichum. White forsythia. Deciduous shrub. Lower and slower growing than true forsythia. Requires less pruning. To encourage new flowering wood, cut ⅓ of old shoots to ground immediately after flowering.

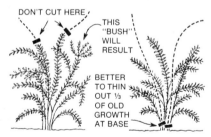

DON'T CUT HERE

THIS "BUSH" WILL RESULT

BETTER TO THIN OUT ⅓ OF OLD GROWTH AT BASE

CUT BACK ⅓ of old growth after flowering to encourage new flowering wood.

ABIES. Fir. Evergreen trees. Slow growing. Unnecessary to prune except for removal of dead, weak, and damaged wood. Conifers generally require more careful pruning (when necessary) than other trees. Before you prune, reread the section on conifers (see page 20).

Two important don'ts to remember: don't cut back into leafless wood, or the whole branch is likely to die; don't cut leader to keep the tree lower, for you'll ruin its natural shape and good looks. If

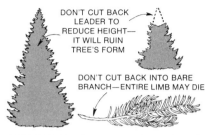

DON'T CUT BACK LEADER TO REDUCE HEIGHT—IT WILL RUIN TREE'S FORM

DON'T CUT BACK INTO BARE BRANCH—ENTIRE LIMB MAY DIE

REMEMBERING two pruning "don'ts" maintains natural shape, good looks of fir.

leader becomes damaged, encourage one of the branches in topmost whorl to replace it by staking and tying branch into upright position.

Never place a fir where it does not have room to grow because you will not be able to keep it small without ruining its natural shape.

ABUTILON. Flowering maple, Chinese bellflower, Chinese lantern. Evergreen, sprawling shrubs. Rapid growers, these require severe thinning and heading back in early spring. Continual pinching of branch tips during growing season will keep shrubs compact and encourage formation of new flower-bearing wood. Can be trained as standards or espaliered formally or informally.

Rejuvenate in spring by cutting oldest stems to ground. If hit by frost, wait until new growth begins; then cut damaged wood back to fresh shoots.

ABYSSINIAN BANANA.
See Ensete ventricosum.

ACACIA. Evergreen shrubs and trees. Most forms can be pruned quite heavily because they are such vigorous growers. Can be pruned anytime, but best time is while in bloom or directly afterwards.

Whether they are trees or shrubs depends on particular species and how they are trained in youth. Cut off lead shoot and it grows as a shrub.

To train as a tree, shorten branches below desired scaffold height and then remove them when trunk is sturdy and self-supporting. Be careful not to damage leader. Stake tree types until deeply anchored. Thin out whole branches on large trees to open interiors, reduce dieback of shaded branches, and prevent wind damage. Thin by cutting selected branches back to trunk.

ACALYPHA. Evergreen tropical shrubs. Control size by pinching new growth whenever necessary, or they will grow

to bulky 10 ft. Thin and head back heavily as needed to keep as house plant.

ACANTHOPANAX sieboldianus (*Aralia pentaphylla*). Deciduous shrub. Can withstand heavy pruning. Renew by thinning out some of the oldest stems each winter or cutting entire plant to ground before new spring growth begins. New growth will quickly follow.

ACANTHUS mollis. Bear's breech. Perennial. Cut plant completely to ground at end of flowering period in mid to late summer for complete renewal of growth. If grown for foliage alone, cut off flower stalks before bloom.

ACER. Maple. Deciduous or evergreen trees or large shrubs. Take many forms; how you prune depends upon the form you want. When grown as trees, they require normal staking and training to single trunk. Very little pruning, aside from removal of dead, weak, and interfering growth, will be required after they have reached maturity. This corrective pruning can be done anytime; however, because most plants bleed profusely, it is best to avoid pruning in spring just before and during period of most active growth. Do not head branches back or you'll encourage unsightly, broomlike growth.

A. buergerianum. Trident maple. Deciduous tree. Low, spreading growth makes it a good bonsai subject. Needs staking and training to make it branch high.

A. campestre. Hedge maple. Deciduous tree. Slow growing, forming dense, compact, and rounded head. Can be trained and sheared into high hedge.

A. circinatum. Vine maple. Deciduous shrub or small tree. Responds well to shaping in a variety of forms. Let it go untrimmed to make natural bowers or espalier against shady side of a wall. Stake and train as a single-trunked small shade tree or as multi-stemmed tree.

A. ginnala. Amur maple. Deciduous shrub or small tree. Stake and train as a single-trunked tree or a multi-trunked tall shrub.

A. griseum. Paperbark maple. Deciduous tree. Thin to emphasize winter silhouette of bare, angling branches.

A. japonicum. Fullmoon maple. Deciduous shrub. Small and slow growing. Best thinned and shaped as shrub.

A. macrophyllum. Bigleaf maple. Deciduous tree. Vigorous grower, needs early staking, training. Too big for most gardens. Roots are greedy and invasive.

A. negundo. Box elder. Deciduous tree. Fast growing, brittle. When young, prune to form good, strong framework. Thin to keep top open; cut out wind-damaged wood.

(Continued on next page)

A. palmatum. Japanese maple. Deciduous shrub or tree. Easy to shape into form and size you want and keep that way. Remove branches that grow in unwanted direction; selectively cut back branches to accentuate its habit of growing in planed, layered branches. Dwarf mounding types can be kept low by heading back branches that show tendency to grow upright. Can be trained as multi-stemmed tree.

A. saccharinum. Silver maple. Deciduous tree. Fast growing. Weak wood and narrow crotch angles make it subject to breakage. Thin out branches when young to avoid crowding; retain best formed, strongest crotches. Also thin top to lessen wind resistance.

ACHILLEA. Yarrow. Perennial. After first bloom, remove stems that have flowered. Cut back to point where fresh growth is coming up. It will bloom again on new growth in late summer or fall.

ACMENA smithii (*Eugenia smithii*). Lilly-Pilly tree. Evergreen large shrub or small tree. Awkward in growth unless trained and shaped when young. Prune after dramatic show of berries in winter.

ACOKANTHERA. Evergreen shrub. Avoid poisonous fruits by removing flowers as they fade. Can be espaliered, grown in a tub as small tree, or let range unchecked as handsome, open shrub. Additional pruning seldom required.

ACROCARPUS fraxinifolius. Deciduous to almost evergreen tree. Somewhat tender; narrow in form. Needs support when young. When necessary, cut out branches which detract from its slender shape.

ACROCOMIA.
See Palm.

ACTINIDIA. Deciduous vine. Rampant grower; can be pruned heavily when necessary to shape or control growth and pattern. Do major pruning while dormant or just as buds begin to swell. Remove some old wood, cutting above buds where you want growth.

ADAM'S NEEDLE.
See Yucca filamentosa.

ADENOCARPUS. Canary Island lupine. Evergreen or semi-evergreen shrub. Can be pruned heavily after flowering if required. Keep faded flowers picked off to prevent seed formation, prolong bloom.

AESCULUS. Deciduous trees or large shrubs. Normal training for form when young, very little pruning when mature except to remove dead, diseased wood. Prune in winter or early spring just before new growth begins.

AETHIONEMA. Stonecress. Perennial. Shear stems back after flowers fade.

AFRICAN BOXWOOD.
See Myrsine africana.

AFRICAN LINDEN.
See Sparmannia africana.

AFRICAN RED ALDER.
See Cunonia capensis.

AFRICAN VIOLET.
See Saintpaulia ionantha.

AGATHIS robusta. Queensland kauri. Evergreen tree. Remove errant branches while young before they dominate and detract from striking, naturally layered form. Accentuate this form by selectively removing unwanted growth as necessary. Also remove any branches tending to form a second leader.

CUT OFF weaker branch when two branches compete to be central leader.

AGAVE americana. Century plant. Succulent. When 10-15 years old, it sends up flower stalk that grows about a foot daily. If allowed to develop and bloom, plant dies. You can save plant by removing stalk as soon as it appears, or you can let it bloom and then propagate by removing and planting some suckers growing around base. No other pruning required.

AGONIS. Peppermint tree, Australian willow myrtle, juniper myrtle. Evergreen trees. Adaptable; how you prune depends on form you want. Train as tree or espalier against a wall. Prune in spring (after danger of frost in cold climate). Freezes to ground in some areas but will come back from stump.

AILANTHUS altissima (*A. glandulosa*). Tree-of-heaven. Deciduous tree. Fast growing with brittle wood; needs selective pruning when young to develop sturdy, desirable form. Suckers profuse-ly; remove suckers, thin out unwanted wood while dormant to keep in control and to maintain desired form.

AJUGA. Carpet bugle. Perennial. Remove faded flowers. Cut back runners drastically whenever necessary to keep from creeping too far. Replant every 3 or 4 years.

AKEBIA quinata. Fiveleaf akebia. Deciduous vine, evergreen in mild winters. Responds well to heavy pruning; can be controlled with annual cutting back to ground (in spring before growth begins) and by pinching back unwanted growth during growing season. Recovers quickly when cut to ground. For open tracery effect when grown on post or column, cut out all but 2 or 3 basal stems.

ALBIZIA julibrissin. Silk tree. Deciduous tree. Commonly called mimosa in eastern states. Rapid grower to 40 ft.; can be held to 10-20-ft. umbrella by heading back upward growing branches. A bit unpredictable in its growth habit. Unpruned, will grow in tiers and usually have several stems. Tends to form branches close to ground if not trained as a tree in its youth by removing branches which are lower than desired. When it is the height you want, top the tree by cutting tip off leader to encourage broader or more umbrella like crown. Prune in winter or early spring. In cold-winter areas, limit pruning to spring when danger of frost is past.

ALDER.
See Alnus.

ALDER BUCKTHORN.
See Rhamnus frangula.

ALLAMANDA cathartica. Evergreen viny shrub or shrubby vine. Will climb to 10 ft. or spread as a shrub, depending on how you train it. Pinch during growing season to control growth and shape it to desired form.

ALMOND. Deciduous tree. Requires normal training for the first 2 or 3 seasons in order to form strong framework (see *Fruit Tree Training,* page 17). Once an almond has reached maturity, you prune it primarily for wood renewal. Almond bears at ends of short spurs which produce for about 5 years, so your pruning objective should be to remove about 1/5 of fruiting wood each dormant season. Also remove dead wood and overcrowded branches as necessary. Rejuvenate older tree by heading branches back to healthy, sound laterals. An almond grows vigorously and a young, healthy tree may throw all its energy into vegetative growth which causes it not to start bearing when it should. In this case, stop pruning for a season or two. This will slow heavy growth and bring tree into bearing.

ALMOND, FLOWERING.
See Prunus triloba.

ALNUS. Alder. Deciduous trees. Tend to grow multiple trunks; make excellent screening plants. To grow as single-trunked trees, select best young trunk and cut all others down to base. Thin crowns selectively to develop strong framework. They do not require much pruning; prune in winter when necessary to shape and to remove dead or crossing branches and sucker growth. Roots can be invasive.

ALOYSIA triphylla (*Lippia citriodora*). Lemon verbena. Deciduous or partially evergreen herb-shrub. Pinch during growing season to shape it as you desire. Makes interesting tracery against wall. Thin out old, weak wood before spring growth begins. No other pruning required.

ALPINIA speciosa (*A. nutans*). Shell flower, porcelain ginger. Perennial. Remove canes that have flowered to make room for new flowering stems.

ALSOPHILA.
See Fern, Tree.

ALSTROEMERIA. Perennial. Cut off ripened foliage and faded flowers to ground level.

ALYSSUM. Perennials. Shear off flower heads after they finish blooming to improve chances of second bloom in the fall. Trimming also helps to keep plants neat and dense by forcing side branches.

AMELANCHIER. Shadblow, shadbush, service berry. Deciduous shrubs or small trees. Prune lightly during winter or just before growth starts in the spring. Look best when allowed to grow naturally with minimum of pruning.

AMORPHA. Indigo bush. Deciduous shrub. Flowers on new wood; remove some of oldest wood each year while dormant to renew. Will recover if frozen back in colder areas.

AMPELOPSIS brevipedunculata. Blueberry climber. Deciduous vine. Vigorous grower. Cut back from windows, doors when necessary. In spring head back some stems and thin out others for good form and spacing.

AMUR CORK TREE.
See Phellodendron amurense.

ANCHUSA capensis. Cape forget-me-not, summer forget-me-not. Biennial. Shear back after first crop of flowers to encourage a second.

ANDROMEDA polifolia. Bog rosemary. Evergreen shrublet. To shape, take out some branches, head back others after spring bloom.

ANEMOPAEGMA chamberlaynii (*Bignonia chamberlaynii*). Yellow trumpet vine. Evergreen vine. Blooms on new wood. Shorten all shoots in spring to ensure growth of lateral shoots and produce flower buds. Thin growth after bloom and cut weak shoots to ground.

ANGEL'S TRUMPET.
See Datura.

ANGOPHORA lanceolata. Gum myrtle. Evergreen tree. Related to eucalyptus and as tough and tolerant. Grows big, needs lots of room. Give it normal training when young (see *Training Young Trees,* page 15). Stake young tree only if it simply cannot stand on its own. As tree matures, prune to shape and to prevent overcrowding of branches. Thin by taking out complete branches back to lateral or main branch. Prune anytime but preferably in late winter, early spring.

ANIGOZANTHUS. Kangaroo paw. Evergreen perennial. Remove dead foliage. Will bloom from late spring to fall if spent flowering spikes are cut to ground. Divide clumps every year or every other year.

ANISACANTHUS thurberi. Desert honeysuckle. Evergreen or deciduous shrub. Looks best when treated as perennial. Cut to ground in winter (if frost doesn't do it) with pruning shears. If frozen, remove dead foliage after new growth appears.

ANNONA cherimola. Cherimoya. Briefly deciduous large shrub or small tree. Very little pruning required except to form well-balanced tree. Overcrowding branches should be removed to provide light to inside growth. Has low-branching habit; remove those below the desired height as tree matures. Good for espaliering. Prune when most dormant.

ANNUALS. An annual is a plant that grows its entire course—from seed to natural death—in one year. Most annuals that you might grow in your garden from seed or nursery plants need little or no pruning during their short but valuable lifetimes. Some, however, do benefit from certain pruning acts. The things you can do are similar to the things you do to the longer-lasting trees, shrubs, and perennials:

1. Pinching tips in early stages of growth makes many lanky or too-open annuals more bushy.

2. Most annuals can benefit from grooming during the peak of their careers. Pick or cut off dead and fading flowers, broken stems, and any branches that spoil the plant's appearance.

3. A few annuals, including petunias, snapdragons, and sweet alyssum, can be cut back hard at the end of what appears to be their complete blooming season, forcing voluminous new growth which in turn will probably produce another cycle of flowers.

ANTHEMIS nobilis. Chamomile. Evergreen perennial. A lawn substitute if mowed or sheared and rolled several times a year to keep low and compact. If not used as lawn, flowering season can be prolonged by removing the faded blooms to prevent the seeds from developing.

ANTHURIUM. Perennial greenhouse or house plant. When plant gets too tall, cut off top 5 or 6 in. of stem and plant this cutting for new plant.

APACHE PLUME.
See Fallugia paradoxa.

APHELANDRA squarrosa. Evergreen house plant. If you keep old flowers picked off, plant will remain colorful for 3-4 months. To make plant bushy and produce more blooms, cut stems back to 1 or 2 pairs of leaves after flowering. A single-stemmed plant will usually produce 2 stems after cutting back. If you pinch tips of these 2 stems when they are a couple of inches long, they will produce 4 new shoots.

APPLE. Deciduous fruit tree. Young tree requires considerable amount of pruning attention to guide it into strong framework (see *Fruit Tree Training,* page 17).

On mature tree, pruning should be mostly corrective (removal of dead wood, weak limbs). You will also want to thin out new growth on mature tree to encourage development of bearing spurs on older wood and to keep tree desired size. Do major pruning during most dormant period. Because apple trees

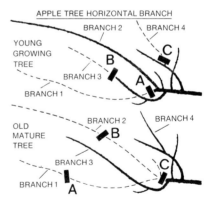

ON YOUNG APPLE TREE, cut A removes weak branch. Branch 2 will grow in length. Cuts B and C subdue branches 3 and 4. On mature tree (with size being maintained), A removes last year's growth; B favors branch 1; C would stimulate replacement wood.

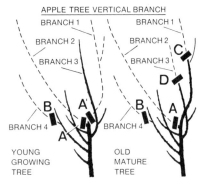

APPLE TREE VERTICAL BRANCH

BRANCH 1 BRANCH 1
BRANCH 2 BRANCH 2
C
BRANCH 3 BRANCH 3
D
B A B A
BRANCH 4 A BRANCH 4 A
YOUNG OLD
GROWING MATURE
TREE TREE

ON YOUNG TREE, cuts at A or A¹ direct growth into uncut branch. B makes branch 1 or 2 more dominant. On old tree, all cuts are to hold back the length.

produce fruit mainly on ends of long-lived spurs, they require considerably less pruning than some of the other fruit trees. The spurs which bear apples develop from vegetative buds on new shoots. As spurs grow, fruit buds which will produce following season's crop form on the ends. A spur therefore begins producing fruit in its second year. The following spring, the spur puts out a little more growth and sets another terminal fruit bud. Sometimes the spur branches, though this occurs more frequently on pears, which have a similar bearing habit. Apple spurs often go through this growing and fruit-setting process over a period as long as 20 years.

APRICOT. Deciduous fruit tree. Unlike apple, pear, or cherry, an apricot tree requires heavy pruning for good fruit production. As with other deciduous fruit trees, major pruning should be done in the dormant period. Most fruit is borne on short spurs that form on last year's growth and remain fruitful for about 4 years. Pruning should be directed toward conserving enough new growth (which will produce spurs) to replace old, exhausted spurs which should be cut out. To stimulate new, produc-

tive growth, cut back older branches to younger, vigorous laterals. For young apricot tree (from planting to 4 years old), see *Fruit Tree Training*, (page 17).

APRICOT, JAPANESE FLOWERING. See Prunus mume.

AQUILEGIA. Columbine. Perennials. Remove faded flowers to encourage longer season of bloom and to help control excessive reseeding. If cut to ground after main bloom period, they may flower again the same season.

ARABIS. Rockcress. Perennial. Cut back enough growth after bloom to remove all seed heads and old flower stalks. Plant will produce new growth, another set of buds, and scattered flowers through summer.

ARALIA chinensis. Chinese angelica. Deciduous shrub-tree. Vertical, slightly spreading habit. In spring, thin out surplus stems at ground level for open effect. Remove diseased or damaged stems whenever necessary.

ARALIA, JAPANESE. See Fatsia japonica.

ARALIA, THREADLEAF FALSE. See Dizygotheca elegantissima.

ARAUCARIA. Monkey puzzle tree, Norfolk Island pine. Evergreen trees. Require only corrective pruning, removal of weak or damaged wood whenever necessary. If leader is damaged, select best branch immediately below and brace it vertically to take its place.

ARAUJIA sericofera. White bladder flower. Evergreen or partially deciduous vine. Very little pruning necessary. Thin out some stems and head back others for desired spacing; shape when necessary.

ARBORVITAE, AMERICAN. See Thuja, Platycladus.

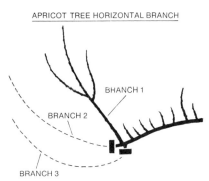

APRICOT TREE HORIZONTAL BRANCH

BRANCH 1
BRANCH 2
BRANCH 3

BRANCHES 2 AND 3 hang down too much. Apricots will form on spurs at right and along Branch 1 (formed last year).

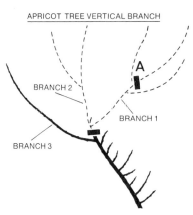

APRICOT TREE VERTICAL BRANCH

A
BRANCH 2
BRANCH 1
BRANCH 3

CUT AT CENTER would make tree more spreading; cut at A would subdue branch 1 so branch 2 could maintain advantage.

ARBORVITAE, ORIENTAL. See Thuja, Platycladus.

ARBUTUS. Evergreen tree and shrub-tree.

A. menziesii. Madrone. Madroña. Evergreen tree or large shrub. Needs only light pruning to shape. Do this in fall or early spring.

A. unedo. Strawberry tree. Evergreen shrub-tree. Plant has interesting trunk and stem pattern that responds well to selective branch removal, shaping, and training. You can train it easily as single-trunked or multiple-trunked tree, or leave unpruned to form dense hedge. Cut out dead branches anytime; prune to shape in spring before active growth starts.

ARCHONTOPHOENIX. See Palm.

ARCTOSTAPHYLOS. Manzanita. Evergreen shrubs. Range in size from creepers to shrubs and small trees. Control growth and shape by frequent tip-pinching during growing season.

A. columbiana. Hairy manzanita. Naturally assumes an interesting branch pattern. Pinch back while young to encourage branching and prevent legginess. Thin to expose branching pattern you want.

A. densiflora. Vine Hill manzanita. Low growing and spreading. Tip-pinch plant while young to shape.

A. d. 'Howard McMinn'. Mounding spreading growth. Tip-pinch after flowering to make it dense. (Don't pinch tips of prostrate branches.)

A. d. 'Sentinel'. Can be trained as small tree by selecting dominant stem or stems and removing others.

A. edmundsii. Little Sur manzanita. Pinch back while young to encourage bushiness.

A. glandulosa. Eastwood manzanita. Sends up many shoots from woody base. To keep it low, pinch out leaders when young and soft.

A. manzanita. Common manzanita. Thin to expose branching pattern you want. Pinch and head back to prevent legginess.

A. patula. Greenleaf manzanita. Thin out unwanted wood to show off beauty of trunk and branches.

A. stanfordiana. Stanford manzanita. If it becomes too dense, carefully thin out center branches.

A. uva-ursi. Bearberry, kinnikinnick. Ground cover. Pinch tips of vigorous growth to induce branching. Shear back when established to thicken.

ARDISIA. Evergreen shrubs or shrublets. Prune only to control size and spread when necessary.

ARECASTRUM romanzoffianum.
See Palm.

ARENGA engleri.
See Palm.

ARISTOLOCHIA. Deciduous vines. Require little maintenance other than directing twining shoots over area you want to cover. If they become too heavy after several seasons, cut back in the winter and train selected new spring shoots to cover. Respond well to heavy pruning.

ARISTOTELIA racemosa. New Zealand wineberry. Evergreen shrub or small tree. Normal training while young for good branch spacing and structure; requires only corrective pruning thereafter. Do this whenever necessary.

ARMERIA. Thrift, sea pink. Hardy evergreen perennials. Require little pruning other than clipping off faded flowers and flower stalks.

ARONIA arbutifolia. Red chokeberry. Deciduous shrub. Large, openly branched, upright growth. Prune to encourage branching while young; prune to shape after berries have dropped.

ARROW-WOOD.
See Viburnum dentatum.

ARTEMISIA. Evergreen or deciduous shrubs or woody perennials.
   A. absinthium. Common wormwood. Perennial. Woody shrub. In spring, cut it back to within 6 in. of the base to renew.
   A. frigida. Fringed wormwood. Perennial. Young plants are compact; to keep their shape, cut back when they become rangy.
   A. pycnocephala. Sandhill sage. Shrubby perennial. Remove flower spikes as they open to keep the plant compact.

ARTICHOKE. Perennial vegetable. After each stem has given its last artichoke, it will seem to fold up, and leaves will die back to a degree. This is the signal for you to cut the stem or stalk back to the base.

ARUNDO donax. Giant reed. Perennial. Cut out dead stems and thin when necessary to avoid overcrowded look. Extremely invasive. Plant only where you can control it.

ASH.
See Fraxinus.

ASH, EUROPEAN MOUNTAIN.
See Sorbus aucuparia.

ASPARAGUS, EDIBLE. Perennial vegetable. When plant turns brown in late fall or early winter, cut stems to ground. In cold winter areas, permit dead stalks to stand until spring before cutting.

ASPARAGUS, ORNAMENTAL. Perennials. Once established, plants need little attention except to remove dead tops when they become noticeable. Remove old stalks at base when brown. Thin stems of vining kinds to prevent tangling. (*A. retrofractus* sheds "needles" on some branches, then grows another crop; don't be too hasty in cutting out brown, dead-looking stalks.)

ASPEN. See Populus.

ASTER. Perennials. Strong growers are invasive. Cut back spreading roots whenever necessary to keep in bounds.
   A. frikartii. Remove faded flowers before they start to go to seed to prolong blooming season. If plants get lanky, or if you want to control their size, cut back to 4 in. from the ground. New growth will come quickly.
   A. novae-angliae; A. novi-belgii. Michaelmas daisy. Pinch when young to induce branching; then, when plant is a foot high, cut back hard if you want lower, bushier plant with more flowers. Continue to pinch out new growth, as with chrysanthemums.
   For better formed plant with more flowers, thin out stalks on plant that hasn't been divided for a year or more, leaving only 6-8 stems (most authorities recommend dividing every year in spring). After it finishes blooming, remove faded flowers and cut plant to ground to prevent seeding and growth of inferior new plants. Some early varieties bloom a second time if you cut back after first flowers fade.

ASTILBE. False spiraea, meadow sweet. Perennial. Cut spent flowers to keep plant looking neat and to induce more bloom. In fall, after leaves die, cut stems to ground; new ones will come up in spring. Protect plant in colder areas by not removing dead foliage until spring growth appears.

ATLAS CEDAR.
See Cedrus atlantica.

ATRIPLEX. Saltbush. Evergreen or deciduous shrubs. Head back and thin to desired shape whenever necessary. Respond well to heavy pruning. Train as shrubs, windbreaks, clipped hedges.

AUBRIETA deltoidea. Common aubrieta. Perennial. Blooms profusely in spring. To maintain brilliance of separate colors, shear back enough growth after bloom to remove old seed heads but always keep some foliage. Plant will produce new growth, another set of buds, and scattered flowers through summer. Trimming also helps keep plant neat and dense by forcing side branches.

AUCUBA japonica. Japanese aucuba. Evergreen shrub. Few plants are easier to hold in check by pruning. Prune in

spring; new growth develops so quickly you hardly notice that shrub has been cut. Shorten plant by cutting back to a pair of buds or to just above leaf joint.

AUSTRALIAN FUCHSIA.
See Correa.

AVOCADO (*Persea americana*). Evergreen tree. Normal training while young. Grown primarily for fruit production, this tree should not necessarily be forced into attractive form. Shape varies with variety and is also affected by weight of fruit forcing branches down. Very little pruning should be necessary for mature tree beyond normal removal of weak, damaged wood. (In fact, commercial avocado growers seldom prune tree.) Dead branches and twigs can normally be snapped off with your hands. A continual inside die-back is normal condition as tree matures. Remove deadwood regularly.
   Bark of avocado is very sensitive to sunlight and sunburns easily so be careful not to remove too much foliage, creating openings through which sunlight can enter and cause damage. Head back upright growth to side branch if you want to keep fruit crop low. (It may be necessary to head back long drooping branches or brace them to prevent their breaking under heavy fruit load.) Best time for any pruning is after harvest or after normal bearing season.

AZALEA.
See Rhododendron.

AZARA microphylla. Evergreen shrub. Can also be trained into single-trunked, small tree. Fanlike, pendulous stems make it natural for espaliering. Responds well to heavy cutting but usually requires only shaping. Prune whenever needed.

BACCHARIS pilularis. Dwarf coyote brush, dwarf chaparral broom. Evergreen shrub. In small plantings prune each year before new growth starts. Thin and head back arching branches and those that grow too tall or out of proportion to rest of plant. Thin out some old wood to rejuvenate. After flowering, remove old flower stems to keep plant looking neat.

BALD CYPRESS.
See Taxodium distichum.

BALLOON FLOWER.
See Platycodon grandiflorum.

BAMBOO. Giant grasses with woody stems. Large group includes *Bambusa*, *Phyllostachys*, *Pseudosasa*. Major pruning concern with bamboos is to keep them controlled. Once established, running kinds grow fast and spread out of their intended area by invasive, underground roots.

(Continued on next page)

screens, or clipped into hedges and screens.

Vertical and giant types can also be planted as groves or used as tall screens and hedges. (On tallest growing kinds you'll have to take out tallest stems to the ground frequently to keep them as low as you want.) An interesting way to prune vertical types is to thin some of the secondary branches back to the main stem. Thinned in this fashion, with ½ to ⅔ of the leaves removed, bamboo makes an attractive plant with an interesting silhouette.

All types — except ground covers — look good when thinned to show off the stems. When cutting stems, take them at or below ground level. When plants get old and dense, cut back heavily; new growth will quickly form a dense mass of foliage farther down.

Root pruning: before strong rhizomes invade flower and shrubbery beds and lawns or pop up into driveways and other paved areas, cut them off at edge of bed with sharp spade. Push spade straight down as far as it will go. In some cases you may have to dig a trench and cut down to double depth. You can also plant in containers or use dividers of galvanized sheet metal, cement, or redwood set 18 in. deep in ground around plants to keep them in bounds.

BAMBOO, HEAVENLY.
See Nandina domestica.

BAMBURANTA.
See Hybophrynium brauneanum.

BANANA.
See Ensete.

BANANA SHRUB.
See Michelia figo.

BAPTISIA australis. False indigo, wild indigo. Perennial. Cut back spent flowers for repeat bloom (unless you want the seed pods to dry for use in winter flower arrangements).

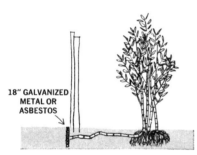

18" GALVANIZED METAL OR ASBESTOS

ABOVE, BAMBOO SPREADS under a fence, pops up in neighbor's lawn. Below, control method: a subterranean fence.

All bamboo should be thinned regularly whenever necessary, and oldest stems removed to make it easier to clean out old leaves. Beyond this, how you prune depends upon growth habit of your bamboo as well as purpose you have in mind. All bamboos can take a good deal of pruning; control them by thinning and shearing. Best time to do heaviest cutting is during young, rapid growing stage in spring.

Bamboos can be divided into 4 general groups: 1) Dwarf or low-growing ground cover types; 2) Clump bamboos with a fountainlike habit of growth; 3) Running bamboos of moderate size and more or less vertical growth; and 4) Giant bamboos.

To keep dwarf types low and compact, shear tops back when required; shorten shoots that grow too high. The hardy clump types have widest use in landscaping and can be grown singly, lined up and left unclipped as informal

TO CREATE INTERESTING SILHOUETTE, side branches have been cut back halfway up main stems of giant bamboo. Do heaviest pruning during rapid spring growth.

BARBERRY.
See Berberis.

BAUHINIA. Evergreen or deciduous trees or half-climbing shrubs.

B. blakeana. Hong Kong orchid tree. Partially deciduous for short period. Train as small tree or allow it to branch at base to form large, multi-stemmed shrub. Prune while most dormant.

B. galpinii. Red bauhinia. Evergreen to semi-deciduous shrub. Often classed as vine, but may ramble into tree. Thin and head back heavily after flowering to keep shape; also pinch back tips at any time except during cold weather. If plant is kept rootbound, it will remain more shrublike. Heavy pruning after flowering encourages new growth that bears flowers. These appear in clusters of 2-10 at about every third joint as new growth elongates.

B. variegata. (Commonly sold as *B. purpurea*.) Purple orchid tree. Partially to wholly deciduous. Stake it, cut off side branches, and selectively thin and head back top to train as single-trunked tree 20-35 ft. tall with nearly equal spread. Without training, it most often grows as multi-trunked shrub. Prune while most dormant.

BAYBERRY.
See Myrica pensylvanica.

BAY, CALIFORNIA.
See Umbellularia californica.

BEARBERRY.
See Arctostaphylos uva-ursi.

BEARD TONGUE.
See Penstemon.

BEAR'S BREECH.
See Acanthus mollis.

BEAUMONTIA grandiflora. Herald's trumpet, Easter lily vine. Evergreen vine. Flowers on old wood; if you cut back too severely, you will reduce the bloom. Thin and head back lightly after flowering to keep in scale but preserve good proportion of 2 and 3-year-old wood.

BEAUTY BERRY.
See Callicarpa.

BEAUTY BUSH.
See Kolkwitzia amabilis.

BEECH, EUROPEAN.
See Fagus sylvatica.

BEGONIA. Perennials. Susceptible to stem rot, so when you cut flowers leave about an inch of flower stem on plants. Stub will cure and fall off naturally. This avoids fresh wound on main stem that would be open to infection. Faded flowers and leaves can also cause rot and should be removed. Pinch out growing tips to encourage branching, keep plants compact.

BELLFLOWER.
See Campanula.

BELOPERONE guttata (*B. tomentosa*). Shrimp plant. Evergreen shrub. Grows into 3-4-ft. mound but can be kept much lower. To shape plant, pinch continuously in early growth until compact mound of foliage is obtained and then let bloom. To encourage continued bushiness, head back stems when flower bracts turn black.

BERBERIS. Barberry. Deciduous and evergreen shrubs. Normally require a minimum of pruning beyond what is needed to keep them neat and shaped. They tolerate pruning well; the more vigorous growers can take a lot of cutting back for growth renewal. Left unpruned, some inner branches die and plants become leggy and ratty. Cut oldest wood to within 4-6 in. of ground to renew before new spring growth starts. Shear hedges whenever required; prune shrubs lightly to shape after bloom and berries have gone.

Sheared, dense plants are susceptible to scale insects. If this becomes a problem, thin plants and take appropriate control measures.

BERGENIA. Perennial, evergreen except in coldest areas. To keep neat, cut or pull off old faded leaves and remove old flower stalks as they finish blooming. Divide and replant whenever crowns appear crowded. Cut back to ground yearly if you wish to prevent legginess.

BETULA. Birch. Deciduous trees. Birches have a habit of growing branches of equal size from the same point, forming weak, narrow crotches. Remove all but one of these shoots to develop strong framework. Birches need normal staking and training in youth to shape to the forms you want. Thin out crowded growth and do major pruning in winter or very early spring. If prun-

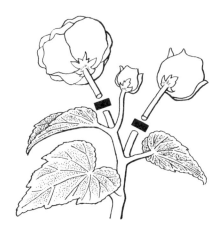

BEGONIAS are an exception to the rule: leave a stub when you cut the flowers.

ing is done at other times, trees will tend to bleed. Although this won't hurt them, it can discolor the bark and possibly cause a secondary trunk infection. Mature trees require little or no pruning except for removal of weak or damaged wood. On many species you also want to remove lower branches to expose the attractive bark.

BIGNONIA. Trumpet vine. Botanists have reclassified plants formerly called *Bignonia*, so that the trumpet vines you knew as *Bignonia* are now placed under other names. Many are still sold under the old names. Since most gardeners still compare one "bignonia" with another when making their selections, we list them below and give the names under which they are described:

B. chamberlaynii. See Anemopaegma chamberlaynii.

B. cherere. See Phaedranthus buccinatorius.

B. chinensis. See Campsis.

B. jasminoides. See Pandorea jasminoides.

B. radicans. See Campsis.

B. speciosa. See Clytostoma callistegioides.

B. tweediana. See Doxantha unguiscati.

B. violacea. See Clytostoma callistegioides.

BIRCH.
See Betula.

BIRD OF PARADISE.
See Strelitzia.

BITTERSWEET.
See Celastrus.

BLACKBERRY. If you don't dedicate yourself to your blackberry plants, caring for them as soon as they need care, or if you have only limited space to plant, blackberries can be sheer disaster. Nothing is better than a perfect crop of aromatic Boysens, but nothing is worse than several hundred square feet of canes gone wild, covered with murderous spines and shooting up new runners everywhere.

Among the most popular blackberries are 'Boysen' and 'Thornless Boysen', with large, aromatic, slightly tart berries; 'Evergreen' and 'Thornless Evergreen', with heavy crops of large, very firm, sweet berries; 'Himalaya', an especially thorny, vigorous plant producing jet black, medium-sized berries over a long season; 'Logan' and 'Thornless Logan', with large, reddish berries that are quite sour and excellent for cooking; 'Nectar', identical to 'Boysen'; 'Olallie', with large, shiny black, firm, sweet berries with overtones of wild blackberry flavor; and 'Young' and 'Thornless Young', which are similar to 'Boysen' but have berries that tend to be a little sweeter and are shiny rather than dull. Other kinds include 'Aurora', 'Cascade', 'Marion', and 'Texas Wonder'.

Blackberries will require some kind of trellis and they need full sun and large amounts of water throughout the growing season. They should not be planted next to a fence because the fence will block sunlight if it's solid and because suckers will come up on the neighbor's side. When planting bare-root berries, spread roots and set plant about an inch deeper than it grew in the nursery. Set plants 3 ft. apart, in rows 5 or 6 ft. apart. Cut back the canes to 4-8 in.

Established berries need only a light trim in late winter. (Do heavy pruning at the end of summer after crop has been gathered.) To do light pruning, trim side branches to 12 in. Small, fruit-bearing branches will grow from these.

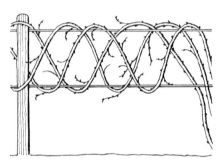

WEAVING CANES onto trellis is one way to train and support blackberry plants.

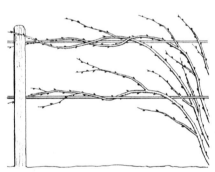

TYING selected canes onto wires is another effective method.

As soon as last of crop is harvested, you should begin heavy annual pruning. Cut to ground level all canes that have borne fruit. Select up to 16 sturdy canes for next year's production and weave or tie these on the trellis. Cut all weak canes to ground.

BLACK-EYED SUSAN.
See Rudbeckia hirta.

BLACK OLIVE.
See Bucida buceras.

BLADDER SENNA.
See Colutea.

BLECHNUM (*Lomaria*). Evergreen ferns.
  B. brasiliense. See Fern, Tree.
  B. gibbum. See Fern, Tree.
  B. spicant. See Fern, Hardy.

BLEEDING HEART.
See Dicentra.

BLUEBEARD.
See Caryopteris.

BLUEBELL CREEPER, AUSTRALIAN.
See Sollya fusiformis.

BLUEBERRY. Deciduous shrub. Should be pruned annually sometime after leaves fall and before it blooms. Most tend to bear so heavily that fruit size is decreased and growth of plant slows down. It must be thinned so that it will produce fewer, but larger berries. How you prune varies somewhat, depending upon whether your blueberry is low and spreading or upright. Spreading types seldom have multiple stems, upright plants have many stems.

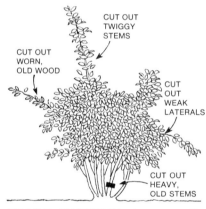

CUT OUT TWIGGY STEMS

CUT OUT WORN, OLD WOOD

CUT OUT WEAK LATERALS

CUT OUT HEAVY, OLD STEMS

PRUNING BLUEBERRY plants annually produces fewer but larger berries.

In general, cut out weak laterals and twiggy growth, as well as from ¼-⅓ of the least vigorous old wood. Heavy old stems that have lost their vitality may be removed at ground level. To limit fruit production, cut branches with many buds back ½-⅔ and cut shoots that have fruited back to 3-5 buds each. Keep first-year plant from bearing by stripping off flowers. On older plants, cut back ends of twigs to point where fruit buds are widely spaced.

BLUE BLOSSOM.
See Ceanothus thyrsiflorus.

BLUE DRACAENA.
See Cordyline indivisa.

BLUE FESCUE.
See Festuca ovina 'glauca'.

BLUE MARGUERITE.
See Felicia amelliodes.

BOG ROSEMARY.
See Andromeda polifolia.

BOSTON IVY.
See Parthenocissus.

BOTTLEBRUSH.
See Callistemon.

BOUGAINVILLEA. Evergreen shrubby vines. Vigorous twining growth to 20 ft. or more; can be restrained and kept lower by pruning. Don't be afraid to prune to renew plants' shape or direct growth, then remove weak growth and cut back heavy canes to basal buds. The buds usually grow fast and flower well, whereas weak growth seldom has good flowers.

Prune heavily in spring after frost risk is over. First remove any branches killed by frost. Where growth is very thick, remove some laterals completely; others can be cut back, leaving short spurs where they join the main stem. Head back extremely long shoots to bring within bounds. On wall-grown plants, nip back long stems during growing season to produce more flowering wood. Shrubby kinds or heavily-pruned plants make good, self-supporting container shrubs for terrace or patio. Without support and with light corrective pruning, bougainvilleas can make broad, sprawling shrubs or bank and ground covers. When growth of plants used as shrubs or a ground cover is slow, cut back to ground the first or second year.

Bougainvilleas are generally pruned more severely (and frequently) in frost-free areas where they are vigorous growers. Too severe pruning in colder regions may result in excessive vegetative growth at expense of flowers. Though tops may be damaged by frost, bougainvilleas usually make a strong comeback if roots have not been hurt.

BOUVARDIA. Evergreen shrubs. Loose, straggly growth habit. Pinch out stem tips on young plants to make them bushier. Cut back after flowering to stimulate new growth, more flowers.

BOX, BOXWOOD.
See Buxus.

BOX ELDER.
See Acer negundo.

BOX SAND MYRTLE.
See Leiophyllum buxifolium.

BOXWOOD, AFRICAN.
See Myrsine africana.

BOXWOOD, OREGON.
See Pachistima myrsinites.

BRACHYCHITON (*Sterculia*). Evergreen to partly or wholly deciduous trees. Normal guidance and training when young; very little pruning (except for removal of dead, weak wood whenever necessary) required on mature trees.

BRACHYSEMA lanceolatum. Scimitar shrub, Swan River pea shrub. Evergreen. Requires only light pruning. Thin out old, straggly stems in spring.

BRASSAIA actinophylla (*Schefflera actinophylla*). Queensland umbrella tree, octopus tree. Evergreen house plant; outdoor shrub/tree in warmest areas. Good bonsai subject. Rapid growing; cut out tips occasionally to induce branching and to keep from becoming leggy. Leggy stems can be cut almost to ground; they will branch and make a better shaped plant. For screening, plant 2-4 ft. apart and keep tipped to encourage bushiness. Prune when necessary.

BRAZIL RAINTREE.
See Brunfelsia calycina.

BREATH OF HEAVEN.
See Coleonema and Diosma.

BRIDAL WREATH.
See Spiraea prunifolia 'Plena'.

BRISBANE BOX.
See Tristania conferta.

BROOM.
See Cytisus, Genista, Spartium.

BROUSSONETIA papyrifera. (Has been sold as *Morus papyrifera*.) Paper mulberry. Deciduous tree. Doesn't need much pruning beyond normal training and shaping for framework while young. Remove weak and crossing branches, deadwood in fall and summer. Cut out suckers when they appear.

BRUNFELSIA calycina. Brazil raintree. Evergreen shrub. Prune in the spring. Remove straggly growth and wood which detracts from desired shape.
B. c. floribunda. Yesterday-today-and-tomorrow. Will reach 10 ft. or more with several stems from the base; may be held as low as 3 ft. by continually removing canes which exceed desired height.

BUCIDA buceras. Black olive; geometry tree. Evergreen or deciduous tree. Thin and head back lightly when necessary to keep small and to accentuate plant's geometric branching pattern. Can be trained into handsome bonsai.

BUCKEYE.
See Aesculus.

BUCKTHORN, ITALIAN.
See Rhamnus alaternus.

BUCKWHEAT.
See Eriogonum.

BUDDLEIA. Butterfly bush. Evergreen or deciduous shrub or small tree.
B. alternifolia. Fountain butterfly bush. Deciduous shrub or small tree. To encourage growth that will produce next season's blossoms, cut back some oldest canes after flowering (on large plant take out a third of them) to bottom two buds (about 4 in. of stem). Can also be trained up into small single or multi-trunked tree.
B. davidii. Common butterfly bush, summer lilac. Deciduous or semi-evergreen shrub. Unlike *B. alternifolia*, this plant blooms on new wood rather than previous season's wood. So you can prune after flowering or you can wait until spring, after danger of frost is past. In cold climates it will freeze to ground in winter but will send up vigorous new growth from roots when the weather warms. For best appearance, cut entire plant to the ground each year after flowering. (In areas where winter frosts come early, wait until spring.)

BUSH ANEMONE.
See Carpenteria californica.

BUSH POPPY.
See Dendromecon.

BUTCHER'S BROOM, CLIMBING.
See Semele androgyna.

BUTIA capitata.
See Palm.

BUTTERFLY BUSH.
See Buddleia.

BUXUS. Boxwood, box. Evergreen shrubs, small trees. Can be cut back and sheared heavily and they will sprout readily from old wood. Type of pruning will depend upon purpose. Prune anytime from spring to fall, during growing season. Remove dead branches back to live wood.

B. microphylla japonica. Japanese boxwood. Grow slowly to 4-6-ft. informal shrubs if not pruned. Most often clipped as low or medium hedge or shaped into globes, tiers, or pyramids. If hedge grows too tall, lop off practically to ground and let it start over. Best time to do this is just as active growth is beginning in spring so that ugly stubs will soon be concealed by new foliage. To keep the rejuvenated plants compact, start shearing when shoots are 6 in. long.

B. sempervirens. Common boxwood, English boxwood. Most often grown as trimmed hedge, they can also be used as container plants, single shrubs, or topiary forms.
Can take any amount of cutting, but be sure to do this early enough in the fall so that new growth is hardy enough to withstand an early frost. Otherwise, pruning should be done after the last frost. Cut tips of branches on the outside of plants to force new growth on inside to fill in bare areas. Susceptible to a canker-causing fungus which results in dead center branches. These should be removed back to live wood.

TOPIARIES of Buxus sempervirens are result of frequent cutting back and shearing. These 20-year-old plants have been carefully pruned throughout their lives.

CALICO BUSH.
See Kalmia latifolia.

CALIFORNIA FUCHSIA.
See Zauschneria.

CALIFORNIA GERANIUM.
See Senecio petasitis.

CALLA.
See Zantedeschia.

CALLIANDRA. Evergreen shrub.

C. inaequilatera (*C. haematocephala*). Pink powder puff. The only pruning required is for shaping to encourage new growth and to get a second flowering. Prune immediately after flowering. Remove dead and crossing branches by cutting back to good laterals. Once mature, selectively cut some of oldest stems to ground each year to renew plant. Makes effective espalier against a wall.

C. tweedii (*C. guildingi*). Trinidad flame bush, Brazilian flame bush. Can be pruned heavily after flowering to open up, thin out, and retain interesting branch pattern. Flower clusters form at branch ends; tip pinch new growth for more branches, blossoms. Cut back overgrown shrub almost to ground or remove entirely and plant new one. Also makes good espalier.

CALLICARPA. Beauty berry. Deciduous shrubs. May freeze to the ground in severe winter, but can be cut to ground in early spring and will come back strong (if roots weren't killed) and produce bloom and berries the same season. Should normally be pruned in late winter or early spring. Heavy spring pruning results in more vigorous growth and heavier fruit set. You should remove dead wood and cut old wood back to new growth.

OLD SHRUB NEEDS SEVERE PRUNING

IF CUT TO GROUND IN EARLY SPRING, WILL PRODUCE BLOSSOMS AND BERRIES IN SAME SEASON

CUT BACK to the ground in early spring, callicarpa will come back strong.

CALLISTEMON. Bottlebrush. Evergreen shrubs or trees. Unpruned plants may become leggy, open, and straggly. Remove dead twigs and head back selected branches in spring for graceful, flower-producing plant. Fast growing, easy to train. Quick wall cover as informal espaliers. Several kinds can be trained as small trees. Some can be used in formal clipped hedges or as informal screens or windbreaks. A few can be trained as ground covers.

C. citrinus (*C. lanceolatus*). Lemon bottlebrush. Massive shrub; grows to 10-15 ft. Make cuts in leafy parts of branches; if cut farther back, die-back often results. Train overgrown shrub into multi or single-stemmed tree. Grown as espalier, it will need occasional selective removal of errant growth.

C. salignus. White bottlebrush. Shrub or tree. Train as small shade tree or plant 4-5 ft. apart as hedge.

C. viminalis. Weeping bottlebrush. Shrub or small tree. Rapid grower. Has pendulous branches. Train as tree by staking main stem; thin surplus branches to prevent top-heavy growth. Also attractive when allowed to grow naturally with branches sweeping to the ground.

CALOCEDRUS decurrens (*Libocedrus decurrens*). Incense cedar. Evergreen tree. To grow as hedge, plant trees about 6 ft. apart. Clip or shear whenever necessary; branches will remain full to ground. If they become overgrown near house or fence as they mature, remove lower limbs and expose 8-10 ft. of trunk to relieve crowding at ground level. When planted alone and the trunk is not cut back, it will grow as tall, columnar ornamental or shade-producing tree.

CALOCEPHALUS brownii. Cushion bush. Evergreen shrubby perennial. Light pruning keeps the plant in shape. Whenever growth gets too dense, thin it by removing some branches. Cut out dead wood at anytime.

CALOTHAMNUS. Net bush. Evergreen shrubs. Thin and head back heavily after flowering to keep plants from getting straggly. Generally not attractive in age, showing more wood than foliage.

CALYCANTHUS. Sweet shrub. Deciduous shrubs.

C. floridus. Carolina allspice. Prune after flowering. Take out oldest stems and branches; thin to shape.

C. occidentalis. Spice bush. Can be trained into multi-stemmed small tree. Will grow to 8 ft. or more with widespreading habit, but can be kept smaller and more compact by selective thinning and pinching of errant growth. Thin arching branches in fall.

CAMELLIA. Evergreen shrubs. Among the most adaptable of plants, camellias can be grown as shrubs, trees and standards, and low hedges. Also good subjects for bonsai, dwarfing, and espaliers.

General pruning rules: best time to prune is when the blooms begin to fade, but good results are obtained even if pruning is delayed into summer and fall. Remove spent flowers to prevent seed formation. Remove undesirable growth at any time of year. Whenever possible, make cuts just above scars that mark spots where one year's growth ended and the next year's began. The scars are slightly thickened, somewhat rough areas where bark texture and color change slightly (see photos below).

PENCIL POINTS OUT where to cut camellia (just above slightly thickened, rough area) to avoid leggy plant.

BUSHY PLANT develops when correct cuts force dormant buds into growth.

Cut just above these areas to force 3 or 4 dormant buds into growth, creating bushier shrubs. Common error for gardeners confronted with leggy camellia is to head it back. Such random cutting normally results in only 1 bud being activated beneath the cut. This causes formation of another long, willowy branch, compounding the problem.

Start pruning and shaping a camellia when the plant is very young, preferably when only a single stem. Continue to control and shape it throughout its lifetime. Drastic pruning can be kept to a minimum if you remove new growth as described above. Overgrown, unshapely, or scraggly camellias are quite tolerant of heavy pruning, except for *C. reticulata*. Most other kinds replace removed wood with new, vigorous growth, provided they have good and healthy root systems.

Some camellias are more vinelike than others and will develop unattractively into leggy, gangly shapes if left to follow their natural bent. To keep them growing straight, stake and then cut to shape them into umbrella forms. If camellias are spreading excessively and growing too close to ground, cut off lowest branches, shorten some downward growing ones, and stake the trunks into upward growing positions.

Pruning container camellias: roots of container-planted camellias should be cut back periodically. A recommended way is to prune ¼ of outer roots each 6 months. With square container, simply shave 1 in. off one side; with round container, take 1 in. off ¼ of the circumference every 6 months. With this control, plant will grow slowly and produce bumper crops of blooms season after season. If a container camellia has been allowed to dry out to the stage where its root ball has shrunk from the side, subsequent watering may flow through gap between root ball and container rather than through root ball. In this case, a form of root pruning will be necessary to save plant. This is the procedure to follow:

1. Remove camellia from container and wash off outside inch of soil.

2. Prune destroyed roots (as many as half the roots may have been destroyed) and repot plant in fresh humus.

3. Prune top of plant by cutting back to main trunk all the long thin branches of old wood that carry no latent buds. Then head back to strong laterals the larger branches that also need to be removed for desired shape. (If plant has lost a great number of leaves during its drought, postpone some top pruning. The injured root system must have leaves to help it grow quickly.)

Pruning overgrown camellias: if your camellia is too big and tall, cut down to size in 2 stages a year or more apart. Starting in late winter or early spring, just before new growth begins, cut all side branches off main stem except for tuft at top (necessary for plant to nourish itself). At the same time, dig 2 trenches on opposite sides of plant. Replace removed soil with soil mixed with ground bark, peat moss, well-rotted sawdust, or other organic matter. Vigorous new shoots will soon appear along bare trunk. Select those needed to form new, lower framework, and rub other shoots off. If next year's growth is vigorous and ample enough, cut off old trunk above top branch of new low clump of foliage. (You may prefer to wait another year for the topping back.) Finally, dig and refill 2 more trenches as illustrated in the drawings below to complete circle of new soil around the plant.

Disbudding: many varieties of camellias (particularly the Japonicas) set more buds than they can properly mature. Some will drop a high percentage of excess buds of their own accord. Reluctant as a gardener may be to deliberately twist flower buds off his choice camellia, it is recommended procedure in many cases because it results in better flowers at blooming time.

CAMELLIA FLOWER BUD being removed. Skinny bud, upper right, is a leaf bud.

Whether or not to disbud, and to what extent, depends upon variety of camellia as well as effect you desire. Reticulatas set fewer buds than Japonicas and are naturally large flowered, so there is no point in disbudding them. Small-flowered hybrid varieties and Sasanquas set large numbers of buds, but heavy disbudding will spoil the free-flowering quality that is part of their appeal. You should be able to distinguish flower buds from long, slender leaf buds at

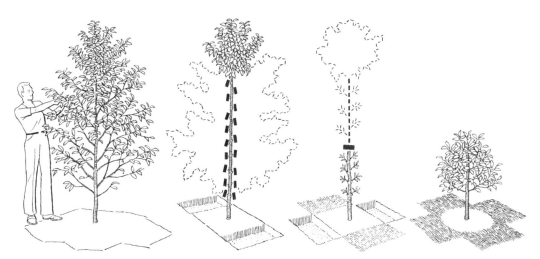

CUT an overgrown camellia down to size in this way: cut off side branches as shown in illustration second from left. Dig two trenches. Refill with conditioned soil. A year later, cut trunk above clump of new foliage (third illustration). Dig and refill two more trenches.

base of each cluster by midsummer, and you can disbud at that time. Before removing any flower bud, find the narrow, pointed leaf bud — it is often hidden among the flower buds—and be careful not to damage it.

CAMPANULA. Bellflower. Mostly perennial, some biennial, a few annual. Pick old, faded flowers off regularly for prolonged bloom, new growth.

CAMPHOR TREE.
See Cinnamomum camphora.

CAMPSIS. Trumpet creeper, trumpet vine. Deciduous vine. Every year in early spring, shorten some branches to 2 or 3 buds and thin out others. Remove dead and weak wood. Remember that blossoms are formed on young new growth, so if you cut off too much wood, you'll reduce flower crop. Pinch vine back frequently during growing season to keep plant bushy and well foliaged at base. Old plant sometimes becomes top-heavy and pulls away from supporting surface unless thinned. Will spread through garden and into neighbors' yards by suckering roots. Persistent; will grow from piece of root left in soil. Can be trained as big shrub, flowering hedge if branches are shortened after first year's growth and then sheared whenever necessary.

CANARY BIRD BUSH.
See Crotalaria agatiflora.

CANDLE BUSH.
See Cassia.

CANDYTUFT.
See Iberis.

CANNA. Tuberous rootstock. After first frost, cut off all leaf stalks and dig up the rootstalks. In warm, frost-free areas, cannas may be left in ground during winter. They will remain green most of the year. In fall, after flower clusters have bloomed, cut stalks to ground.

CANTUA buxifolia. Magic flower, sacred flower of the Incas. Evergreen shrub. Scraggly, open growth. Thin after flowering to shape as desired.

CAPE FORGET-ME-NOT.
See Anchusa capensis.

CAPE FUCHSIA.
See Phygelius capensis.

CAPE HONEYSUCKLE.
See Tecomaria capensis.

CAPE PLUMBAGO.
See Plumbago auriculata.

CARAGANA arborescens. Siberian peashrub. Deciduous shrub or small tree. With heavy pruning, you can keep it any height you want. Pruning regularly helps curb leggy tendency, promotes dense growth. When trained to grow as small tree, it will reach 18 or 20 ft. with 12-ft. spread. Prune after flowering, trim off blooms as soon as they fade and before seeds ripen and scatter; you'll avoid later nuisance of many volunteer seedlings. Use as windbreak, clipped hedge, cover for wildlife. Attractive small tree.

CARICA papaya. Papaya. Evergreen tree or greenhouse plant. If cut back to 2 or 3 ft. from ground in spring, the normally straight, branchless trunk will send out side shoots that thicken and bear fruit. Keep only 2 or 3 of these side shoots; if you let all develop, fruits will be small.

CARISSA grandiflora. Natal plum. Evergreen shrub. Can be heavily pruned and may be trained as clipped hedge, espalier, or ground cover, or grown as single shrub. Beware of spiny stems. Naturally sprawling, but young plant can be trained to open-form shrub by cutting off low-growing stems and encouraging balanced framework of branches. Shape by removing unwanted growth when necessary. Older shrub may send out erratic shoots, making the plant lopsided. Cut these off as they appear, to bring the plant back into balance. Spring

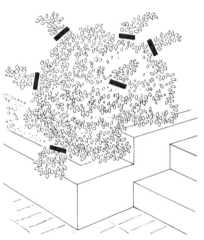

MAINTAIN PLEASING SHAPE of carissa by removing errant growth.

is best time to prune in order not to interfere with fruit and flower production. Do not prune after September where there is danger of frost. Important: remove old twiggy or dead growth. Thin some old wood yearly or plant becomes very woody. Plant can be restrained to 3-5 ft. with annual pruning.

CARMEL CREEPER.
See Ceanothus griseus horizontalis.

CARNATION.
See Dianthus.

CAROB.
See Ceratonia siliqua.

CAROLINA ALLSPICE.
See Calycanthus floridus.

CAROLINA JESSAMINE.
See Gelsemium sempervirens.

CAROLINA LAUREL CHERRY.
See Prunus caroliniana.

CARPENTERIA californica. Bush anemone. Evergreen shrub. Prune after flowering to restrain growth or shape. Because leaves tend to discolor in cold weather, many faded leaves and branchlets make plant look somewhat untidy during winter and early spring. New foliage will hide them, but you may want to trim these off as soon as frosts are past.

CARPET BUGLE.
See Ajuga.

CARPINUS. Hornbean. Deciduous trees. Respond well to heavy pruning but rarely require it. Prune in late winter or early spring before new growth appears. Adaptable; can be trained and clipped into large or small hedges or screens if desired.

CARROT WOOD.
See Cupaniopsis anacardioides.

CARYA illinoinensis (*Carya pecan*). Pecan. Deciduous tree. Needs only normal early training and guidance. Prune mature tree only to shape or to remove dead, weak wood. Do this anytime.

CARYOPTERIS. Bluebeard. Deciduous shrubs. Will freeze back in colder areas. Cut frost-damaged tops back in spring. New growth will appear quickly when weather warms. In areas where they don't freeze back, cut back to ground in early spring to keep them compact and encourage strong new growth and better bloom.

CARYOTA.
See Palm.

CASIMIROA edulis. White sapote. Evergreen or erratically, briefly deciduous tree. Unpruned, it will reach 30 ft. in height, with an equal spread, but you can keep the tree lower by selectively thinning out some branches and heading back those that grow higher than you want whenever necessary. Normally branches almost to ground, but you can train it as umbrella-shaped shade tree by pinching out terminal buds to encourage lateral branching and by removing lower branches as the young tree spreads out. Thinning in spring may reduce crop during main bearing season, but it stimulates the tree into producing a second crop and stretches the bearing season to 4 or 5 months.

CASSIA. Senna. Evergreen, partially evergreen, or deciduous shrubs, trees. You prune all of them after flowering, though some need more than others.

C. alata. Candle bush. Deciduous shrub. Prune freely after flowering.

C. artemisioides. Feathery cassia. Evergreen shrub. Prune this plant lightly after flowering. Stems tend to be long and sprawly unless the plant is kept trimmed.

C. bicapsularis. Evergreen shrub. Prune heavily after flowering.

C. corymbosa. Flowery senna. Large evergreen shrub. Prune hard after flowering.

C. excelsa (*C. carnaval*). Crown of gold tree. Partially evergreen tree. Fast growing; prune hard after flowering.

C. nairobensis. This one is a stump sprouter and should be cut back regularly. To induce longer bloom period, remove flowering stems one at a time, as soon as blossoms fade.

C. splendida. Golden wonder senna. Evergreen shrub. This name has been applied to a number of cassias of varying growth habits. All require much thinning after flowering.

C. surattensis (*C. glauca*). Evergreen shrub. Does not need to be pruned heavily; grows fast to 6-8 ft. and spreads wider.

C. tomentosa. Woolly senna. Evergreen shrub. Vigorous, rank growth; prune heavily after flowering.

CASTANEA. Chestnut. Deciduous trees. Give normal training and guidance for form and strong framework when young. Need only corrective pruning when mature. Some are susceptible to a fungus; remove blighted parts completely whenever they appear. Do major pruning in dormant period.

CASTANOPSIS. Chinquapin. Evergreen trees and shrubs. Little care after established, though they respond well to pruning at any time.

C. chrysophylla. Giant chinquapin. Tree or shrubby tree. Adaptable, can be trained from start into desired form.

C. c. minor. Golden chinquapin. Shrubby, very adaptable to pruning. Makes good, dense hedge.

C. sempervirens. Bush chinquapin, Sierra chinquapin. Shrub to 8 ft. Grows naturally in thickets, useful as low, ground-covering shrub. Can be kept under 8 ft. by removing upright growth.

CASTOR BEAN.
See Ricinus communis.

CASUARINA. Beefwood, she-oak. Evergreen trees. Give young trees normal training; then prune only as required to shape. Thin out center branches as necessary to let air and light inside. Can be pruned anytime.

CATALINA CHERRY.
See Prunus lyonii.

CATALINA IRONWOOD.
See Lyonothamnus floribundus.

CATALPA. Deciduous tree. Catalpas branch close to the ground. If you're growing one to live under, train a 10-12-ft. whip to produce trunk of desired height before heading it back to force side branching. Do major pruning during dormant season.

C. bignonioides. Common catalpa. Train as above to get tree tall enough to walk under. Needs very little pruning thereafter, except to remove damaged wood. Can be pollarded (see page 23).

C. b. 'Nana'. (Almost always sold as *C. bungei*.) Umbrella catalpa. This variety is grafted 6-7 ft. from ground to form dense, umbrellalike head. Cut it back each winter to old wood to keep in scale, retain its tight formal outline. Winter form after pruning is nothing more than a bare stick with switches on the end.

C. speciosa. Western catalpa. Train and selectively prune tall trunk and umbrella-shaped crown.

CATHA edulis. Khat. Evergreen shrub. Start pinching early to shape it. Can grow as high as 20 ft. but can be kept from 3-8 ft. high by selectively thinning and heading back upright growth. Effective when trained as espalier. Prune when necessary.

CATMINT.
See Nepeta mussinii.

CATNIP.
See Nepeta cataria.

CAT'S CLAW.
See Doxantha unguis-cati.

CEANOTHUS. Wild lilac. Mostly evergreen shrubs, small trees, or ground covers (a few are deciduous). Prune after flowering. Shape during growing season with frequent pinching out of undesirable, errant growth. Best to avoid drastic, annual pruning because heavy pruning of some species leads to fungus attack, with resulting dieback and possible loss of plant. Try to limit pruning cuts to branches no thicker than a pencil. (Do not prune in rainy, wet weather, as the fungus is spread by rain.) You should, of course, cut out diseased wood by cutting well back into healthy tissue. Treat these pruning cuts with a wound dressing, disinfect your pruning tools, and discard cuttings in an area where they cannot infect healthy plants.

C. arboreus. Feltleaf ceanothus. Large shrub or small tree. Prune lightly but frequently to shape.

C. a. 'Ray Hartman'. Big shrub or small tree. Easily shaped into single or multi-stemmed tree. Heavy pruning will inhibit flowering for a year.

C. cyaneus 'Sierra Blue'. Shrub. Has neat erect form and ability to withstand

clipping. Useful as hedges and high screens. Can be shaped lightly into attractive informal screen.

C. delilianus. Deciduous shrub. Flowers on new wood, looks best with annual pruning in late winter or early spring. Shorten main branches back 12-18 in. and cut secondary branches back to 2-6 buds.

C. 'Gloire de Versailles.' Deciduous shrub. Prune as you would *C. delilianus* (above). Can also be trained against wall where space is at a premium.

C. gloriosus. Point Reyes ceanothus. Ground cover. You can keep plant flat and as low as 8 in. if you pinch out tips of upright shoots.

C. griseus horizontalis. Carmel creeper. Ground cover. In its natural environment, Carmel creeper is kept low and spreading by coastal winds. In garden environment, prune as follows to get effect you want: for low spreading effect, thin and cut back as often as necessary branches that tend to grow upright. For more upright, bushy plant, do less shortening and thinning of stronger growing branches. Heaviest pruning should be done in late summer just before new growth starts in fall. This rampant grower may tend to get leggy with age. Shape with frequent pinching out of unwanted growth.

C. impressus. Santa Barbara ceanothus. Shrub. Pinch growing tips frequently to induce bushiness, prevent legginess.

C. i. 'Mountain Haze'. Shrub. Responds well to clipping and pruning.

C. 'Julia Phelps'. Shrub. Pinch to shape when young. Prune lightly after bloom. Can be trained as big screen planting, or single shrub.

C. 'Mary Lake'. High ground cover. Prune lightly when young. Trailing branches take root; pull them out to control.

C. prostratus. Squaw carpet, Mahala mat. Ground cover. Forms dense mat that spreads by rooting branches. Prune only as needed to control.

C. pumilus. Low shrub, ground cover. Habit and pruning requirements same as *C. prostratus*.

C. thyrsiflorus. Blue blossom. Shrub or small tree. Variable in growth. Pinch to shape when young.

C. t. repens. Creeping blue blossom. Ground cover. Keep it flat by pinching back upright growth.

CEDAR.
See Cedrus.

CEDAR, INCENSE.
See Calocedrus decurrens.

CEDAR, WESTERN RED.
See Thuja plicata.

CEDRELA. Deciduous or evergreen trees. Normal training for shape and to form good branch structure when young; as trees mature, prune only to shape when necessary.

CEDRUS. Cedar. Evergreen trees.

C. atlantica. Atlas cedar. Needs very little pruning. On young tree, branches may often appear to get too long and heavy. This may sometimes be corrected by pinching or cutting back the tips, but don't be in too much of a hurry to do this. As the tree matures, what first appeared to be an ungainly form often turns out to be shapely. Branches occasionally mat together, cutting out light and air circulation from body of tree, resulting in dieback. Thin out by cutting selected, unwanted branches back to trunk. Do major pruning in spring.

C. deodara. Deodar cedar. Most gardeners will want to plant this tree in area large enough for natural growth to display its grace and charm. However, annual pruning in late spring will keep shape you want. To control spread of tree, cut new growth of side branches halfway back in late spring. This will

SIDE PRUNE a deodar cedar by cutting the branches back to top-facing shoots.

make tree more dense. You can keep this naturally tall-growing tree as low as 4-6 ft. by cutting leader back each year and taping a suitable side branch into vertical position as new tip. Will also tolerate shearing.

C. libani. Cedar of Lebanon. Slow growing. Pruning should be done in spring and kept to minimum.

CELASTRUS. Bittersweet. Deciduous vines. Vigorous, rampant vines capable of strangling young trees if not checked. Will become tangled mass of intertwining branches unless pruned on a regular basis. Cut out fruiting branches in winter, pinch out tips of vigorous branches during the summer. Old plants can be renewed by cutting them to ground while dormant.

CELTIS. Hackberry. Deciduous trees. Normal training for good form and structure while young. Need only thinning, removal of unwanted wood when mature. This corrective pruning can be done anytime.

CENTRANTHUS ruber (*Valeriana rubra*). Jupiter's beard, red valerian, gate lilac. Perennial. Cut off old stems after flowering to shape plant and prolong bloom.

CENTURY PLANT.
See Agave americana.

CEPHALOTAXUS harringtonia. Korean yew. Evergreen tree. Shrubby and slow growing. Useful as a hedge or screen. Very little pruning required except to shape it in form desired. Do this anytime.

CERASTIUM tomentosum. Snow-in-summer. Perennial. How far it spreads or hangs down is up to you. Clip back or pull out whenever it gets out of bounds. In desert gardens don't shear heavily during the hot season. After flowers turn brown, you have three choices: shear back tops with hedge shears, leaving plant clean of dead flowers but shorn of its usual softness; pull dead flowers out of their sockets individually or by the handful (though a tedious and slow job, this keeps the attractive mounding form intact); or just ignore the dead flowers. In a couple of months, the foliage mass will grow enough to swallow them up. Looks shabby in cold winters, but revives rapidly in spring.

CERATONIA siliqua. Carob, St. John's bread. Evergreen large shrub or tree. Tends to branch low to the ground. Easily trained to form high crown by heading trunk at about 7 ft., forcing side branches at that point. Though it can stand heavy pruning and reshaping, drastic cutting isn't necessary if you thin and shape regularly each winter from the start. Allowed to grow naturally, it maintains a bushy form with branches to ground. Often multi-stemmed. Use this way as a big hedge, informal or trimmed. Train it as a compact hedge by topping stems low and letting it spread.

CERATOSTIGMA plumbaginoides. (Often sold as *Plumbago larpentae*.) Dwarf plumbago. Perennial ground cover. Cut declining top growth to the ground after flowering.

CERCIDIPHYLLUM japonicum. Katsura tree. Deciduous tree. Slow growing. Give normal training and guidance when young; very little pruning required when established. May form multiple trunks. For a slender, more upright tree, remove all but one of the multiple trunks.

CERCIDIUM. Palo verde. Deciduous trees. Require pruning only when necessary (regardless of season) to shape them. Watch out for sharp spines.

CERCIS. Redbud. Deciduous shrubs or trees. Confine pruning to removal of dead and weak branches and cutting out any off-balance growth. Best time to prune is in spring before new growth appears. To train tops to canopy shapes, cut upright branches back to good laterals. Remove branches competing with leaders but never cut leaders.

CERCOCARPUS. Mountain-mahogany. Evergreen or partially deciduous tall shrubs or small trees. Will take heavy pruning, which may be necessary to maintain the form you desire. Can be trained as dense screening plants or as trees. Cut old, straggly plants back to ground to renew. Best time to prune is early spring.

CEREUS peruvianus. Cactus. Corrective pruning when necessary is all that is normally required.

CESTRUM. Evergreen shrubs. May freeze back in heavy frosts. Wait until after spring growth starts to remove frost-damaged wood. Fast growing, inclined to be rangy and top-heavy unless thinned out and headed back frequently. Nip back growing tips regularly for compactness and cut back severely after flowering or fruiting.

C. nocturnum. Night jessamine. Cut flowering (new) wood back to about 6 in. immediately after bloom. This will usually bring on new growth and flowering in fall.

CHAENOMELES. (Some formerly called *Cydonia*.) Flowering quince. Deciduous shrubs. Left alone, quince can grow into a thicket, their flowers nearly hidden by the tangles. Start training them as young shrubs. Select main branches as skeletons of plants and remove the rest. Because flowering quince blooms on wood that is one or more years old, it is one of the few spring-flowering shrubs you can prune in winter and still get blooms. With an eye to maintaining their delicate, open symmetry, cut back new growth at least ⅓, thin out weak or crossing branches, and remove suckers. On older or neglected quince, remove weak branches, suckers, and crossed limbs. Shorten strong branches you wish to keep. Reclaim old bushes gradually over a period of several seasons by cutting out oldest wood.

Many gardeners like to prune in the tight bud season in winter, using cut branches for indoor arrangements. The new growth that follows will bear next year's flowers. Plants also respond well to consistent summer pruning to divert growing strength into main branches and into formation of next year's flowers. Each summer, as soon as your shrubs have made most of their new growth, cut back by half on the main shoots and trim laterals back to 2 or 3 leaves. Slow down subsequent growth by rationing late summer water and keep fertilization to a minimum.

CHAMAECYPARIS. False cypress. Evergreen trees, shrubs, and shrublets. Stimulate new growth, control size and shape by pinching branch tips in spring.

C. lawsoniana. Lawson cypress, Port Orford cedar. Normally grows to more than 60 ft. but can be topped and held at 10 ft. As a hedge plant, it takes shearing very well. Shear in early spring and later as needed.

C. l. 'Forsteckensis'. Forsteck cypress. Makes a dense, informal hedge.

C. obtusa. Hinoki false cypress. Splendid bonsai subject. Prune to shape when necessary.

C. o. 'Crippsii'. Conical growth to 30 ft. but can be kept lower by pruning as necessary. Effective with branches spaced at various levels.

C. pisifera (*Retinospora pisifera*). Sawara false cypress. Head back or shear heavily to force new growth, hide dead foliage on inner branches.

C. p. 'Plumosa'. Plume false cypress. Leave it unpruned as tree or carefully prune it into big shrub. Remove lower branches which die or lose vigor. Can also be sheared to shape it.

C. p. 'Plumosa Aurea'. Pinch tips frequently to restrain growth, promote density.

C. p. 'Squarrosa'. Moss cypress. Should be thinned out as it ages to give more character.

CHAMAEDOREA.
See Palm.

CHAMAELAUCIUM uncinatum. (Sometimes sold as *C. ciliatum*.) Geraldton waxflower. Evergreen shrub. Cut freely for arrangements or cut back after

flowering to maintain a better balanced shape.

CHAMOMILE.
See Anthemis nobilis.

CHASTE TREE.
See Vitex.

CHERRY. Deciduous fruit tree. Young cherry trees tend to grow long, pendulous branches without properly placed laterals. As trees develop, new growth should be pinched or headed back to encourage proper branching. Mature cherries bear fruit on short spurs which have a productive life of 10-12 years or more. These spurs grow very slowly, and because of their longevity, mature cherry trees require less pruning than other deciduous fruit trees. About all that is required is removal of dead or weak wood. Take out no more than 10 percent of oldest wood each dormant season. Another good way to prune is to pinch soft tips of new growth in summer.

CHERRY, BRUSH.
See Syzygium paniculatum.

CHERRY, CATALINA.
See Prunus lyonii.

CHERRY, FLOWERING.
See Prunus.

CHESTNUT.
See Castanea.

CHILEAN JASMINE.
See Mandevilla laxa.

CHILOPSIS linearis. Desert willow. Deciduous large shrub or small tree. Tends to be ragged and undisciplined; needs some heading back and thinning out to keep it in shape. Do major pruning while dormant.

CHIMONANTHUS praecox (*C. fragrans, Meratia praecox*). Wintersweet. Deciduous shrub. Cut branches back to good lateral or promising bud during bloom or right afterwards (or you can cut branches in bud to force into flower indoors). Like most other spring flowering plants, wintersweet bears its flowers on last season's wood. Thorough pruning, as described above, will stimulate new growth during spring and summer and produce more flowers next season. After it reaches 8-10 ft., you can make a small, multi-trunked tree out of it by cutting weakest trunks to the ground and removing the twiggy growth from bottoms of trunks that remain.

CHINA-BERRY.
See Melia.

CHINA FIR.
See Cunninghamia lanceolata.

CHINESE ANGELICA.
See Aralia chinensis.

THREAD SAWARA FALSE CYPRESS (Chamaecyparis pisifera 'Filifera'), like other varieties of Sawara cypress, can be clipped and opened out into layered mounds.

CHINESE BELLFLOWER.
See Abutilon.

CHINESE LANTERN.
See Abutilon.

CHINESE PISTACHE.
See Pistacia chinensis.

CHINESE TALLOW TREE.
See Sapium sebiferum.

CHINESE WITCH HAZEL.
See Hamamelis mollis.

CHINQUAPIN.
See Castanopsis.

CHIONANTHUS. Fringe tree. Deciduous trees. Use as slow-growing, airy shrubs or attractive small trees. Once established in forms you want they don't require much pruning. Thin and head back as needed to control size and shape. Cut some of oldest stems to ground, if trained as shrubs, to renew. Prune after bloom, as flowers are borne on tips of branches. Heading back in winter and spring will reduce bloom.

CHIRANTHODENDRON pentadactylon (*C. platanoides*). Monkey hand tree. Evergreen tree. Fast growing with brittle wood and undisciplined habit. Thin out and head back regularly to promote bushiness. Tree tends to be top-heavy and may topple in a strong windstorm. To lessen this danger, thin out selected branches so that the wind can pass through.

CHLOROPHYTUM comosum (*C. capense*). Spider plant. Evergreen perennial. When used as a ground cover, keep it in bounds by removing the long, arching flower stems before they take root in adjacent garden bed.

CHOISYA ternata. Mexican orange. Evergreen shrub. A fast grower, it will respond well to heavy pruning. Prune after flowering and pinch tips throughout growing season as required to shape. Thinning out older branches in center of plant encourages production of new wood. Cut freely for decoration when in bloom. After blooming, remove spent flowers but don't shear. Older, very woody plant benefits from severe cutting back and will sprout from the stump.

CHOKEBERRY, RED.
See Aronia arbutifolia.

CHORISIA speciosa. Floss silk tree. Evergreen to briefly deciduous tree. Prune only when required to shape. Remove dead wood when needed.

CHORIZEMA. Flame pea. Evergreen shrubs. Keep plants bushy and free blooming by thinning and heading back heavily after they flower.

CHRISTMAS BERRY.
See Heteromeles arbutifolia.

CHRYSANTHEMUM. Annuals, perennials. Procedure for cutting plants back after bloom in fall depends on whether or not you live in frost-free area. In cold winter areas, let plants fade after flowering. Then cut back in stages by first removing faded flowers, then top half of stems, and finally remaining stalks to within 8 in. of ground. This gradual cutting back helps to minimize shock to plants. Before late fall or early winter, all plants should have been cut down, ready for lifting and storing. If you live in a mild climate (and soil is well drained) you can cut plants back to ground after bloom and leave roots in ground.

Chrysanthemums need growth control. Allowed to grow unchecked, they'll be sprawling by blooming time. For sturdy plants and big flowers, pinch them frequently, beginning at planting time by removing tips of new plants. Select 1-4 lateral shoots which will form continued growth. Continue pinching all summer, nipping top pair of leaves on every shoot that reaches 5 in. On some early-blooming cushion varieties, or in coldest regions, pinching should be stopped in mid-August. Stake plants to keep them upright. To produce big, showy blooms, disbud by removing all flower buds except for 1 (or 2) in each cluster. If you want masses of color, leave buds alone.

TO DISBUD CHRYSANTHEMUM, remove all buds except two shown. When the end bud is bigger, remove the other one.

C. balsamita. Costmary. A weedy perennial. Spreads rapidly; pull up rooted stems to thin. Keep it at 8-10 in. by cutting back vigorously. Or just cut back the leggy stems to encourage attractive basal leaves.

C. coccineum (*Pyrethrum roseum*). Painted daisy, pyrethrum. Bushy perennial. Early bloomer. If cut to ground after bloom, may flower again in late summer.

TREE CHRYSANTHEMUM. Lower shoots removed in spring, tops pinched 4 times.

C. frutescens. Marguerite, Paris daisy. Perennial. Start pinching or cutting back marguerite as soon as small plant is set out to make it branch. Keep it up through summer. If left alone, it frequently takes on lopsided shape and becomes woody. Then if you cut back very hard, it may never recover, for marguerite can't withstand shock of heavy trimming. Blooms almost all year if protected from frost and if you pick off faded flowers. Keep healthy and productive by pruning lightly at frequent intervals. Remember to cut green wood only; you can kill plant by cutting into hard wood since it seldom produces new growth. (This is especially true in hot climates.)

C. maximum. Shasta daisy. Perennial. Commercial growers cut plants back after peak bloom period in spring to get another flush of new growth and second crop of blooms. Home gardeners preferring continuous bloom should keep old flowers picked off regularly. In mild areas this will result in year-round bloom; in colder areas, it will keep plant blooming from early spring until killing frosts.

CHRYSOLARIX amabilis (*Pseudolarix amabilis, P. kaempferi*). Golden larch. Deciduous conifer. Slow growing, needs only normal training while young, very little pruning later. Makes good bonsai or container plant when young. Confine pruning to most dormant period.

CIGAR PLANT.
See Cuphea ignea.

CINNAMOMUM camphora. Camphor tree. Evergreen tree. Slow to moderate growth, needs only early training, little pruning later. Subject to root rot, causing twigs and branches to show brownish discoloration. Cut out damaged wood at any time.

CINQUEFOIL.
See Potentilla.

CISSUS. Evergreen vines. Climb by tendrils. Outdoors in mild climates, prune when necessary to avoid tangling or overgrowth and to remove dead or damaged wood. If you grow them as house plants, tip-pinch to control stem length and promote branching.

CISTUS. Rockrose. Evergreen shrubs. Generally, rockroses tend to resent heavy pruning (though there are instances where drastically pruned plants came back as vigorously as before). Happily, their form and growth make heavy pruning generally unnecessary. If you want to give plants a neater appearance, remove a few branches at a time, enabling these to start new growth before you cut back other branches. All branches should have some foliage left, or they may not grow again. Rockroses can be kept in bounds either by constantly pinching back or by a light annual pruning right after flowering. Some gardeners don't prune at all, preferring to let the plants grow naturally in tumbled masses. But you may find it necessary to remove deadwood occasionally.

CITRUS. Evergreen trees and shrubs. These do not require as much pruning as deciduous fruit trees. Because citrus fruits are borne at ends of current season's growth, it's not necessary to prune for large amounts of wood renewal. Pruning requirements vary within the group and are also somewhat determined by whether you are growing your citrus as an ornamental or for fruit production (probably a compromise in most home gardens). Specific pruning directions for citrus forms that need it are given at the end of this section.

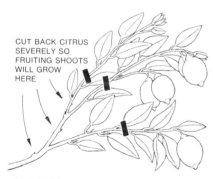

CUT BACK CITRUS SEVERELY SO FRUITING SHOOTS WILL GROW HERE

CUT OFF branch ends to encourage fruit to be borne nearer center of tree.

When young, all citrus must be pruned and shaped for form. Some vigorous growers will send out branches unevenly beyond the mass of the tree. If you want even growth (in youth as well as maturity), cut shoots way back to a good lateral or to main branches at

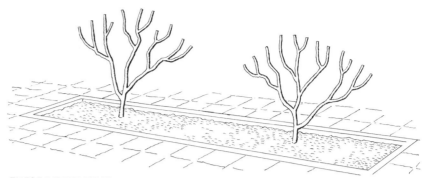

THESE WERE LANKY, overgrown tangerine plants. Cut back to 12-inch stubs in March.

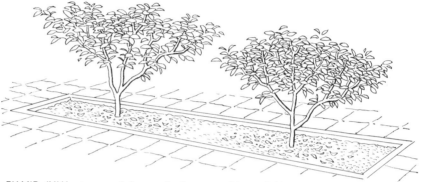

BY MID-JULY, new growth forms a leafy canopy 2 feet tall. No crop for several years.

any time. Constantly pinch back tips of any new growth that threatens to take off alone. Most citrus growers strive for compact, bushy trees. Prune anytime in frost-free areas; wait until danger of frost is past in colder areas.

PRUNING TO REINVIGORATE OLD CITRUS TREES

As orange and lemon trees get older, they tend to lose vigor, fill up with deadwood, and produce less and less new growth capable of good fruit production. This is the time to prune them all heavily to encourage new growth and better fruit production. Here are some things you can do:

Topping: Remove top limbs that keep light from lower branches. Removing 2 or 3 limbs each year won't reduce crop.

Brushing out: Remove deadwood; this lets more light through the branches and forces some growth all over tree.

Hedging: Cut back side branches of tree 1-3 ft. This encourages new growth.

In frost-free areas, these jobs can be done in January. Wait until all danger of frost is past in inland and desert areas.

PRUNING DWARF CITRUS

Same general pruning rules apply to dwarf citrus, except that they require less pruning per tree than normal-sized plant. But here too you may want

to renew an old plant and develop stronger, lower, more compact branch framework. To do that, prune heavily. If you have healthy plant with sound root system, you can expect normal growth response to this renewal pruning, just as in other varieties.

Your approach can be drastic, cutting all trunks back to 12-in. stubs (do this only in spring, after danger of frost is past); or you can accomplish the same thing gradually and maintain more attractive, leafy plant. To accomplish this, prune successively in spring, summer, and fall, removing about ⅓ of the plant each time. Whichever method you use, follow-up care—especially during first 2 years after pruning—is extremely important.

A few weeks after pruning, closely spaced new shoots appear along stems, mostly toward the tips. Remove up to ½ of these; those you keep should be rather evenly spaced along the stems. Cut off any new growth from below bud union. Later, cut off a few more fastest growing shoots. To force remaining new growth to branch out, prune back tips when about 8 in. long. The resulting new branches should be tipped back, in turn, after they've grown about 8 in. long. At the same time, remove crowded branches; too-dense growth shades center of plant and restricts future flower and fruit production. Citrus pruned this heavily won't produce crop for 2 or 3 years.

(Continued on next page)

BARK PROTECTION ON PRUNED CITRUS

To protect newly exposed bark from sunburning, either coat it with white protective paint (often called "tree white") or build cloth-covered wood frame to shade plant from hot afternoon sun. Because of drastic reduction in size of plant, it requires much less water.

PRUNING ORNAMENTAL CITRUS

Generally, if you are growing your citrus mainly for appearance, prune them lightly as you would other broadleafed evergreens, removing wood that detracts from plant's shape and encouraging growth in direction you want it to take. Remove dead, damaged wood, too. But if you want good fruit production — especially with lemons — you'll have to prune more in the manner of the commercial growers. One obvious difference (apparent when you look at a commercial grove) is that producers usually leave lower branches on citrus even if they touch ground. Most of fruit crop comes on lower branches and it is easier to pick down there. Then, too, lower branches filter out light necessary for weeds so there are fewer of them to hoe.

Because citrus trees are sensitive to sunburn, you should avoid making large openings in the leaf canopy. Delay pruning out frost-damaged wood until danger of frost is past. Then cut back gradually until you come to live, green wood. The object is to prune out first live bud and leave next lower one to develop.

LEMONS

Lemons generally have a more scraggly, undisciplined growth habit than other citrus fruits and must be pruned more heavily to be kept under control. Lemons also respond much better to pruning cuts and produce new wood more readily. Young nursery tree should be headed back to about 3 ft. and 3 or 4 laterals selected. Head these back quite severely to balance top with reduced root system. As tree matures, encourage a few more well spaced laterals and strive for strong, compact structure.

A vigorous young lemon tree usually produces fair crop of strong growing, upright suckers each year. They emerge from trunk and run vertically up center of tree. Most of them should be snapped off. If tree has gaps in branch structure, however, you can turn a sucker into new scaffold branch quite simply. A sucker of the right age is limber enough to bend without snapping off if you grasp it

about a foot above point where it joins trunk. Slowly bend it in large arc toward the ground. Ordinarily, it will stay in desired position after you release it. If it's a bit too old, it might spring back; if it does, weight it with a small stone. New lateral shoots will grow out along top of arc to fill the gap in tree.

The awkward growth habit typical of lemons often results in long, pendulous branches carrying foliage at very end. These should be cut back severely to encourage fruiting shoots closer toward center of tree.

ORANGES

Once established, oranges require very little pruning beyond the removal of dead, crowded, twiggy growth. But they do require careful early training and pruning to help them establish strong framework.

Starting with young nursery tree, head back central leader (to about 3 ft.) as with the lemon, but head back laterals only lightly. In first 2 or 3 years, aim for strong framework with upright branches, keeping in mind that weight of foliage and fruit will bend branches down. Allow lower branches to remain on young tree, removing gradually to get clean trunk to height you want. As tree matures, remaining lower limbs will droop; keep the lowest high enough so that they clear the ground.

Sour orange, Seville orange (Citrus aurantium). These have dense and bushy growth and can be trained as trees, container plants, or (with heavy clipping and pruning) attractive hedges.

GRAPEFRUIT AND OTHER CITRUS

Prune as you do oranges: train to strong framework when young; very little pruning later.

CLADRASTIS lutea. Yellow wood. Deciduous tree. Training is important when tree is young. Occasionally in early summer shorten side branches that tend to spread widely. This shortening will also force a strong leading shoot. For a taller trunk, remove lower branches while tree is still young. Prune mature tree as required after bloom.

CLEMATIS. Deciduous, evergreen vines, sprawling perennials. When and how you prune depend upon time of flowering.

Clematis fall into three general groups: spring flowering, summer flowering, and those that flower in spring and then again in summer. The first group flowers on wood formed the previous season, the second blooms on new wood formed since spring growth started, and the third group flowers on year-old wood in spring

'EUREKA' LEMON trained as an espalier. To remain presentable, it needs regular pinching of vertical growth and occasional thinning of branchlets and twigs.

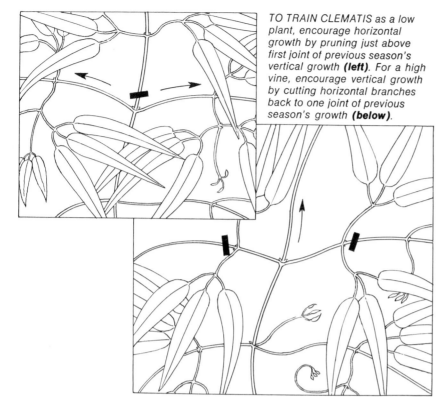

TO TRAIN CLEMATIS as a low plant, encourage horizontal growth by pruning just above first joint of previous season's vertical growth **(left)**. For a high vine, encourage vertical growth by cutting horizontal branches back to one joint of previous season's growth **(below)**.

and on new wood in summer. Prune heavily, just after flowering, those that flower only in spring. This will give the wood that will bear next spring's flowers the longest possible time to develop. You have two choices with those that bloom in summer. You can cut back after flowering in the fall, or you can wait until the buds swell in early spring. Cut to within 6-12 in. of the ground or to 2 or 3 buds for the first 2 or 3 years. Cut older plants to 2 ft. or less. Those types blooming both in spring and summer should have flowered portions pruned immediately after spring bloom; then prune in fall or early spring to remove unruly or excessive growth.

These basic techniques apply to all types. If you want a low plant with a maximum number of flowers, prune just above the first joint of the previous season's growth. For a higher vine, train the first leader to the height you want, and then cut back the side branches each year. Always leave one joint of previous year's growth on side branches. You can train clematis in many ways: on wire mesh frames in containers, on a fence or wall as a handsome tracery, twining up a tree, around a deck support or lamp post, or draping down a partly shaded bank.

C. armandii. Evergreen clematis. This evergreen vine blooms in spring, needs constant pruning after flowering to prevent tangling and buildup of dead thatch on inner parts of vine. Keep and tie up

stems you want, and cut out all others. Frequent pinching will hold the foliage to eye level. Normally makes a dense, heavy growth, but you can train it to produce a sharply defined outline. Cut out brown die-back.

C. chrysocoma. Deciduous vine. Blooms in spring on old wood, later blooms in summer from new wood.

C. 'Crimson King'. Flowers in early spring, again in summer.

C. davidiana. See *C. heracleifolia davidiana.*

C. dioscoreifolia (*C. paniculata*). Sweet autumn clematis. Blooms in late summer and fall. After bloom or in early spring, prune year's growth to 1 or 2 buds.

C. 'Duchess of Edinburgh'. Blooms in early spring, again in summer.

C. 'Ernest Markham'. Blooms in summer only.

C. 'Gypsy Queen'. Blooms in summer/fall only.

C. 'Hagley Hybrid'. Blooms in summer only.

C. heracleifolia davidiana. Blooms in summer only.

C. integrifolia. Flowers in June-July. Prune after bloom.

C. jackmanii. All flower in summer on new wood and do well with severe pruning in early spring as buds begin to swell. Freezes to ground in cold-winter areas. Can climb to 20 ft. in a single summer but is easily kept to 6 ft. by pruning.

C. lanuginosa. Blooms on old wood in spring, new wood in summer. After first flush of flowers, cut back flowered portions promptly for another crop later in summer. Then in early spring, prune lightly, removing only dead or weak growth.

C. 'Lasurstern'. Blooms in spring and again in summer.

C. lawsoniana. Spring and summer blooms.

C. 'Lord Neville'. Flowers in spring and summer.

C. macropetala. Downy clematis. Blooms in early spring followed by showy seed clusters, so delay your pruning until they fade. Then to remove dead, weak wood prune lightly in early spring as buds begin to swell.

C. 'Mme. Baron-Veillard'. Blooms in summer only.

C. montana. Anemone clematis. Flowers in early spring on old wood so it can be heavily thinned and cut back immediately after flowering to rejuvenate or to reduce size. A vigorous grower, it has a habit of climbing quickly to the top of its support and then growing into an untidy tangle. To avoid this, start training vine to grow horizontally when still young.

If an old vine seems hopelessly tangled, a good time to prune it is early spring, as soon as swelling buds indicate which stems are living, which dead. Cut out all deadwood, as well as poor, weak canes or stalks. (If stems are badly tangled, cut out deadwood in short sections rather than tugging at the whole stem.)

C. m. 'Rubens'. Less vigorous than above. Prune lightly after spring bloom.

C. m. 'Tetrarose'. More vigorous than above. Prune after spring bloom.

C. 'Mrs. Cholmondeley'. Vigorous, blooms in summer only.

C. 'Nelly Moser'. Blooms in spring and summer. Use where you want light tracery.

C. 'Ramona'. Spring and summer blooming.

C. 'Susan P. Emory'. Blooms both spring and summer.

C. tangutica. Golden clematis. Blooms in summer. After bloom, or in early spring, prune year's growth to 1 or 2 buds.

C. texensis. Scarlet clematis. Blooms in summer only.

C. 'The President'. Blooms in spring and summer.

C. viticella. Blooms in summer only.

CLERODENDRUM. Glorybower. Evergreen or deciduous shrubs, trees, or vines.

C. bungei (*C. foetidum*). Cashmere bouquet. Evergreen shrub. Rapid grower, suckers readily. Thin and head back thoroughly in spring and pinch back through the growing season to keep compact. Will form thicket if not restrained. Remove suckers when they appear.

C. thomsoniae (*C. balfouri*). Bleeding heart glorybower. Evergreen shrubby vine. Thin and head back heavily after bloom to keep a shrubby plant and to produce more flowers next year.

C. trichotomum. Harlequin glorybower. Deciduous shrub-tree. You may prune after flowering, but this will remove showy fruit. To enjoy both, delay pruning until plant becomes dormant. Keep it as a shrub by heading back and by removing tall branches. To train as tree, cut off all but strongest shoot you want to develop as main trunk. Remove suckers as they appear.

CLETHRA. Deciduous shrub and evergreen tree.

C. alnifolia. Summersweet, sweet pepperbush. Deciduous shrub. Has naturally upright habit, which fits it for hedging. But clipping results in twiggy growth at expense of pleasing natural form and flowers. Cut out overgrown old growth to renew. Prune to shape while dormant.

C. arborea. Lily-of-the-valley tree. Evergreen tree. Small, moderate rate of growth. Requires only normal training while young for form and structure and very little pruning thereafter, though it will tolerate it. If damaged or frozen back, it will grow from old wood or from the roots.

CLEYERA japonica (*Eurya ochnacea*). Evergreen shrub. Needs training and shaping when young to develop into desired form. Continue to shape as it matures with selective cutting and pinching back in spring.

CLIANTHUS puniceus. Parrot-beak. Evergreen, shrublike vine. After bloom, cut out deadwood and thin out and head back older canes and weak branches. This will encourage strong growth for next season's bloom. Train either as vine on walls, fences, or trellises or as a tall shrub or standard.

CLIFF ROSE.
See Cowania mexicana stansburiana.

CLIVIA miniata. Kaffir lily. Evergreen perennial with tuberous roots. If dead, outside leaves come off easily, pull them off; remove old flower stalks to prevent fruit from forming.

CLYTOSTOMA callistegioides (*Bignonia violacea, B. speciosa*). Violet trumpet vine. Evergreen. Strong, clambering grower. Stems need some support and training in direction you want. Blooms in spring and summer; prune after each flowering to control growth, prevent tangling.

COBAEA scandens. Cup-and-saucer-vine. Perennial. Vigorous growth to 25 ft. or more if not trimmed. Start pinching back new growth on plant from the time it is 6 in. tall to make it bushy.

COCCOLOBIS uvifera. Sea grape, seaside plum. Evergreen shrub. Very adaptable; can be pruned any time. Can be trained to single trunk, planted in a row as windbreak, or espaliered. For a good espalier, start with a very young plant, fasten branches in design you want, and trim off stray whips that break desired pattern.

COCCULUS laurifolius. Evergreen shrub or small tree. Makes a good informal espalier. Needs frequent pruning to keep it in bounds because it wants to grow as high as 20 ft., spreading as wide. Early thinning as plant develops will prevent legginess. Don't head back; instead, thin entire branches to main trunk. Regular selective reduction of new and old growth (except main structural members) will produce healthier, greener foliage. Prune whenever required; will respond rapidly if growing in rich soil. It can be staked and trained as a single-trunked, umbrella-shaped tree.

COFFEA arabica. Coffee. Evergreen house or patio plant, outdoor shrub. Prune to shape when young; corrective pruning as necessary as plant matures.

COFFEEBERRY.
See Rhamnus californica.

COLEONEMA and DIOSMA. Breath of heaven. Evergreen shrubs. Trim back lightly with hedge shears each year after main bloom to keep plants compact. Limit severe pruning to old plants that have had no attention. To renew neglected, old plants, thin out straggly or dead growth and cut plants back about half way. Plants don't always recover from this heavy pruning.

COLEUS blumei. Coleus. Perennial. Left alone, coleus becomes tall and leggy topped with spikes of pale blue flowers. For compact growth and luxuriant foliage, pinch out growing tips regularly during summer to encourage branching. Remove flower buds to keep plant growing vigorously.

COLOCASIA esculenta (*Caladium esculentum*). Taro, elephant's ear. Perennial with tuberous roots. Remove old leaves when they begin to yellow. Cut frost-damaged stalks to ground in spring after danger of frost is past.

COLUMBINE.
See Aquilegia.

COLUTEA. Bladder senna. Shrub. Cut back to the ground each year in spring

after last frost. This promotes new growth. For a larger plant, remove weak wood and cut other stems back only halfway.

COMAROSTAPHYLIS diversifolia. Summer holly. Evergreen shrub or small tree. Train as dense, compact shrub by pinching back tips during growing period or shape into small tree by removing lower limbs.

CONVOLVULUS. Evergreen shrub, evergreen perennial, and an annual.

C. cneorum. Bush morning glory. Evergreen shrub. Rapid growing. Thin and head back thoroughly in late winter to renew plant; pinch tips of new growth. Can get leggy if left alone.

C. mauritanicus. Ground morning glory. Evergreen perennial. Trim back in late winter to keep from getting woody. Pinch tips during the growing season.

COPROSMA. Evergreen shrubs. All respond well to heavy pruning, shaping.

C. kirkii. If ground cover plantings get too high or too uneven, cut them back with hedge shears. Late spring or early summer is a good time.

C. repens (*C. baueri*). Mirror plant. A fairly fast grower that will take all the pruning you want to give it. Can be pruned anytime. An open, straggly shrub if neglected but a beautiful plant when cared for. Two prunings a year should be sufficient to keep it dense and at height you want. Take out some stems to the base; cut others back to lateral you want to retain. Where shrub receives ocean wind, little pruning is necessary. Use as hedge, screen, wall shrub, informal espalier.

CORAL BELLS.
See Heuchera sanguinea.

CORAL BERRY.
See Symphoricarpos.

CORAL TREE.
See Erythrina.

CORDYLINE. Evergreen palmlike shrubs or trees. (Often sold as *Dracaena*.)

C. australis (*Dracaena australis*). Will grow into 20-30 ft. tree, rather stiff like Joshua tree. For more graceful plant, head back when young to force multiple trunks or plant in clumps, cutting a few back to ground each spring until all develop multiple trunks.

C. indivisa. Blue dracaena. Removal of lower leaves as they die is only pruning requirement.

C. stricta. Will grow to 15 ft. but can be kept lower by cutting tall canes to ground whenever they exceed desired height. New canes will replace them.

Long cuttings will root quickly if you stick them into ground.

C. terminalis. Ti. Cut back anytime to encourage branching. Will survive even when chopped to ground. Start new plants with cut portions.

COREOPSIS. Annual and perennial. Prolong bloom on all types by removing old flowers. Cut perennial types back to ground when they finish blooming in fall.

CORNUS. Dogwood. Deciduous shrub or tree. Tree forms require only normal shaping and training for structure when young and very little pruning later. Prune lightly as necessary to maintain shape; remove dead and weak wood in spring after flowering. Shrub forms generally require more pruning than trees.

C. alba. Tatarian dogwood; and **C. a. 'Sibirica'.** Siberian dogwood. Shrubs. In cold-winter areas, the blood red, bare twigs are very colorful. New wood is brightest, so cut some of older wood back to side branches in spring to force new growth.

C. controversa. Giant dogwood. Tree. Lower branches often sweep ground. Remove them if you want to use as shade tree to sit under or as street tree to walk under.

C. florida. Flowering dogwood, Eastern dogwood. Tree. Lowest branches often sweep ground, giving natural protection. In cold-winter areas, don't cut off these low branches. If they don't branch low naturally, they may need special protection during coldest weather when morning sun can crack and split frozen bark. Protect with shrubs planted around it or place evergreen boughs against the east side of tree trunks. Unprotected bark, in defense, may send out leafy sucker shoots. If you remove these suckers, the bark may crack and die.

C. f. 'Welchii'. Tricolor dogwood. You can let it grow as a big shrub with foliage to the ground or train it into tree form (see *Training Young Trees*, page 15).

C. mas. Cornelian cherry. Shrub or tree. Grows naturally as airy, twiggy shrub but can be trained to form small, finely branched tree (see *Training Young Trees*, page 15).

C. nuttallii. Pacific dogwood, Western dogwood. Give only normal training while young (see *Training Young Trees*, page 15) because this tree reacts unfavorably to pruning. If protecting trees or shrubbery don't shade trunk, tree tends to send out suckers on sunny side. Pruning these off may cause sunscorched bark of tree to split, inviting insects and diseases which can eventually damage and kill the tree. Protect from bark injury by planting a buffer strip of shrubbery around its base.

C. sanguinea. Bloodtwig dogwood. Shrub. Grows as many-stemmed shrub. Remove oldest stems at ground in spring to produce new red branches and twigs for winter color.

C. stolonifera. Redtwig dogwood, red-osier dogwood. Shrub. Remove oldest, darkest stems to ground in early spring to encourage fresh new ones and to hold plant in check. Cut back if it gets too tall. Spreads rapidly by underground stems. To control, use a spade to cut off roots that have gone too far. Cut off branches that touch ground.

COROKIA. Evergreen shrubs. Naturally picturesque plants. You don't normally have to prune them to achieve this effect, except occasionally when upright stems develop in the center of plants. Remove these at the base whenever they appear in order to keep plants in proper balance.

CORONILLA varia. Crown vetch. Perennial. Tenacious ground cover that goes dormant and looks ratty during coldest weather unless it is covered with snow. Mow it in spring to get lush green summer cover.

CORREA. Australian fuchsia. Evergreen shrubs. Prune very lightly after flowers have faded to keep the shrubs compact and the size you want. Pinch back regularly to keep from spreading. Since they don't sprout readily from old wood, they should not be heavily pruned.

CORTADERIA selloana. Pampas grass. Evergreen giant ornamental grass. Difficult to prune because its leaves are sharp and cut your hands easily, but it is more attractive if cut back from time to time to keep it under control. Cut off fluffy plumes before they go to seed because they get messy. Most efficient way to control it is to burn it to the ground periodically if you are in an area where this can be done. If burning is not permitted, shear it to ground.

CORYLOPSIS. Winter hazel. Deciduous shrubs. Slow growing, rather open structures and delicate branching patterns. Little pruning required; thin and shape as necessary after bloom.

CORYLUS. Filbert, hazelnut. Deciduous shrubs or small trees. Need only early training or shaping. If necessary, thin by cutting unwanted stems at bases when dormant. If trained as a tree, select best trunk and remove its side branches to desired height. Also remove suckers as they appear.

CORYNOCARPUS laevigatus. New Zealand laurel. Evergreen shrub or small tree. Will withstand heavy pruning though it's seldom required. Slow growing, keeps attractive form for years.

Older specimens can grow as high as 30 or 40 ft., but you can control height by thinning and heading back selectively. Small orange fruits are extremely poisonous.

COSTMARY.
See Chrysanthemum balsamita.

COTINUS coggygria (*Rhus cotinus*). Smoke tree. Deciduous. Thin lightly when dormant; remove dense growth or deadwood. Can be trained as a single or multi-trunked tree or shrub.

COTONEASTER. Evergreen, semi-deciduous, and deciduous shrubs. These range all the way from ground covers to upright small shrubs to taller shrubs and trees of fountainlike growth with graceful, arching branches.

Vigorous growers, they all respond well to pruning, though they don't normally require much beyond shaping and removing branches that have carried berries — cut them just above an unberried side branch. (Cutting the berries for indoor decoration is usually enough pruning.)

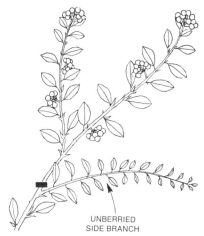

REMOVE berried cotoneaster branches; cut back to an unberried side branch.

For deciduous types, major pruning is normally done in winter or early spring. Evergreen types should be pruned just before new growth begins. Cotoneasters all need elbow room. To avoid having to prune severely and frequently, choose a type that will fit your space. Some medium and tall growers can be sheared, but they look best when allowed to maintain natural fountain shapes. Prune only to enhance graceful arch of branches.

Keep low growers looking young by cutting out portion of oldest wood each year. Prune ground covers to remove dead or awkward branches. Don't plant where branch ends need shearing (near a walk or drive) because stubbed branches are unattractive.

(Continued on next page)

COTONEASTER PANNOSA—a type that is evergreen to half-evergreen—normally grows as a 10 by 10 foot shrub. This one has been fastened to wall and pruned often.

Neglected shrubs can be cut back heavily to renew. New vigorous growth sprouts readily from old wood. If a neglected shrub has become a brambly eyesore, transform it into a gnarled, picturesque tree with a pruning saw. Lop off branches that grow out between ground level and shoulder height to reveal pleasing trunk lines hidden under excess branch growth.

Cotoneasters are susceptible to fireblight. Examine them carefully as soon as buds begin to expand in spring; dead branches may indicate the disease in areas where it's a problem. Prune out dead branches to lessen chance of infecting new growth. Sterilize pruning tools.

C. parneyi. Cotoneaster, red clusterberry. (Plants sold under this name are usually *C. lactea*.) Evergreen. This hardy shrub will endure heavy pruning, responding with vigorous growth from old wood. Such severe treatment should be necessary only when periodic pruning has been neglected. Heavy pruning will cost you one crop of berries.

Holds its foliage near the ground, a characteristic that makes it good as freestanding shrub or hedge, or even as espalier or shrub for container. It is one of the few plants that can be woven through a chain link fence.

If you wish, you can confine pruning to removal of berried branches for display indoors. Remove branches at point just above a lateral. When there are no such side branches, cut just above ground level. Through such heading back and thinning, you can preserve the overall character of the shrub and keep it a profusely berrying plant. It has such flexible branches that you can lead it into any pattern you want. You can espalier it, training the branches by fastening them to wires strung between nails driven in the wall.

Or use it as a ground cover. Start with small plants that show a low, spreading growth habit. Set 3-4 ft. apart, peg branches to the ground with inverted U made of wire. To make a standard, select a plant with a vertical stem. Keep it staked for 2-4 years. When stem reaches 3-4 ft., pinch out tip to force branching. Grow as clipped hedge. By pruning you can control it at any height up to about 6 ft. If let grow naturally, it forms a graceful 6-ft.-high shrub.

COTTONWOOD.
See Populus.

COWANIA mexicana stansburiana. Cliff rose. Evergreen shrub. Trim off some branches and straggly growth to show off smoky pink trunk bark. Prune as required to shape after flowering and fruiting.

COYOTE BRUSH, DWARF.
See Baccharis pilularis.

CRABAPPLE, FLOWERING.
See Malus.

CRABAPPLE, FRUITING.
See Apple.

CRANBERRY, HIGHBUSH.
See Viburnum opulus.

CRANBERRY, MOUNTAIN.
See Vaccinium vitis-idaea.

CRAPE MYRTLE.
See Lagerstroemia indica.

CRASSULA. Succulents including jade plant. Easy to prune and shape, but they grow slowly and retain their shape many years without excessive pruning. Some pruning may be necessary to prevent plants from becoming top-heavy and falling over or to bring symmetry to lopsided plants. Remove growth at any time to control shape and height and for use in flower arrangements. Remove whole stems or cut cleanly just above a node. Prune anytime.

CRATAEGUS. Hawthorn. Deciduous trees. Require very little pruning. They are much prettier if you don't interfere with the natural, dense growth. Some types have a tendency to grow tops that are too dense. An annual spring thinning will minimize the danger of being uprooted by wind. Beyond this, restrict pruning to removal of suckers from trunk and around the base and thinning excess twiggy growth. Never cut back shoots.

For a hedge, start with young unbranched trees planted 3 ft. apart. Kept trimmed, they will grow into a dense, somewhat thorny flowering hedge. Keeping them closely clipped means that you sacrifice some flowers so wait to prune until after flowering. Susceptible to fireblight in some areas. Cut out blighted branches well below dead part; clean pruning tools with disinfectant between each cut.

CREAM BUSH.
See Holodiscus discolor.

CREEPING FIG.
See Ficus pumila.

CRINODENDRON patagua (*C. dependens, Tricuspidaria dependens*). Lily-of-the-valley tree. Evergreen tree. Needs early training and shaping (see *Training Young Trees*, page 15) to make an attractive tree. Left on its own, it tends to become shrubby. Keep a single-trunk tree clean of extra growth. Thin out brushy growth toward the center whenever necessary; remove branches that tend to hang down.

CROTALARIA agatiflora. Canary bird bush. Evergreen shrub. Fast, rank grower, not particularly attractive unless thinned and headed back consistently. Criss-cross growth needs frequent cleaning out. Prune heavily three times during the growing season: after the heavy fall blooming period, prior to late spring growth, and again in midsummer. In coldest areas, frost does some of the pruning. Cut out freeze-damaged wood. New growth will sprout from stump.

CROWN OF GOLD TREE.
See Cassia excelsa.

CROWN VETCH.
See Coronilla varia.

CRYPTOCARYA rubra. Evergreen tree. Grows with multiple trunks; remove all but one trunk to train as a single-trunk tree. Easily restrained as a small tree or in the confined space of a container.

CRYPTOMERIA japonica. Japanese cryptomeria. Evergreen tree. Needs very little pruning—just the removal of errant branches whenever necessary.

C. j. 'Elegans'. Plume cedar, plume cryptomeria. Can be pruned for oriental effect by taking out some branches to give a tiered look, or by leaving clusters of foliage on tips of branches in a pompon effect.

CUNNINGHAMIA lanceolata. China fir. Evergreen tree. Responds well to pruning, though all that is required is normal training and guidance (see *Training Young Trees,* page 15) and removal of dead branches. Remove suckers that form at base.

CUNONIA capensis. African red alder. Evergreen large shrub or small tree. Buy as tree form or as dense shrub. By thinning and heading back selectively whenever necessary, you can hold plant to about 6 ft.

CUP-AND-SAUCER VINE.
See Cobaea scandens.

CUPANIOPSIS anacardioides (*Cupania anacardioides*). Carrot wood, tuckeroo. Evergreen tree. Prune whenever necessary to enhance structure; remove excess branches. Never stub back; always cut to a side branch. Interesting when trained as multi-stemmed tree.

CUP FLOWER.
See Nierembergia.

CUPHEA ignea. Cigar plant. Perennial. Cut back after flowering to encourage

more bloom. Tends to sprawl, but you can keep it relatively compact by pinching out growing tips. Cut older plant back severely in late fall, early spring.

CUP-OF-GOLD VINE.
See Solandra hartwegii.

CUPRESSOCYPARIS leylandii. Evergreen tree. Grows extremely fast. Responds well to light or heavy pruning as needed.

CUPRESSUS. Cypress. Evergreen trees.
C. forbesii. Tecate cypress. Very fast growing. Thin out some of top when necessary to keep from becoming top-heavy for size of its root system. Can be trained as hedge.

C. glabra. (Often sold as *C. arizonica.*) Smooth Arizona cypress. Fast grower. Train it as tree (see *Training Young Trees,* page 15) or tall screen.

C. macrocarpa. Monterey cypress. Grows naturally into picturesque form. Little pruning required except to remove deadwood whenever necessary.

C. sempervirens. Italian cypress. Branches often pull away from main body of plant. Don't attempt to tie them back in place. Cut branch off a little inside of where it grows away from column. This will force side growth to fill in bare area and maintain a sturdy plant. For formal hedging, you can shear it lightly anytime.

CURRANT. Deciduous shrub. Currants bear at the base of year-old wood and on spurs on 2 and 3-year wood. Prune while dormant so that you keep balance of 1, 2, and 3-year canes. Prune out older canes and weak growth.

CURRANT, INDIAN.
See Symphoricarpos.

CURRANT, ORNAMENTAL.
See Ribes.

CUSHION BUSH.
See Calocephalus brownii.

CYPERUS alternifolius and C. papyrus. Umbrella plant, papyrus. Perennials. Pruning these tropicals is a matter of grooming and control. Clean up at least twice a year. Cut back overgrown and brown flower heads at base of long stems. To keep plants from spreading, chop off above ground the basal stems that keep spreading out. What is left will sprout and make more compact plants.

Prune out overripe foliage down to bases before active growth in spring. Unless these stems are cut down, they turn brown and make clump look ugly, messy, and overcrowded. In colder areas, frost may cut them down to ground. New growth will appear in spring.

CYPRESS.
See Cupressus.

CYPRESS, BALD.
See Taxodium distichum

CYPRESS, FALSE.
See Chamaecyparis.

CYTISUS, GENISTA, SPARTIUM. Brooms. Evergreen or deciduous shrubs and shrublets. To grow brooms successfully, prune right after flowering every year. If you cut brooms all the way back into old wood, the limbs will probably die; however, there have been cases

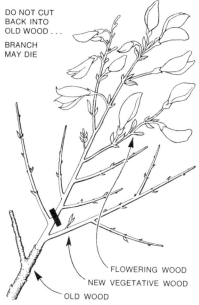

DO NOT CUT BACK INTO OLD WOOD . . . BRANCH MAY DIE

FLOWERING WOOD
NEW VEGETATIVE WOOD
OLD WOOD

PRUNE BROOMS by cutting off flowering wood and half of new vegetative wood.

where some types have come back from the root crown after being cut to the ground.

Old plants that have become coarse and leggy from neglect cannot be made trim and vigorous again. It's best to discard them and start with new ones. Each spring, cut off all flowering wood and up to half new vegetative wood. If you remove spent flowers before they have a chance to set seeds, you will minimize volunteer seeding and spreading.

In colder areas, unpruned brooms can be damaged by snow. Once the weight of snow has pinned limbs to the ground, they will have a stiff and somewhat awkward shape when they rise again. You will find the same condition if children or pets play in them.

DAHLIA. Perennial grown from tuberous roots. Bushes, summer hedges, screens, and low borders. When tall-growing dahlias are 4-5 in. high, thin in spring to strongest shoot or 2 shoots (make cuttings of removed ones). When plants reach 8-12 in. and 3 or 4 sets of leaves have formed, pick off tips just above

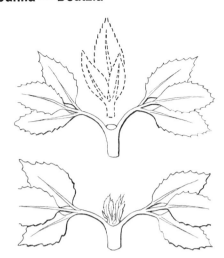

FOR BUSHY DAHLIAS, pinch out tips. Initial growth response shown below.

the topmost pair of leaves. This procedure, known as "crowning-out," will encourage side branching and produce rounder, bushier plants with well-distributed blossoms.

Without pinching, dahlias tend to become lanky and top-heavy, having all their flowers at the top. For even bushier plants, tips of subsequent laterals can also be pinched out.

Disbudding: You will get the best possible flowers if you remove surplus flower buds on decorative types—normally there are 3 buds at the tip of each branch. (Many types such as Tom Thumb need no disbudding.)

In early morning or evening, buds are brittle and snap off with a flick of your finger. When they are the size of small peas, snap off 2 buds at the sides of the tip so that terminal bud will get benefit of plant's energy and reach maximum development. At the next node below the terminal bud, 2 other buds will develop. Snap these off, too. By the time terminal bud has matured and bloomed, flowers on lower laterals will be showing color. Repeat disbudding as buds emerge.

TO MAKE BIGGER dahlia flowers, disbud 2 outer flower buds. Middle one benefits.

If you don't crown-out and disbud dahlias, they will form one large bloom at top of plants and increasingly shorter stems on lower side branches.

Cutting flowers: Cut dahlias only after flowers are fully open (buds don't develop well after being cut). For a second batch of flowers, cut stems that have flowered back to one joint on the main stalk.

Fall cutback: When dahlia tops have been cut by frost or have died down, cut tops to 4 in., lift the clumps of tubers, and store in a cool, dry place until time to divide and plant in the spring.

D. imperialis. Tree dahlia. Cut back to ground in fall after bloom or after frost kills it. Grows each year from permanent roots.

DAIS cotinifolia. Pompon tree. Briefly deciduous. Form may be a bit gross, but you can improve it markedly by removing unwanted, erratic growth when leafless to reveal some of its branching form. Naturally multiple trunked, it looks best if you remove all but one and train to single trunk.

DAISY BUSH.
See Olearia haastii.

DAISY, MICHAELMAS.
See Aster novae-angliae.

DAISY, TRANSVAAL.
See Gerbera jamesonii.

DALEA spinosa. Smoke tree. Deciduous tree. Prune only to shape as required.

DAPHNE. Evergreen and deciduous shrubs. Daphnes can withstand severe pruning, but they seldom need it except to reshape plants. (*D. mezereum,* February daphne, may not bloom again for a year after pruning.) Daphnes can be pruned whenever their shoots get out of bounds, but normal procedure is to prune during and after bloom.

A good way to shape plants is by cutting small clusters of flowers to wear during the flowering season (late winter). If you want big cut branches, make cuts just above growth buds or small shoots. Cutting to outward facing buds results in spreading plants; cutting to inside facing buds will tend to produce erect plants. Daphnes can also be cut in bud and brought indoors for forcing into bloom.

DATE PALM.
See Phoenix.

DATURA. Angel's trumpet. Evergreen shrubs. Strong, vigorous growth and soft wood make it necessary to trim, shape, and clean out shrubs at least once a season. Do serious pruning in early spring, after last frost. Cut back branches to 1 or 2 buds.

DAUBENTONIA tripetii. Scarlet wisteria tree. Deciduous shrub or small tree. Prune heavily in early spring; thin and shorten side branches. Blooms from May through summer. Pods that follow blossoms should be removed to prolong flowering. Often trained to flat-topped standard tree on 6-ft. trunk.

DAVIDIA involucrata. Dove tree. Deciduous. Prune plant lightly to maintain desired shape. Remove crossing, rubbing branches; dead or diseased wood. Prune after flowering, leaving no stubs; remove entire twig or branch back to base. Wounds are susceptible to disease, rot. Treat cuts ½ in. or wider with wound dressing.

DAYLILY.
See Hemerocallis.

DELPHINIUM. Perennials, biennials, annuals. When new shoots develop in spring, remove all but 2 or 3 strongest (you may leave more on older, better established plants). When first large flower spikes finish blooming, cut stalks to within 6 or 8 in. of ground. Leave stubs of old stalks until new shoots from bases are several inches high and then remove them. New shoots will bloom in late summer and early fall. Blooms will continue to come all summer if you cut off faded flower stalks.

D. cheilanthum. Sturdy, bushy perennial. Should be treated a bit differently, for many flowering stems branch off main stalk. When all flowers have faded, cut plant to ground, and new growth will shoot up.

DENDROMECON. Bush poppy. Evergreen shrubs. Will withstand almost any amount of pruning, though light and infrequent pruning to remove deadwood and renew oldest wood is all that is normally required. Cut off long shoot growths to prevent legginess. Do major pruning after bloom. Cut *D. rigida* back to 2 ft. after flowering.

DEODAR CEDAR.
See Cedrus deodara.

DESERT CANDLE.
See Eremurus.

DESERT HONEYSUCKLE.
See Anisacanthus thurberi.

DESERT WILLOW.
See Chilopsis linearis.

DEUTZIA. Deciduous flowering shrubs. Respond well to heavy pruning right after bloom. Thin twiggy growths any time. Some pruning while plants are blooming will provide good display of color for the house. Cut flowering branches back to strong side branches of new growth. Cut oldest stems of low and medium growing kinds to ground to force new shoots. Prune tall-growing kinds severely by cutting back wood that has flowered (cut to outward facing side branches).

It's good practice to prune deutzias before the flowers are all gone. New growth will start well out on blooming branches, and by the time growth starts, you'll need a steely heart to cut away all the wood you should. Cut flowering branches far back into center of plants. Later in summer, cut back the new growth if necessary. Cut back unwanted shoots and suckers that emerge from ground around plants.

DIANELLA tasmanica. Perennial. Groom by removing shabby leaves and dead fruiting stalks whenever necessary.

DIANTHUS. Carnation, pink. Perennials, biennials, annuals. For long bloom, shear off spent flowers frequently. Cut plants back to about half size in fall to encourage new bottom growth and keep from becoming straggly.

D. 'Beatrix'. Perennial. Give full year to become established and trim foliage back halfway in late fall to keep plant full and shapely.

D. caryophyllus. Carnation, clove pink. Perennial. For large flowers, leave only terminal bloom on each stem. Pinch out all other buds down to fifth joint, below which new flowering stems will develop. Do not disbud if you want lots of flowers. Carnations tend to become straggly when permitted to grow at will. Pinching will reward you with bushy plants. When cuttings are about 7 joints high, nip out growing tips to encourage side branching. Pinch out growing tips on side shoots if they get out of line. (Don't pinch out top growth later or you'll remove current season's flowers.) When you cut blooms for arrangements, take flowers with long stems, cutting back to main stalk.

D. chinensis. Chinese pink, rainbow pink. Biennial or short-lived perennial. Pick off faded flowers along with bases to prolong bloom.

D. 'Little Joe'. Perennial. Will bloom from May to November if dead blooms are removed.

D. 'Rose Bowl'. Perennial. Blooms almost continually if spent blooms are removed regularly.

DICENTRA. Bleeding heart. Perennials. Cut back after flowering for second growth and sometimes repeat bloom.

DICKSONIA.
See Fern, Tree.

DIEFFENBACHIA. Dumb cane. Evergreen indoor foliage plant. When plant gets tall, it loses most lower leaves, so you may want to start new plant by rooting cuttings in water.

DIGITALIS purpurea. Common foxglove. Biennial, sometimes perennial.

After first flowering, cut main spike. If all cultural conditions are to the plant's liking, side shoots will then develop and bloom in summer.

DIMORPHOTHECA ecklonis.
See Osteospermum.

DIOSMA.
See Coleonema.

DIPLACUS. Shrubby monkey flower. Shrubby perennial or evergreen shrub or shrublet. If pruned after first flowering, will bloom again in fall. Prune also in spring before new growth starts.

DIPLOPAPPUS filifolius (*Aster fruticosus*). Shrub aster. Evergreen shrub. Bushy, densely branched. Shear off dead flowers after bloom, then thin by taking out whole branches and dead weak wood.

DISTICTIS. Evergreen vines.

D. laxiflora (*D. lactiflora, D. cinerea*). Vanilla trumpet vine. More restrained than most trumpet vines, needs only light pruning whenever necessary.

D. 'Rivers'. (Sometimes labeled *D. riversii*.) Royal trumpet vine. Much more vigorous and needs heavy pruning to keep it tidy. Prune whenever it gets out of bounds.

DISTYLIUM racemosum. Evergreen shrub. Resembles Japanese privet (*Ligustrum japonicum*). Can tolerate heavy pruning or shearing. Can be trained either as dense clipped screen or as espaliered wall plant. Prune any time in milder areas, but wait until spring in colder parts of country.

DIZYGOTHECA elegantissima. (Often sold as *Aralia elegantissima.*) Thread-leaf false aralia. House plant (juvenile stage); evergreen garden shrub (mature form).

CUT TALLEST STEM TO BASE EACH YEAR TO MAKE PLANT BUSHY WITH FOLIAGE ALONG WHOLE PLANT

BUSHY PLANT, lacy leaves, staggered stem heights are maintained by pruning.

In subtropical areas, gardeners who grow it as landscape plant usually cut it back every year or so in spring to keep delicate juvenile leaves coming along. Can become small tree with 10-12-ft. spread if not pruned severely.

If plant has several trunks, you can maintain them at staggered heights by cutting back tallest one to base each year or so. A single shoot will sprout quickly from trunk base beneath the cut and grow straight up. This pruning method puts foliage along whole plant rather than just at top of long bare stem. It also assures a good crop of lacy, juvenile leaves. Unpruned plant eventually develops coarser, thicker, mature leaves.

DODONAEA viscosa. Hop bush, hopseed bush. Evergreen shrub. Left on its own, it will become an attractive, informal, leafy wall, needing only occasional thinning and pinching back of errant growth. Do this at any time. Can also be sheared into neat, compact, formal hedge or trained as espalier. Fast growing with many upright stems, it can be trained as a tree by cutting out all but a single stem. In this case, keep well staked and remove side shoots up to desired height of clear trunk when they appear on main stem.

DOGWOOD.
See Cornus.

DOLICHOS lignosus. Australian pea vine. Perennial twining vine. Evergreen in mild winters. Vigorous, rapid grower that must be cut back heavily if it gets out of control. If overgrown or freeze damaged, cut back to ground in spring and start over with new growth.

DOMBEYA wallichii. Evergreen shrub. Fast growing with brittle wood and undisciplined habit. Needs regular thinning out and heading back for bushiness. Faded flower clusters tend to hang on and look untidy unless removed. Can be espaliered or trained over arbors to display flowers. Prune anytime.

DORONICUM. Leopards bane. Perennial. If you cut back flower stalks as soon as blooms have faded, you encourage second flowering.

DOUGLAS FIR.
See Pseudotsuga menziesii.

DOVE TREE.
See Davidia involucrata.

DOVYALIS caffra (*Aberia caffra*). Kei apple. Evergreen shrub. Thin out some stems and head others back in spring to keep to size you wish. Can be kept anywhere from 1-8 or 10 ft. high and as little as 12 in. wide. If pampered with water and fertilizer, it will grow taller and rangier, requiring cutting back of straggly branches.

DOXANTHA unguis-cati. Cat's claw, yellow trumpet vine. Partly deciduous vine. Prune heavily after bloom to keep in bounds. Remove all old and weak shoots, cut back some stems nearly to ground to stimulate new growth lower down. Control size by pinching new growth during growing season.

DRACAENA draco. Dragon tree. Evergreen foliage plant. Clusters of flowers form at branch ends. After blossoms drop, stemmy clusters remain. Trim off to keep plant neat. Strip off dead leaves.

DRAGON TREE.
See Dracaena.

DRIMYS winteri. Winter's bark. Evergreen tree. Usually multi-stemmed but easily trained to single trunk. May require pruning for shape whenever necessary to maintain pleasing symmetry of outline.

DUCHESNEA indica. Indian mock strawberry. Perennial. Grows rapidly as a ground cover, can become a nuisance if neglected. Shear surface and trim edges whenever necessary to keep under control.

DUMB CANE.
See Dieffenbachia.

DURANTA. Evergreen shrubs. Need continual thinning and heading back to control. Remove to ground (or to strong unflowered laterals) all branches after they have produced berries. Tip cutting should be avoided, for it will result in bushy growth just below cuts.

DUSTY MILLER.
See Senecio cineraria.

EASTER LILY VINE.
See Beaumontia grandiflora.

ECHEVERIA. Succulents. All the pruning that the low, squatty types (represented mostly by plant called hen and chicks) need is to have old, dead leaf rosettes and flower stalks removed. With tall kinds, your concern will be what to do with them when they get leggy. It's simple. Just cut off the top and insert its stem into sand. The big cutting will form new roots, and new growth will sprout from the remaining base.

ECHINACEA purpurea (*Rudbeckia purpurea*). Purple coneflower. Perennial. Cut to the ground after bloom.

ECHIUM fastuosum. Pride of Madeira. Shrubby perennial. After each spike finishes blooming, cut stalk off a few inches down in foliage. Whenever necessary, lightly trim plant to keep bushy. If you cut back too hard, it may not survive. If, on the other hand, you don't do any cutting or pinching, the plant's

vigor soon turns it into bizarre, treelike shrub.

ELAEAGNUS. Deciduous and evergreen large shrubs or small trees. All are tough, grow fast (when young), and typically can exist a lifetime with no pruning at all. Pruning becomes necessary when the plants get too big or—infrequently—when they become unattractive. When you must prune, plant will respond well to selective branch removal and cutting back. Prune at any time of year. Plants can be shaped like bonsai.

E. angustifolia. Russian olive. Small deciduous tree. Varies greatly in growth habit. In selecting one look for form you want; otherwise you'll have to do a lot of training and shaping. Should be pruned at least every 2 or 3 years during the dormant period. Limbs that have grown too long may break from wind or the weight of snow; cut these back. Tree can be trained as clipped or informal hedge or screen or grown as well-groomed tree.

E. fruitlandii. Fruitland silverberry. Evergreen shrub. Much like *E. pungens*. Grows dense, full, firm, and tough. Requires only minimum of pruning whenever necessary. Natural shape is good when given plenty of room. Excellent for large bank planting. Best grown naturally or sheared as a foliaged screen.

E. pungens. Silverberry. Large evergreen shrub. Naturally sprawling, it will take any amount of pruning and direction you give it. By encouraging angular nature of stems, you can make picturesque container plant. Can be trained as small tree completely clothed in foliage or directed toward a more formal small standard. Clipped, makes an excellent hedge. With pinching and heading back of errant growth, it will form flat wall cover, either full foliaged or with open pattern of spiny branches and shimmery leaves.

ELDERBERRY.
See Sambucus.

ELEPHANT'S EAR.
See Colocasia esculenta.

ELEPHANT'S FOOD.
See Portulacaria afra.

ELM.
See Ulmus.

EMPRESS TREE.
See Paulownia tomentosa.

ENGLISH LAUREL.
See Prunus laurocerasus.

ENKIANTHUS. Deciduous shrubs. Prune only to remove dead or broken branches. Short spurs tend to develop along stems of old plants, detracting from their interesting, angular forms. Keep these spurs snipped off.

ENSETE. Big, palmlike perennials. Evergreen in mild areas, die back in winter and regrow in spring in colder climates.

E. ventricosum (*Musa ensete*). Abyssinian banana. When older, bottom leaves begin to droop and turn yellow. Cut these off at base using sharp knife. After flowering, plant dies to roots. Cut stalk off at base so that new growth will sprout.

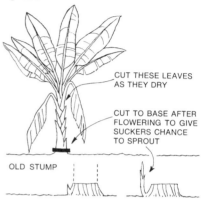

CUT THESE LEAVES AS THEY DRY

CUT TO BASE AFTER FLOWERING TO GIVE SUCKERS CHANCE TO SPROUT

OLD STUMP

PRUNING for new growth is a two-stage process for ensete.

EPAULETTE TREE.
See Pterostyrax hispida.

EPIDENDRUM. Epiphytic or terrestrial orchids. Flower on new growth. To keep new blooms coming all year, cut flowering stems back to within 1 or 2 nodes of ground after flowers have faded. Besides more flower stems, you'll get more compact growth. This applies to reed-stemmed terrestrial species only. Some epidendrums have pseudobulbs and need no pruning.

EPIMEDIUM. Perennials. In early spring, after danger of frost is past, cut off old foliage to make room for new growth.

EQUISETUM hyemale. Horsetail. Perennial. Can get out of hand so fast that it should be grown in concrete or metal-lined container. In the garden, you'll have to chop back invasive roots and shoots. Cut oldest canes to base as they begin to fall over and become messy.

ERANTHEMUM nervosum. (Sometimes sold as *E. pulchellum*.) Evergreen shrub. Pinch back stem tips 2 or 3 times early in growing season to keep plant compact and encourage more flower production. Cut leggy plant to ground to stimulate fresh new growth.

EREMURUS. Foxtail lily, desert candle. Perennials. Cut flower stalks to base as soon as last blooms fade. If allowed to set seed, plants are usually weakened and may not bloom for several years.

ERIOBOTRYA japonica. Loquat. Evergreen tree. Can tolerate any amount of pruning but may require none at all. Normally seen as single or multi-stemmed tree and espalier. It can be trained to hedge form. Trained as espalier, branches are quite rigid and need firm tying. Left to grow naturally, tree becomes compact and round. For maximum fruit, thin to admit light. Prune in spring before new growth starts. Thin fruit some to reduce chances of fruit-laden branches breaking in storms.

Susceptible to fireblight in some areas. Watch for it as buds begin to expand; dead branches may indicate the disease. If leaves and stems blacken from the top downward, prune back 12 in. or more into healthy wood. Discard prunings (burn them if possible) and sterilize shears between cuts.

ERIOGONUM. Wild buckwheat. Annuals, perennials, shrubs. You can do some pruning to shape if you start when plants are young. If they've had no attention and have become straggly, better replace them.

ERYTHEA.
See Palm.

ERYTHRINA. Coral tree. Mostly deciduous (some nearly evergreen) trees or shrubs. Can be pruned at any time of the year since they don't have a true dormant period. The important thing is to distinguish old wood from new wood, and to know if the kind of coral tree you are pruning blooms on new or old wood. It's wise to prune before new growth starts, because pruning then doesn't weaken the tree and because then you can direct new growth where you want it to go. Most corals look best with multiple trunks or 2 or 3 low trunklike branches.

E. bidwillii. Deciduous shrub. Closely related to *E. crista-galli,* and you can prune it in the same way—heavily, before new growth begins.

E. caffra. Kaffirboom coral tree. Briefly deciduous. One of the really big corals, it almost never needs pruning except to eliminate branches when they grow too low. A pruning can actually stop tree from blooming for several years. It takes that long for branches to get old enough to produce blooms. The tree's shape is naturally that of a spreading horizontal tree.

E. coralloides. Naked coral tree. Deciduous. Blooms before any leaves show in spring, so its bare structure is important. Left alone, it can get pretty scraggly, with branches going every which way (sometimes even in circles).

Properly pruned, it can be open, airy, and architectural. Prune so that most remaining branches are horizontal and spreading. Prune by removing whole branches, not by tipping the ends where the blooms appear. You may need to do some pruning every year.

E. crista-galli. Cockspur coral tree. Deciduous shrub or tree. Can have as many as 3 distinct flowering periods, spring through fall. Cut back old flower stems and deadened branch-ends after each wave of bloom. This stimulates new growth, resulting in another good crop of blooms.

E. humeana. Natal coral tree. Deciduous, sometimes evergreen. Blooms off and on all summer, so unless you must shape the tree don't cut off anything except dead flower spikes.

ESCALLONIA. Evergreen shrubs. Vigorous growers, they can stand any amount of pruning or shaping. They tend to get woody and rangy if not pruned. After bloom, remove about a third of old wood to ground, snip back leggy stems, and cut off old seed clusters that hang on long after flowering. Escallonias look best if you don't clip them closely, but even if you trim them as formal hedge you'll get some flowers because they bloom on new wood. You can train the taller growing forms into trees; as the plants age, trunk structures become more interesting. Tip pinch smaller kinds to keep them compact.

EUCALYPTUS. Evergreen trees and shrubs. Though eucalypts can take heavy pruning, they generally don't require much. Most can live a lifetime with no pruning. However, many kinds do grow extremely fast and may need some early training (see *Training Young Trees,* page 15). The trunk of a young tree you select at a nursery should be sturdy enough not to need staking. If it isn't, bend it down to the ground, making an arch. Hold the trunk in this arched position by wiring to a rock or a short stake. New sprouts will then grow from the base and a new trunk, probably huskier than the original, will

develop. About a year later, cut off the old, arched trunk.

There are about 150 different kinds of eucalyptus grown in the milder parts of the Western and Southwestern United States. They can be grouped broadly into three forms: the mallees, or shrubby, multi-trunk species; the medium or intermediate size with single trunk or many trunks; and the tall, single trunk forest trees.

The mallees—the shrubby forms—are usually best left alone. They'll normally form dense clumps on their own and pruning may make them look awkward. If you have a mallee with rangy, leggy stems, you can cut it to the ground to force multiple shoots and shrubby growth from the ground. Later, select 3 to 5 of the strongest new shoots for the framework and cut out the rest.

Medium or intermediate size types like *E. lehmannii* can grow either as single or multi-trunk trees. If you want to encourage a single trunk, cut off side shoots (but not immediately after planting — leave them on for a while, to help nourish the tree). If you want to encourage a multi-trunk, cut off the top at 2 ft. if there are plenty of side shoots beneath. Or bend it to the ground as described previously and start over with the new sprouts.

Tall, forest type, single-trunk eucalyptus seldom need pruning except to train in the early stages as outlined previously. At times on any big single trunk species, you (or a commercial tree pruning man wearing safety equipment) may have to cut out storm damaged or weak wood.

Mature tree types that have grown too tall are often cut back to stumps. They have a great capacity for regrowth and will respond by sprouting several new trunks. With proper shaping and

---

EUCALYPTUS GROWTH TYPES

The commonly grown eucalyptus species can be divided into the following groups:

Mallee	Intermediate	Forest Tree
E. caesia	E. cinerea	E. calophylla
E. eremophila	E. cloeziana	E. camaldulensis
E. erythronema	E. erythrocorys	E. citriodora
E. grossa	E. ficifolia	E. cladocalyx
E. kruseana	E. forrestiana	E. cornuta
E. macrocarpa	E. lehmannii	E. globulus
E. orbifolia	E. leucoxylon	E. globulus 'Compacta'
E. orpetii	E. leucoxylon macrocarpa 'Rosea'	E. gunnii
E. preissiana	E. linearis	E. maculata
E. pyriformis	E. macrandra	E. maculosa
E. rhodantha	E. megacornuta	E. melliodora
E. tetraptera	E. microtheca	E. nicholii
	E. niphophila	E. pauciflora
	E. perriniana	E. robusta
	E. platypus	E. rudis
	E. polyanthemos	E. saligna
	E. pulverulenta	E. sideroxylon
	E. spathulata	E. viminalis
	E. stellulata	
	E. torquata	

training, you have one or several new, smaller trees in just a few seasons.

If pruning is necessary, the best time to do it is spring and summer (after bloom where flowers are important). If possible, cut back to just above a side branch or bud. If you can't find a promising growth point, cut right into a smooth trunk; if the plant is established, new growth will break out beneath the cut. Later, remove all excess new branches—keep only those that are mechanically well placed.

EUONYMUS. Evergreen or deciduous shrubs, evergreen vines, ground covers. They all withstand heavy pruning (any time in mild areas, in spring after danger of frost is past in colder climates). The type of pruning and training you do depends on plant type and how you're using it.

EUONYMUS JAPONICA needs clipping twice a year to keep neat tree shape.

E. alata. Winged euonymus. Deciduous shrub. Slow growth, dense, twiggy. Prune for form in early spring, much as you would lilac.

E. fortunei. (Formerly *E. radicans acuta.*) Evergreen vine or shrub. This versatile plant will grow as a vine, attaching itself with minimum of assistance if given wall to climb on or tumble over. Without some kind of support to climb, it doesn't send out long vining stems but instead becomes low growing, bushy, mounded shrub. Keep top growth cut to train as ground cover. It can take heavy pruning but seldom needs it once established. Cut deadwood back to

healthy growth and shape in spring. On variegated form, cut out all-green shoots. As plant gets older, remove some center stems occasionally.

E. japonica. Evergreen euonymus. Evergreen shrub. Upright growth to 8-10 ft. can be held lower by pruning. Older shrubs make attractive trees if you thin to reveal curving trunks, angled stems. After you have formed it into the tree you want, pinch back tip growth to keep it compact. If plant is too compact and dense in wet areas, it may mildew badly. To prevent this, thin growth in center of plant.

E. kiautschovica (*E. patens*). Evergreen shrub. Spreading shrub; lower branches will sometimes root in moist soil. Can be trained as hedge, screen, sheared formal plant, espalier.

EUPHORBIA. Spurge. Shrubs, subshrubs, perennials.

E. biglandulosa. Evergreen perennial or subshrub. Stems die back after seeds set and should be removed. New ones come up to take their places.

E. epithymoides. Cut back to ground in fall in areas where winters are not severe enough to cause normal dieback.

E. pulcherrima. Poinsettia. Evergreen or deciduous shrub. Poinsettia must be pruned heavily in spring after bloom so that it will make rapid comeback and produce strong framework for following winter's flowers. It should not be pruned at any other time of year. Pruning is usually done in April or May, but the best time will depend upon your climate as well as when you want show of color to be at peak. If show of color is premature, peaking before Christmas holidays, you pruned too early. Delay pruning next time, even if plant begins to look straggly and spindly.

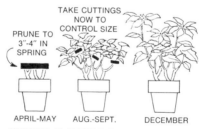

WINTER-FLOWERING poinsettia is result of early pruning, beginning in spring.

Cut plant almost all the way back, leaving 2 or 3 buds or leaf scars at base of each stem to produce growth for following season. Keep stump as compact as possible. If growth is very crowded, it may be necessary to remove some large stems to base. Sufficient new growth will come from rest of stump to make up for loss of older stems. (You can start a supply of new plants by making cut-

tings from stems you cut off.) As new growth proceeds, pinch back growing tips to encourage bushiness. This will produce more flowers.

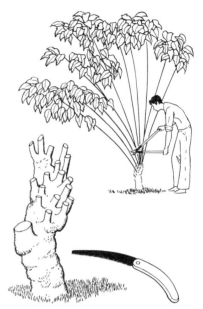

CUT POINSETTIA back heavily. Stubs on stump have 2 or 3 buds each.

To care for Christmas gift plants: when leaves fall in late winter or early spring, cut stems back to 2 or 3 buds, withhold water, and store in cool place. When danger of frost is past (or in late spring), set pots in sun outside. Train as they grow by pinching back growing tips as described previously.

EUROPEAN BEECH.
See Fagus sylvatica.

EUROPEAN MOUNTAIN ASH.
See Sorbus aucuparia.

EUROPEAN PLUM.
See Plum.

EURYA emarginata. Evergreen shrub. Slow growing, spreading, but easily kept at 3-4 ft. and compact by heading back to bud or side branch when required. Can be trained to almost any shape. Natural for miniature espalier effect.

EURYOPS. Shrubby evergreen perennials. Keep old blooms picked off, prune to keep neat after flowering.

EVERGREEN PEAR.
See Pyrus kawakamii.

EVODIA hupehensis. Hupeh evodia. Deciduous tree. Rapid grower when young; prune to shape as required. Branches are brittle; thin out some to minimize snow, sleet, and wind damage.

EXOCHORDA. Pearl bush. Deciduous shrubs. Generally, pruning after bloom is required only to control size and form. Head branches back occasionally if you want more bushiness.

FAGUS sylvatica. European beech. Deciduous tree. Requires only normal training while young (see *Training Young Trees,* page 15). Will grow naturally into conical-shaped tree with branches almost to ground. If you want standing or sitting room under it, remove lower branches. No other pruning required.

FALLUGIA paradoxa. Apache plume. Partially evergreen shrub. In fall when fruits have turned to seed, head back wood produced during current season.

FALSE CYPRESS.
See Chamaecyparis.

FALSE DRAGON-HEAD.
See Physostegia virginiana.

FALSE INDIGO.
See Baptisia australis.

FALSE SPIRAEA.
See Astilbe.

FATSHEDERA lizei. Evergreen vine, shrub, ground cover. This hybrid between *Fatsia japonica* and *Hedera helix* comes from nursery both as a single and multi-stalked plant. It can be trained as a shrub, as a small tree, as a vine, as a ground cover, shaped into a pillar, potted as a container plant, or strung out as an espalier. A rampant plant, it has an erratic growth pattern that can get out of control but can be shaped if you are persistent.

Pinch tip growth to force side branching. If plant gets away from you, cut it back to the ground; it will regrow quickly. If you want to use it as a ground cover, cut back vertical growth every 2-3 weeks during growing season. Fatshedera tends to become unruly foliage mass unless you constantly pinch and cut back to keep it controlled.

FATSIA japonica (*Aralia sieboldii, A. japonica*). Japanese aralia. Evergreen shrub. Responds well to severe pruning, but once established it requires little care. Established plant often suckers freely. You can remove them or keep 1 or 2 as new main stems. Old, tired, spindly plant can be cut back to about 6 in. in spring. Rush of new growth will come from stub. For bigger, lustier leaves, cut flowers off as soon as they appear. Attractive when trained and trimmed as single-stemmed tree.

FEATHER BUSH.
See Lysiloma thornberi.

FEIJOA sellowiana. Pineapple guava. Evergreen shrub or small tree. Normally a many-stemmed shrub, it can take any amount of pruning and can be held to almost any height and trained to grow in almost any shape: espalier, screen, hedge, small tree.

If you want to train to tree form, select good single-trunk specimen at nursery. As it grows, remove all secondary stems at ground level and thin out crossing branches. Control top growth by pinching back tips of branches you wish to retard.

Will usually recover nicely if killed back by frost. Do major pruning in late spring after new growth begins.

Tree also has exceptional potential as multi-stemmed specimen. Allow to grow naturally as shrub with many trunks for 2-3 years (depending on location and culture). Then start training by selectively removing base growth, leaving from 2-5 trunks desired for tree form; questionable trunks can be removed later on. Annually raise open area 9-12 in. and selectively prune upper growth.

FELICIA amelloides (*F. aethiopica, Agathaea coelestis*). Blue marguerite. Shrubby perennial. Vigorous and likely to overgrow and look ragged; trim severely for cut flowers and prune back hard in late summer to encourage new blooming wood. Keep seed heads removed to prolong bloom.

FERN, HARDY. Perennial plants. All ferns look best well groomed. Cut back old or unattractive fronds after new growth has started in spring. Ferns make root growth in the fall and need old fronds for food reserves at that time. (Fronds also form protective mulch for spring growth.) After new growth is well started and danger of frost is past, cut off old fronds right at soil line. (Be careful not to injure new growth.) If well protected, maidenhair and sword ferns respond well to cutting back to ground level in spring—just before new growth starts. If ferns should revert (throw plain fronds from plants that normally have crested or finely divided fronds), cut mavericks off close to plants. (Root disturbance can cause plants to revert.)

FERN PINE.
See Podocarpus gracilior.

FERN, TENDER OR EXOTIC. Perennials. Tender ferns grown indoors need only grooming to keep them looking good. Grooming includes removing dead or damaged fronds when they appear and dividing plant when surplus crowns or an excess of creeping stems give plant a crowded look. Where exotic ferns grow out of doors in mild-winter climates, delay removing fronds and trimming until spring (see Fern, Hardy).

FERN, TREE. Perennials. Groom by cutting off dead or unsightly fronds near the trunk, leaving a short stub. They are usually the oldest fronds, growing from farthest down on the trunk. In Australian tree fern (*Alsophila cooperi, A. australis*) stubs will eventually drop off, leaving a smooth trunk with attractive diamond patterning. With others, stubs will remain a long time, giving a rugged, shaggy look.

FESCUE.
See Festuca ovina 'Glauca'.

FESTUCA ovina 'Glauca' (*F. glauca*). Blue fescue. Ornamental grass. Necessary to trim festuca back almost to ground (2-3 in.) each year to prevent it from getting shaggy and to encourage new growth. In late spring or early summer when it starts to go to seed, give plant a close haircut. Easiest tool to use for few plants is pruning shears; hedge shears are best for larger numbers of plants. (A power rotary mower with blades set 2 in. high will work on extensive area.) Trimmed grass will look shabby and stubby for few weeks; then it will put out fresh, new spiky growth in typical blue fescue color.

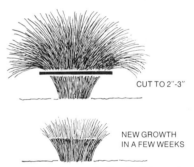

CUT TO 2"-3"

NEW GROWTH IN A FEW WEEKS

FESTUCA before and after its late spring haircut. This shearing keeps it fresh.

FICUS. Ornamental figs. Evergreen or deciduous trees, vines, shrubs, house plants. These take wide variety of shapes and sizes, most tolerating pruning well. Prune anytime except when approaching cold weather could harm tender new growth. (They will usually recover nicely from frost damage, though.) Wait until weather warms and danger of frost is past to prune frozen, winter damaged wood from plants.

F. benjamina. Weeping Chinese banyan. Evergreen tree, house plant. Can be damaged by frost in marginal areas but recovers quickly as weather warms. Tolerates pruning well. You can easily keep it confined to container, for it is easiest of group to keep pruned to small size.

Tree has good potential for multi-stem use. Follow same procedure as described for *Feijoa sellowiana*.

(Continued on next page)

RUBBER PLANT trained against wall thrives in this protected entry. Branches are fastened to the wall and pruned whenever necessary to keep plant in bounds.

F. elastica. Rubber plant. Evergreen shrub or tree, house plant. Can be pruned whenever necessary to shape. If potted plant gets too tall and leggy, cut off top and select side branch to form new main shoot.

F. e. 'Variegata' (*F. doescheri*). Pruning procedure is same as above.

F. lyrata (*F. pandurata*). Fiddleleaf fig. Evergreen tree or large shrub, house plant. Vertical growth habit; can be trained as vine. To increase branching, pinch back tips when plant is young.

F. pumila (*F. repens*). Creeping fig. Evergreen vine, house plant. Cut back to ground soon after planting to make new growth that will take off fast. Once it begins to climb, there is almost no limit to size of this vine and area it will cover. Unless restrained, it can in time envelop a 3 or 4-story building. If you use it on a house, cut it to ground every few years. Or control by removing fruiting stems from time to time as they form. Roots are invasive, have to be pruned to be contained. *F. p. 'Minima'* is not as invasive but should be watched.

F. retusa. Indian laurel fig. Evergreen tree. Serves well as patio or street tree. Excellent for training into multi-stemmed, canopy form. With regular care, will provide good shade, throwing interesting shade and light patterns. Slim trunk supporting massive crown may be concealed by lower trailing branches if these are not trimmed off regularly. You can keep it more shrub-like or train it as formal hedge.

F. r. nitida. Tolerates pruning well at any time of year. You can form it to almost any size or shape you want. Well suited to formal shearing. An attractive house plant if given a lot of shaping. Also good in multi-stem, canopy form.

F. roxburghii. Briefly deciduous. Usually takes form of large spreading shrub. Must be kept under control by pruning because it is so vigorous it can take over an entire planting area. If large overgrown plant is cut back to 5-ft.-high stem, new leaves will soon fill it out. Best time to prune is summer, early fall. (Don't prune any later than September in areas where there is danger of frost.)

FIG, EDIBLE. Deciduous tree. Vigorous plant, fig can take a good deal of pruning without appreciably reducing fruit crop. It can also grow an appreciable fruit crop every year with no pruning at all. An understanding of the fig's bearing habit will help you to prune it correctly when necessary. It normally bears two crops of fruit each year—first in early summer, next in late summer. The first crop is always carried on last year's wood; the second crop is carried farther out on branches, on new wood grown during summer after harvest of the first crop. On unpruned tree, figs form farther and farther out on branches or on new laterals.

Method of pruning a fig will vary somewhat depending upon whether you're pruning for looks or for fruit crop. If growing a fig for looks and you don't care how big it gets, let grow naturally except for removing unattractive branches. If growing a fig for looks and you wish to control size, select branches for most attractive placement and remove others. Do heaviest pruning in winter and then lightly prune vigorous growth 2 or 3 times during summer to keep plant presentable.

For best fruit, prune to encourage formation of new wood. Retain young side branches that break from main trunk and train as part of framework. Some light summer pruning will be necessary to keep plant in bounds. Avoid heavy cutting between fruit crops because this not only seriously reduces second fruit crop but also removes wood that will carry next season's first crop. Pinch back runaway shoots any time.

To espalier a fig, plant bare root plant as close as possible to support, cutting main stem back to where you want first side branches to form. As laterals break from the main stem, support those you want to keep and remove all others. This diverts all growth into basic framework.

FIG, ORNAMENTAL.
See Ficus.

FILBERT.
See Corylus.

FIR.
See Abies.

FIR, DOUGLAS.
See Pseudotsuga menziesii.

FIRETHORN.
See Pyracantha.

FIREWHEEL TREE.
See Stenocarpus sinuatus.

FIRMIANA platanifolia (*F. simplex*). Chinese parasol tree. Deciduous tree. Slow growing. When tree is dormant, thin out branches as necessary to get good branch spacing, good form.

FITTONIA verschaffeltii. Fittonia. Evergreen house plant. Pinch back new growth to encourage branching and to keep the plant low.

FLAME BUSH, TRINIDAD OR BRAZILIAN.
See Calliandra tweedii.

FLAME PEA.
See Chorizema.

FLAME TREE.
See Brachychiton.

FLAME TREE, CHINESE.
See Koelreuteria.

FLAME VINE.
See Pyrostegia venusta.

FLANNEL BUSH.
See Fremontodendron.

FLAX, NEW ZEALAND.
See Phormium tenax.

FLOWERING MAPLE.
See Abutilon.

FLOWERING QUINCE.
See Chaenomeles.

FORSYTHIA. Deciduous shrubs. Most bushes need no trimming during the first few seasons in your garden. When they reach the size you wish to maintain, take out a third of stems as soon as shrubs finish blooming. If they have 6 major stems, remove two each spring, at the same time cutting out weak or crowded growth. To maintain plant's graceful form, remove old, woody branches at ground. Don't head back because it will force brush of suckers from the cuts. You can, of course, start pruning while plants are flowering and use branches for indoor arrangements. Well-budded branches can be forced into bloom several weeks early indoors. If you have old, neglected, overgrown shrub, you can cut it to within 6 in. of ground in early spring to renew. This will sacrifice a season's flowers.

FORSYTHIA, WHITE.
See Abeliophyllum distichum.

FORTNIGHT LILY.
See Moraea iridiodes.

FOTHERGILLA. Deciduous shrubs. To preserve plants' natural grace, an occasional thinning in center of shrubs may be necessary. Cut unwanted stems to ground. This pruning is best done in winter, when plants are dormant. You may also prune, if required, after flowering in spring.

FOUNTAIN GRASS.
See Pennisetum setaceum.

FOXGLOVE, COMMON.
See Digitalis purpurea.

FOXTAIL LILY.
See Eremurus.

FRAGRANT SNOWBELL.
See Styrax obassia.

FRANKLINIA alatamaha (*Gordonia alatamaha*). Deciduous tree. Normal training while young (see *Training Young*

Trees, page 15). Prune while dormant to remove dead, weak wood.

FRAXINUS. Ash. Deciduous trees (*F. uhdei* is semi-evergreen, holds leaves all winter in mild areas). These are fast growers, requiring some attention during their early years to shape into trees you want. Remove lower side branches to get clean, single trunks and then head back laterals you want to keep to promote branching and to form the desirable rounded, dense tops. Cut out any long, whippy, lanky branches that tend to throw trees off balance.

Mature trees that have been well trained while young (see *Training Young Trees,* page 15) will require little pruning beyond the removal of dead, damaged wood. Shamel ash (*F. uhdei*) and Modesto ash (*F. velutina* 'Modesto') tend to form deep, V-shaped crotches that are weak and likely to split under stress of windstorm. Prevent these weak formations by literally "nipping them in the bud."

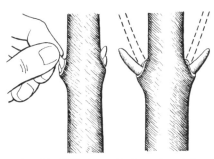

TO PREVENT deep, V-shaped crotches (shown by dotted lines) on Shamel and Modesto ash, remove upper buds. Lower buds will then form stronger crotches.

One-year-old twigs form two pairs of buds at each node. The top pair are primary buds, the ones that form narrow crotches. Only if you pinch these off will you stimulate dormant lower, or secondary, buds into growth. These lower branches will grow at a much wider (and stronger) angle from main branch. If branches do develop from primary buds, these can still be removed after 1 or 2 seasons of growth to stimulate secondary bud into growth.

FREMONTODENDRON (*Fremontia*). Flannel bush. Evergreen shrubs or small trees. Fast growers; will get rangy if not pinched and pruned regularly from the start. Respond well to heavy pruning right after flowering.

FRINGE TREE.
See Chionanthus.

FUCHSIA. Evergreen to deciduous shrubs or shrublets. Fuchsias should be pruned when most dormant—November to February. Pruning may force the

development of tender new shoots, though, so if you live in areas subject to frost in winter, postpone pruning until danger of frost is past. (To protect plants in winter areas, you can prune back in fall and mulch ground heavily.)

Many fuchsias in older gardens have gone unpruned for years, but these plants get a little larger each year and ultimately most get too big (and maybe too rangy) to be attractive any longer. Because they bloom on new wood, fuchsias can be cut back severely. Some fuchsia growers cut all the way back to one node on past summer's growth; more cautious pruners make cuts just above second node.

In cold winter areas where plants are to be stored, prune lightly; remove leaves and twiggy growth before bringing in. Then in spring cut out any broken branches. Cut hanging basket types back to perimeter of container. Frequently pinch back tips as new growth sprouts to develop better branching, bushier growth, and more flowers. If you want spectacular show of color for some special occasion in summer or fall, continue to pinch until about 6 weeks before the date you're aiming at, and then let flower buds develop and bloom.

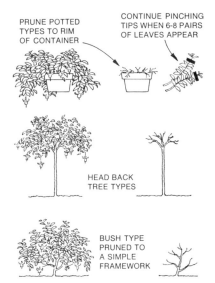

PRUNE POTTED TYPES TO RIM OF CONTAINER

CONTINUE PINCHING TIPS WHEN 6-8 PAIRS OF LEAVES APPEAR

HEAD BACK TREE TYPES

BUSH TYPE PRUNED TO A SIMPLE FRAMEWORK

CONTAINER, tree, or bush fuchsias take heaviest pruning when dormant.

FUCHSIA, AUSTRALIAN.
See Correa.

FUCHSIA, CALIFORNIA.
See Zauschneria.

FUCHSIA, CAPE.
See Phygelius capensis.

GAILLARDIA aristata. Perennial. Nip off faded blossoms every few days to prolong flowering.

GAMOLEPIS chrysanthemoides. Evergreen shrub. Regular pinching and thinning during blooming season will control untidy, leggy tendencies and also insure summer-through-winter show of flowers. Plant usually grows from 2-4 ft. high with as much as 3-4 ft. spread but can be kept lower with constant shaping. Can also be used as clipped hedge.

GARDENIA. Evergreen shrubs. Require little or no pruning. But to maintain vigorous growth, you should remove weak wood and thin out some shoots when plants are in bloom. Plants are easily reshaped, if necessary, by careful thinning. For best flower production, hold plants to about 30 in. Remove old flower clusters as they fade. When plants become old and straggly, cut oldest, weakest stems back to 6 or 8 in. from ground before spring growth begins. This will stimulate new growth from base. Remove more of oldest wood during following season to renew plants gradually.

GARRYA. Silktassel. Evergreen shrubs. Can be trained as small trees. Respond well to training and shaping whenever necessary. Because some tend to become rangy, you'll have to trim to keep them neat. Remove old tassels after flowering.

GAULTHERIA shallon. Salal. Evergreen shrub. Only neglected plant needs pruning. Can be pruned at any time of the year, but best time is spring, when old growth looks shaggy and new growth is just starting. Do not shear it but head back each branch, as you would a rose, to just above a leaf node. In this way, a planting that has become thin or leggy through neglect can be restored to its thick, lustrous best. Cut freely for use in house. Foliage stays green a long time in arrangements.

GAURA lindheimeri. Gaura. Perennial. Blossoms drop off cleanly when spent, but seed-bearing spikes should be cut.

GAZANIA. Perennials. Shear overgrown or weary-looking plants back heavily in early spring to stimulate fresh new growth (fertilizer and water are also required).

GEIJERA parviflora. Australian willow, wilga. Evergreen tree. Prune this graceful tree only to correct form when necessary.

GELSEMIUM sempervirens. Carolina jessamine. Evergreen vine. Tolerates heavy pruning when necessary to control. If vine gets top heavy, cut back severely. Usually well behaved, its stems seldom get thick and woody and are easy to prune and shape. Used in some areas as a ground cover, kept to a height of about 3 ft. by trimming back

vertical growth. Do most pruning immediately after flowering.

GENISTA.
See Cytisus.

GEOMETRY TREE.
See Bucida buceras.

GERALDTON WAXFLOWER.
See Chamaelaucium uncinatum.

GERANIUM. For common geranium, ivy geranium, Lady Washington or Martha Washington geranium, and scented geraniums see *Pelargonium*.

The true geraniums are hardy perennials for borders or rock gardens. They require no more than grooming and occasional division when clumps become crowded and blooms drop off.

GERBERA jamesonii. Transvaal daisy. Perennial. When you pick flowers for the house, cut stems at base or pull stems off as you would those of rhubarb. Stubs of cut stems remaining on plant have sharp points that can cause painful cuts. Keep dead leaves and flowers picked off plant. Do not let dirt pile up around base.

GERMANDER.
See Teucrium.

GEUM. Perennials. Keep dead flowers picked off to prolong bloom. If cut back after spring bloom, they will flower again in fall.

GIANT REED.
See Arundo donax.

GINGER LILY.
See Hedychium.

GINKGO biloba. Maidenhair tree. Deciduous tree. Graceful, slow growing. Needs early staking and training (see *Training Young Trees,* page 15), very little pruning afterwards except to remove dead, weak, or damaged wood. Prune while dormant. Tree sometimes produces upward-growing shoots which are parallel with central leader. Remove unwanted shoots back to lateral or to branch they grew on.

GLADIOLUS. Corm. Cut gladiolus flower stalks about where 3rd and 4th leaves cross stem, making sure you leave at least 4 or 5 leaves on plant. These are vital for manufacture of next season's corms. Cut leaves off only after they have turned brown and you have harvested corms.

GLAUCIUM flavum. Yellow horned poppy. Perennial or biennial. Cut back each year to new basal leaves when healthy and growing. This encourages new growth.

GLEDITSIA triacanthos. Honey locust. Deciduous tree. Will withstand heavy pruning and shaping. Do major pruning while dormant. Stake and train young tree to get basic branch pattern you want. Large spikes and thorns on trunk and branches can be hazard to children and gardeners. Remove these spikes as soon as they appear. Thin crowded branches. 'Sunburst' variety has tendency to grow unruly branches. Head back to produce better balanced tree.

A YOUNG 'Sunburst' honey locust (Gleditsia) that's been pruned to best form.

GLORIOSA DAISY.
See Rudbeckia hirta.

GLORYBOWER.
See Clerodendrum.

GOATNUT.
See Simmondsia chinensis.

GOLDENCHAIN TREE.
See Laburnum.

GOLDEN LARCH.
See Chrysolarix amabilis.

GOLDENRAIN TREE.
See Koelreuteria.

GOLDEN TRUMPET TREE.
See Tabebula chrysotricha.

GOOSEBERRY.
See Ribes.

GRAPE. Deciduous vine. You shouldn't let a grape vine run wild. A badly trained, badly pruned vine will tangle, tend to get mildew, always bear disappointing crops of fruit—and never grow into anything that's much to look at.

If you want a neatly trained vine as well as good fruit production, best way to prune is usually one of two methods shown in the illustrations, depending on which kind of grape you have planted. The sketches take you through a grape vine's first 4 years, from planting to maturity. Devote the first 3 years to training the vine. After it has matured, treat it the same way each pruning season (December 1 to March 1).

To be sure of large, good-flavored grapes, you have to thin out some of crop each year. Until the vine matures, never let more than half a dozen bunches develop; cut off rest as soon as fruit forms. After maturity, let about half the bunches develop.

WHICH PRUNING METHOD?

How to prune depends on the variety of grape. One of the two methods is called spur pruning and the other long-cane pruning. If you follow either system or if you train a vine on an arbor, do the same thing for the first year and a half: always start out by following the 3 steps you see illustrated below.

Spur pruning. This method works for most European grape varieties except 'Thompson Seedless'; use it, for example, for 'Cardinal', 'Muscat', 'Perlette', 'Red Malaga', 'Ribier', 'Tokay', and the California wine varieties. The sketches show the vine trained on a simple wire support. You can train a vine like this on top of a fence or similar structure.

Long-cane pruning. Use this method for 'Thompson Seedless' and for most American grapes (for example, 'Concord', 'Delaware', 'Niagara', 'Pierce'). These kinds don't produce much fruit when cut back to short spurs. They bear most of their fruit from buds farther out on the canes (the part that's cut off when branches are spur pruned). Train them on the same type of structures as spur-pruned vines.

Arbors. If led in the right direction, almost any grape can climb up and over an arbor. Spend the first few years getting the vine to cover the structure, then prune annually using the method (spur or long cane) that's best for the variety.

Starting a grape vine ... planting to second spring

At planting time

Soak roots if dry. Cut plant back to three buds, trim roots to 6 inches. Bury whole thing except top two buds. Water. Mound light soil over top (buds grow through).

First winter after planting

Time to start training and pruning. Until now object has been to let plant sprawl, develop strong roots. Cut off all but strongest cane. Cut that to three buds. Tie.

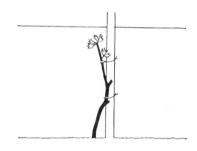

Second spring

New shoots grew from buds left after pruning. When shoots are a foot long, select most vigorous to serve as a permanent trunk, cut off others. Tie to stake loosely.

This is spur pruning

Second summer

When main shoot reaches foot above wire, cut it back even with wire. When top two buds sprout, train shoots horizontally. Tie each one to wire about foot from tip.

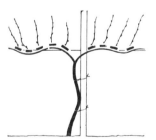

Second winter

Cut off all branches from two main side arms (don't injure bud at base of each branch). You aren't pruning for fruit yet. The object is to develop a strong framework.

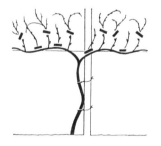

Third winter

Now begin pruning for fruit production. First cut out all weak and crowded branches. Then select strong canes 6 to 10 inches apart; cut each one back to two-bud spur.

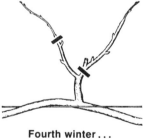

Fourth winter ... and after

Two canes grew from last winter's spurs and had fruit. Cut off outer cane at base. Shorten one closest to trunk to two buds. Repeat process each winter from now on.

(Long-cane pruning illustrated on next page)

Grape — Gymnocladus

This is long-cane pruning

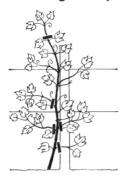

Second summer

Pinch out tip of stem a foot above the top wire. Let side shoots grow on upper third of plant; cut off shoots on bottom two-thirds. Tie vine near the top and at the middle.

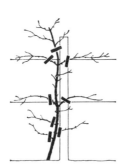

Second winter

Cut off stem right through bud just above wire. Remove side branches below midpoint. Above, remove all but two to four side shoots; cut back to the two-bud spurs.

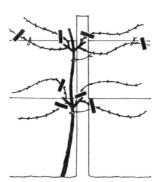

Third winter

Last winter's spurs now long branches. Cut two as fruiting canes (leave 8 to 12 buds). Train in fan shape. Cut two to four as two-bud spurs. Cut off the other canes.

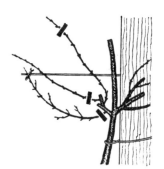

Fourth winter... and after

Cut off old fruiting canes. Each spur sent out two shoots; cut upper as fruiting cane (8 to 12 buds), lower as spur. Keep 4 to 6 spurs, and the same number of canes.

This is how you train a grape vine on an arbor

Second summer

Unlike above methods, don't stop stem. When tip of it reaches top of support, tie down over corner. Encourage stem to grow long by pinching back side shoots.

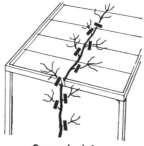

Second winter... and following spring

Cut back main stem to pencil-sized wood. Cut off side branches. In spring, when new shoots are 6 inches long, thin to foot apart. When 18 inches, tie down at midpoint.

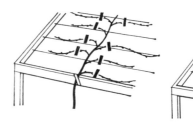

Third winter ... and after

Spur-pruned varieties: Cut back shoots to two buds. Next year, prune as in drawing at bottom right of previous page. Long-cane pruning: Alternate spurs with fruiting canes (8 to 12 buds). Next year, cut off canes; prune spurs as in drawing at top right of this page. With both methods, you can leave strong canes about 4 feet long every 3 feet to become part of the permanent framework.

GRAPE, EVERGREEN.
See Rhoicissus capensis.

GRAPEFRUIT.
See Citrus.

GRAPE, OREGON.
See Mahonia aquifolium.

GREVILLEA robusta. Silk oak. Evergreen tree. Branches tend to be brittle and subject to wind damage. Head tree back hard at planting time to strengthen framework. Then prune it lightly each year after flowering. Avoid heavy pruning; if cut too severely, wood may fail to heal properly. Young plant can be confined in tub for few years.

GREWIA caffra. Lavender starflower. Evergreen shrub. Fast growing and sprawling, it takes kindly to pruning and is easily kept under control. Pinch back tips regularly to make dense. Tends to form natural espalier if given some support. Can also be used as clipped hedge or screen, as ground cover (prune out upright growth), trained and staked as single-trunked tree, or tied and trained to cover arbor or trellis. After first heavy bloom, head back to keep new flowering wood coming into continued bloom through autumn; then thin and head back again after flowering.

GRISELINIA littoralis. Evergreen shrub. Neat, compact, and well groomed. Only pruning it needs is heading back each spring, just before new growth begins, to encourage dense branching habit. Good espalier subject.

GUAVA, STRAWBERRY.
See Psidium cattleianum.

GUM.
See Eucalyptus.

GUM, SWEET.
See Liquidambar.

GUNNERA. Perennial. Improve appearance of plant by cutting leaves to base each winter. In cold winter areas, leaves die back completely in winter; elsewhere, old leaves remain green for more than one year.

GYMNOCLADUS dioica. Kentucky coffee tree. Deciduous tree. Often naturally grows with 3 or 4 upright main stems from trunk into narrow, round-headed tree. Young tree needs normal staking and training (see *Training Young Trees,* page 15); mature tree requires little pruning aside from removal of weak and damaged wood. Prune while dormant.

PRUNING SAW is used to remove unwanted branches of common witch hazel. They sprouted from rootstock on which this Chinese witch hazel was grafted.

GYPSOPHILA. Annuals, perennials. To prolong bloom, cut back flowering stems before seed clusters form. Cut back to ground in fall after main bloom period ends.

HACKBERRY.
See Celtis.

HAKEA. Evergreen shrubs, trees. Pinching tips while young will promote bushier growth. Beyond that, little pruning required. Can be trained into tree forms but should not be sheared, for they will not recover quickly.

HALESIA carolina (*H. tetraptera*). Snowdrop tree, silver bell. Deciduous tree. Prune to single stem when young unless you want to let it grow as a large shrub. If headed back to fork at 4 or 5 ft. height, it will form attractive structure. Once established, very little pruning will be required. Do any necessary pruning after bloom period.

HALIMIUM. Evergreen shrublets. Shear plants back after spring flowering to encourage fall bloom.

HAMAMELIS mollis. Chinese witch hazel. Deciduous tree or shrub. Prune lightly in winter to keep open branch pattern. You can do this when you cut flowers for indoors. Will eventually grow into 12-15-ft.-high shrub. Can be kept small by heading unwanted growth back to side branches. New growth can be promoted by thinning out oldest wood.

Because Chinese witch hazel is difficult to propagate, growers often graft it to the root stock of our common native witch hazel, *H. virginiana*. If you notice that your Chinese witch hazel has some branches with different shaped leaves and flowers that don't appear when the others do, then shoots from the grafted rootstock have sprung up and been allowed to grow. These should be cut out close to the ground.

HARDENBERGIA. Evergreen shrubby vines. Pinch back during growing season to shape. Cut back after blooming to prevent tangling. Remove old, weak growths to keep from getting leggy.

HARPEPHYLLUM caffrum. Kaffir plum. Evergreen tree. Easy to train while young. New growth can be erratic, but with patience, stems and branches can be shaped into almost any form. Tends to have dense head, but tree can be opened up by thinning out inside branches. Can be pruned into many interesting shapes. Recovers quickly from pruning and damage of freezing. Prune to shape and to remove winter-damaged wood in spring after danger of frost.

HAWTHORN.
See Crataegus.

HAZELNUT.
See Corylus.

HEAVENLY BAMBOO.
See Nandina domestica.

HEBE. Evergreen shrubs. Prune after blooming, shortening flowering branches considerably to keep plants compact and bushy. Flowering branches can be cut to ground each year after they fade. Plants withstand heavy pruning, sprout readily from old wood.

HEDERA. Ivy. Evergreen woody vines. May be pruned as lightly or as heavily as you wish at almost any time of year, though pruning should be avoided in late fall and winter because regrowth is very slow then. Most ivy ground covers need trimming around edges with hedge shears, machete, or sharp spade 2 or 3 times a year. Ivy on fences and walls need shearing or trimming 2-3 times a year. (If you are trying to retain pattern effect, you will have to trim every time pattern gets out of line—as often as every 2 weeks.)

Overgrown leggy beds can be mowed with a heavy-duty rotary power mower or cut back with hedge shears. Do this in spring so new growth will quickly cover the bald look. If you want clusters of berries on your English ivy (*Hedera helix*) in winter, direct some of it to upright growth and allow it to go its own way. It will ultimately produce stiff-branched clusters of small, ivory green flowers in fall. Tiny berries that follow will last well into winter and lend themselves to holiday decorating.

HEDYCHIUM. Ginger lily. Perennials. After bloom, remove old flower stems. As soon as cold weather approaches, plants become shabby looking and should be cut back to ground. Forms that die down to ground each year can be treated much like cannas: cut stems back to ground after frosts in spring.

HELENIUM autumnale. Common sneezeweed. Perennial. Pinch back tips of all shoots until mid-June to keep plants compact and to produce more bloom. Trim off faded blossoms to encourage more blooms.

HELIANTHEMUM nummularium. Sunrose. Evergreen shrublets. In cold sections, helianthemums will die back to roots almost every winter. They will come back in spring. Remove dead portions in early spring. In less severe winters, leaves will die but stems will grow new leaves again. Shear plants back after they bloom in spring and early summer to encourage fall bloom. Occasionally nip off seed pods to encourage scattering of blooms into late fall.

HELICHRYSUM petiolatum (*Gnaphalium lanatum*). Shrubby perennial. In mild winter areas, prune plant back occasionally to keep it tidy. In colder areas, plant is apt to be cut back by frost, so prune to remove deadwood only after weather warms in spring. If you cut back a helichrysum too severely, you may lose it.

HELIOTROPE.
See Heliotropium arborescens.

HELIOTROPIUM arborescens (*H. peruvianum*). Common heliotrope. Perennial. To make plant bushy, pinch back tip growth when stems are 4-5 in. high. With this early pinching, the rather sprawling, bushy plant can be kept below 18 in. Trimming off some stems when removing faded flowers keeps plant compact and encourages new crop of blossoms.

HELLEBORE.
See Helleborus.

HELLEBORUS. Hellebore. Perennial. When flowering season is over, new growth comes from roots. Cut off (don't pull) all dead or dying leaves near ground only after new foliage starts. After that, avoid cutting the foliage; it's needed to manufacture food for next flower crop.

HEMEROCALLIS. Daylily. Perennial, evergreen and deciduous. Snap off faded flowers daily; cut back severely after bloom to stimulate new growth. Remove dead foliage on deciduous varieties in late winter or early spring before new growth appears. Can be transplanted successfully by trimming off broken, bruised roots and about ⅔ of the top growth.

HEMLOCK.
See Tsuga.

HERALD'S TRUMPET.
See Beaumontia grandiflora.

HETEROMELES arbutifolia (*Photinia arbutifolia*). Toyon, Christmas berry, California holly. Evergreen shrub or small tree. Will stand any amount of pruning to keep it low or to prevent loose straggly growth. Even if cut back to ground, will sprout up from roots.

Can be pruned and trained to spread out over bank, form informal hedge, or grow as a small, single-trunked tree. Best time to prune is in late winter or early spring when new growth appears. If trimmed to produce abundance of year-old wood, it will produce more berries.

Susceptible to fireblight: as soon as buds begin to expand in spring, look for dead branches indicating disease. Cut these out to lessen chance of infecting new growth. Sterilize pruning tools after cutting any diseased wood.

HEUCHERA sanguinea. Coral bells. Perennial. Requires little care beyond removal of spent flowers by snapping off stems at base. If cut to ground after main bloom, it may bloom again same year.

HIBBERTIA scandens (*H. volubilis*). Guinea gold vine. Evergreen twining vine. Needs little pruning. To keep stems from tangling, cut out frost-damaged wood in spring. If vine gets top-heavy, cut back a few oldest stems to force out new, lower growth.

HIBISCUS. Perennials, deciduous, and evergreen shrubs.
  H. huegelii. Blue hibiscus. Evergreen shrub. Needs only occasional pinching or pruning after danger of frost is past to keep compact.
  H. moscheutos. Perennial hibiscus, rose-mallow. Perennial. Each fall after flowering, cut plant to within 3 in. of ground.
  H. rosa-sinensis. Chinese hibiscus, tropical hibiscus. Evergreen shrub. Should not be pruned in winter (except in tropical climates) because chilly weather slows it down and lowers its vitality.

After weather warms, don't be afraid to prune old wood severely, for showy flowers are produced on new wood. Young plants seldom need pruning, but nipping growing tips of branches will help to increase flowering wood.

Progressively cut back old shrubs with unproductive, woody branches; starting in spring, cut out 1 or 2 oldest stems. Do this once a month until August. Do not shear like a hedge. Instead, cut few forward branches, not all same height. When these have leafed out, treat back growth the same way. Continued pruning throughout growing season will encourage more branching, control size of plant, and eliminate drastic pruning the following season. Don't prune after mid-September in areas where there is danger of freezing because new growth is susceptible to frost.

Plan for yearly removal of one or more old branches, cutting back from ⅓-⅔ of last season's growth. This encourages new shoots, leafage low down on plant, more bloom. Strong growers ('Agnes Galt', 'Kona', 'San Diego Red',

'White Wings') must be pruned severely every spring or they will become thick-trunked, sprawling and so high you won't be able to see flowers carried at ends of branches. Best procedure is to remove crossing or conflicting branches, leaving strongest and those providing best framework. Cut rank growth back severely and remove some laterals, particularly those growing toward inside of plant.

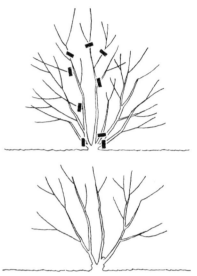

PRUNE SHRUB-FORM hibiscus as shown in top drawing. Result is shown below.

Leave about 3-6 well-placed laterals on each main branch, cutting back to 2 or 3 buds. Prune as growth begins in spring. If frost blackened foliage during the winter, or if cold weather stopped plant growth and flower production, cut stems back to about 6 in. from ground.

  H. syriacus. Rose of Sharon, shrub althaea. Deciduous shrub. Needs only light pruning to shape; for bigger flowers, though, prune more severely in winter, cutting back previous season's growth to 2 buds.

HIGHBUSH CRANBERRY.
See Viburnum opulus.

HIPPOCREPIS comosa. Perennial ground cover. If used as lawn substitute, mow once a year, just after flowers fade.

HOHERIA. Evergreen tree and deciduous tree or shrub. Can be trained as single or multiple-stemmed plant. Only light pruning required once form has been established. Prune after flowering.

HOLLY.
See Ilex.

HOLLY, CALIFORNIA.
See Heteromeles arbutifolia.

HOLLY, COSTA RICAN.
See Olmediella betschleriana.

HOLLY, GUATEMALAN.
See Olmediella.

HOLLYLEAF CHERRY.
See Prunus ilicifolia.

HOLLYLEAF SWEETSPIRE.
See Itea ilicifolia.

HOLLY, SUMMER.
See Comarostaphylis diversifolia.

HOLODISCUS discolor. Cream bush, ocean spray. Deciduous shrub. Can get ragged, needs pruning for neatness. Do major pruning after bloom—head longest branches back to laterals, remove all seed clusters. In spring, prune off freeze-damaged portions.

HOMALANTHUS populifolius. Queensland poplar. Evergreen or semievergreen small tree. To train as a full-sized tree, cut off lower branches in winter when young. When mature, remove lower branches if necessary, cutting off straggling upper limbs. Thin out heavy top growth to keep the tree's shape attractive. Remove all of the deadwood and suckers.

HONEY BELL.
See Mahernia verticillata.

HONEY BUSH.
See Melianthus major.

HONEY LOCUST.
See Gleditsia triacanthos.

HONEYSUCKLE.
See Lonicera.

HOP BUSH.
See Dodonaea viscosa.

HOP, COMMON.
See Humulus lupulus.

HOPSEED BUSH.
See Dodonaea viscosa.

HORNBEAM.
See Carpinus.

HORSECHESTNUT.
See Aesculus.

HORSETAIL.
See Equisetum hyemale.

HOSTA (*Funkia*). Plantain lily. Perennials. All forms go dormant in winter. Shear leaves off after they turn brown; remove old flower stalks. New, fresh-looking leaves sprout from perennial roots in early spring.

HOWEIA.
See Palm.

HUCKLEBERRY.
See Vaccinium.

HUMMINGBIRD FLOWER.
See Zauschneria.

HUMULUS lupulus. Common hop. Perennial vine. Cut stems to ground after frost turns them brown. Regrowth comes from ground the following spring. Twining stems should be trained by hand in June and July.

HYACINTH SHRUB.
See Xanthoceras sorbifolium.

HYBOPHRYNIUM brauneanum (*Bamburanta arnoldiana*). Bamburanta. Perennial. Thin or divide when clumps get too thick. In most cases cut old stalks to ground when leaves become shabby. Also remove old flower stalks.

HYDRANGEA. Deciduous shrubs, vines. Though all forms are deciduous, many hold their leaves all year where winters are mild. Hydrangeas make two kinds of flower heads—full, round heads and the kind where big flowers form only around the edge. The latter are called "lace cap" hydrangeas. Keep them from going to seed by removing their flowers as soon as they have bloomed. Hydrangeas can also be cut back each spring to point just above bases of previous year's growth. For plants that have not bloomed well, try removing spent flowers to help force remaining buds. Cut stems just above round pair of leaves below flower heads.

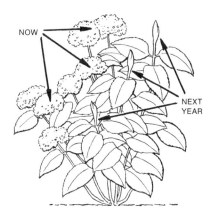

CUT HYDRANGEA BRANCHES when flowers fade. Notice that some branches will flower next year (save them).

H. anomala petiolaris (*H. petiolaris*). Climbing hydrangea. Deciduous vine. Only pruning normally required is shortening of new growth that sometimes swings out from wall in summer and may loosen vine from its support. Left unpruned, climbing hydrangea can cover jumbled rockery.

H. arborescens. Smooth hydrangea. Deciduous shrubs. Need heavy pruning in spring. Remove crowded and dead stems; head back live wood to 2 or 3 buds to stimulate new growth.

H. macrophylla (*H. hortensia, H. opuloides, H. otaksa*). Bigleaf hydrangea, garden hydrangea. Deciduous shrubs. Strong, rank growers; should be pruned heavily as flowers fade. Cut stems back to strong laterals or promising buds. In early spring remove frost-damaged wood; thin out half of oldest woody stems by cutting them to the ground. Cut back stems that bloomed last season to within 2 pairs of buds from ground level. When neglected, plants tend to become woody or stubby; prune to ground and let them start over. (Winter damage to buds may cause plants to produce foliage but no flowers. If this happens, prune in summer after normal flowering and *do not* prune following winter or spring.)

H. paniculata 'Grandiflora'. Pee gee hydrangea. Deciduous shrub or small standard tree. Can grow high and wide or be kept as a 3 or 4-ft. hedge by pruning. For fewer but larger flower clusters, prune heavily in early spring, heading back year-old wood to 3 or 4 spurs. If trained to one stem, cut back to 2 or 3 growth buds on well-placed branches.

H. quercifolia. Oakleaf hydrangea. Deciduous shrub. If pruned to ground each spring, makes compact, 3-ft. shrub. Thinned to well-spaced branches, makes distinguished container plant.

HYMENOSPORUM flavum. Sweetshade. Evergreen small tree or large shrub. Early training necessary (see *Training Young Trees,* page 15) because developing branches tend to create weak crotches that are likely to split. Thin out weak branches and prune to space out remaining branches. Strengthen branches by frequent pinching and shortening. When planted in small groves, tree grows well without staking or pruning. Prune to shape whenever necessary.

HYPERICUM. St. Johnswort. Shrubs and perennials, evergreen or semi-evergreen. Will respond well to heavy pruning during dormant season or in spring when new growth begins. Remove crowded, weak, dead branches; cut others back to 2 or 3 buds. If neglected, plants become straggly, twiggy, untidy. Cut back severely to give them room to produce new growth.

H. calycinum. Aaron's beard, creeping St. Johnswort. Evergreen shrub, ground cover (semi-deciduous where winters are cold). Spreads by underground runners and fills in quickly. Vigorous underground runners often need chopping back with sharp spade. To thicken, shear or mow off tops at least every 2 or 3 years while most dormant.

(Continued on next page)

H. 'Sungold'. Twiggy, rounded shrub. Little pruning required other than removing oldest wood every 2 or 3 years to rejuvenate.

IBERIS. Candytuft. Annuals, perennials. For neat appearance, remove spent flower clusters by shearing lightly after flowering to stimulate new growth.

I. sempervirens. Evergreen candytuft. Perennial. Planted close together, they make solid, rather formal miniature hedge or ground cover. Keep low with heavy annual shearing.

ICE PLANT. Succulent perennials, subshrubs, or annuals. Chop or shear expanding edges or burgeoning tops whenever necessary to keep the planting under control.

Lampranthus. Cut back lightly after bloom to eliminate fruit capsules, encourage new leafy growth.

ILEX. Holly. Evergreen shrubs or trees. All types will withstand heavy pruning any time of the year, and can be used as sheared hedges, topiary, bonsai, shrubs, or trees. One of best times to prune berried hollies is during Christmas season so that you may use berried greens indoors (only female plants have berries).

When they grow large, they tend to droop to the ground and root, creating an impenetrable jungle underneath. Best to remove branches up a bit on trunks, high enough so that drooping branches do not touch ground. Important to have enough clearance to get rake underneath to keep them cleaned out. When cutting back holly, do not leave leafless stubs.

I. altaclarensis 'Wilsonii' (*I. wilsonii*). Wilson holly. Shrub or tree. Fast, strong grower, can be shaped as standard tree, espalier, shrub, screen, or clipped hedge. Regular pruning of shrub type will keep it bushy and increase amount of berry wood. May grow to 20 ft., but can be kept as low as 6 or 8 ft. tall with annual prunings.

I. aquifolium. English holly, Christmas holly. Shrubs, trees. Will take great deal of cutting, thinning, or shearing. If young trees develop two main trunks, remove one to avoid danger of splitting.

To give shrubs solid compact look, pinch tips of new growth back in spring to force branching. (Remember, however, that dense growth tends to increase scale insect problems, and that unfruited tips of last season's growth produce berries for coming year.) When cutting holly for decorations, consider each branch tip—whether 3 in. or 20 in. long—a holly spray. Make cuts to enhance regular form of trees, rather than being concerned with size of sprays.

I. cornuta 'Burfordii'. Burford holly. Shrub or small tree. Not a fast grower so it doesn't require as much attention as English holly. Occasional thinning and heading back will keep it in shape.

I. c. 'Rotunda'. Dwarf Chinese holly. Because of compact habit and slow growth, you'll find little need for pruning. Makes excellent low, trimmed hedge.

I. crenata. Japanese holly. Shrub. Left alone, shrub becomes rather tall, slim, densely-foliaged spire. However, it can be trained and shaped by pruning to almost any form you want. In Japan it is used frequently for topiary. Naturally neat and low growing, it can be kept even lower.

I. c. 'Convexa'. (Often sold as *I. c. bullata*.) Plant has a pleasing shape whether it's clipped or left to grow naturally. Trimmed, looks like boxwood. Will grow to 6 ft. but can be kept lower by pruning.

I. c. 'Helleri'. Dwarf. Makes excellent low trimmed hedge with minimum of pruning. Attractive left unpruned.

I. c. 'Microphylla'. Capable of growing to tree size. It can be kept to 2-4 ft. by cutting back or even shearing like hedge.

I. pernyi. Shrub or small tree. May grow to height of 20 ft., becoming open and gangly as it matures, but form is easily controlled by pruning.

IMPATIENS oliveri. Oliver's snapweed, poor man's rhododendron. Perennial. In colder areas, frost kills to ground; it will grow again in spring. Where frost does not kill it, you can cut it to the ground in fall for new growth in spring.

INCENSE CEDAR.
See Calocedrus decurrens.

INDIA DEVIL TREE.
See Rauwolfia samarensis.

INDIAN CURRANT.
See Symphoricarpos.

INDIAN LAUREL FIG.
See Ficus retusa.

INDIAN MOCK STRAWBERRY.
See Duchesnea indica.

INDIGO BUSH.
See Amorpha.

INDIGO, FALSE.
See Baptisia australis.

IOCHROMA cyaneum (*I. lanceolatum, I. purpureum, I. tubulosum*). Evergreen shrub. Prune it hard after bloom. Softwooded, it looks best espaliered or tied up against wall. Take out some oldest shoots to ground annually.

IPOMOEA. Morning glory. Vining perennials. Train on fence, trellis, or use as ground cover. Cut to ground annually in fall. New growth will appear in spring.

IRIS. Bulbs, rhizomes. Dormant plants, with dead outside leaves and yellowed leaf tips, are unsightly and serve as winter hiding place for insects, snails, and slugs. Remove old leaves, always pulling off outermost dried leaves first. Do not cut back green leaves except when transplanting.

ITALIAN BUCKTHORN.
See Rhamnus alaternus.

ITEA ilicifolia. Hollyleaf sweetspire. Evergreen shrub or small tree. Graceful, open shrub, requires only minimum of pruning for shaping, removal of deadwood. Normally grows to about 10 ft. but can easily be kept to 4 or 5 ft. with occasional thinning. Prune whenever necessary to shape.

IVY.
See Hedera.

IVY, BOSTON.
See Parthenocissus.

IVY GERANIUM.
See Pelargonium peltatum.

JACARANDA acutifolia (*J. mimosaefolia*). Jacaranda. Deciduous to semievergreen tree. Very adaptable, can be trained to form single or multi-trunked plant. Once you have the form you want, little pruning is necessary beyond cleaning out deadwood and occasionally heading back growth that departs from desired form. In cases where tree is frozen badly, a number of shoots will develop at base of trunk. For single-stemmed tree, select most vigorous shoot and encourage it. For clump-type tree, select 3 or 4 of strongest shoots. To convert a single-trunked tree into a multi-trunked one, lop off trunk 2 ft. or less above ground. New branches will break below cut, and tree can be trained to 3 or 4 main trunks. Pinch out growing tips every 3 ft. or so to force more branching. If tree gets rangy, cut it back.

JACOBINIA carnea. Brazilian plume flower. Evergreen shrub. In colder climates, cut back to ground each fall, or frost will do it for you. (You can, of course, grow it in container and bring indoors in winter.) In milder areas, grow as evergreen shrub, cutting back every 2 or 3 years to keep neat. Heavy pruning just as plant starts to grow in spring results in more vigorous, compact growth and a better crop of flowers. As plant grows pinch developing stems once or twice to increase the number of branching stems.

JADE PLANT.
See Crassula.

JAPANESE ARALIA.
See Fatsia japonica.

JAPANESE KNOTWEED.
See Polygonum cuspidatum.

JAPANESE PAGODA TREE.
See Sophora japonica.

JAPANESE SPURGE.
See Pachysandra terminalis.

JASMINE.
See Jasminum.

JASMINE, CHILEAN.
See Mandevilla laxa.

JASMINE, STAR.
See Trachelospermum.

JASMINUM. Jasmine. Evergreen or deciduous shrubs or vines. All jasmines need frequent pinching, thinning, and shaping to control growth. Do this whenever necessary.

J. grandiflorum (*J. officinale grandiflorum*). Spanish jasmine. Semi-evergreen to deciduous vine. Can be pruned and trained as a vine or as a shrub.

J. humile. Italian jasmine. Evergreen shrub or vine. Erect willowy shoots form tall, arching shrub. Can be trained as vine.

J. magnificum. See *J. nitidum*.

J. mesnyi (*J. primulinum*). Primrose jasmine. Evergreen shrub. Long, arching branches form 6-10-ft. shrub. Will grow taller if trained against wall.

J. multiflorum. (Often sold as *J. gracillimum*.) Pinwheel jasmine. Evergreen shrub or vine. Will get bare and leggy if not headed back regularly to force bushiness.

J. nitidum. (Often sold as *J. magnificum*.) Angelwing jasmine. Evergreen or semi-deciduous vine. Versatile, very receptive to training. If planted 3-5 ft. apart and left to grow as it likes, will make good, solid ground cover in couple of years. Trained up trellis or wall, it weaves stems into screen of solid green. By pinching or clipping straying branches, you can turn it into handsome low-growing shrub.

J. nudiflorum. Winter jasmine. Deciduous viny shrub. Prune hard by thinning ⅓ of wood each year after bloom. This keeps the plant in bounds and forces new flowering growth. An easy way to keep it in bounds is to consistently pick twiggy side branches before buds bloom and bring them indoors (they last well in water).

J. officinale. Common white jasmine, poet's jasmine. Semi-evergreen to deciduous twining vine. Very fast growing; it often rambles to over 50 ft. if not controlled. Requires constant shaping and heading back during growing season.

J. parkeri. Dwarf jasmine. Evergreen shrub. Normally low-tufted plant with many twiggy branches. Keep it lower and more spreading as ground cover by shearing tops after bloom.

J. polyanthum. Evergreen vine. Head back and thin branches each year after bloom.

J. sambac. Arabian jasmine. Evergreen shrub. Will get bare and leggy if not headed back regularly to force bushiness.

JERUSALEM SAGE.
See Phlomis fruticosa.

JERUSALEM THORN.
See Parkinsonia aculeata.

JESSAMINE, CAROLINA.
See Gelsemium sempervirens.

JESSAMINE, ORANGE.
See Murraya paniculata.

JETBEAD.
See Rhodotypos.

JOHNNY-JUMP-UP.
See Viola tricolor.

JOJOBA.
See Simmondsia chinensis.

JUGLANS.
See Walnut.

JUJUBE, CHINESE.
See Zizyphus jujuba.

JUNIPER.
See Juniperus.

JUNIPER MYRTLE.
See Agonis.

JUNIPERUS. Juniper. Evergreen shrubs and trees. Junipers respond well to pruning. If they look straggly or lopsided, remove unwanted growth to improve the shape before new growth starts. Shrub types can be developed into thick, well-shaped plants by cutting tips of branches back to first fork (or farther if more drastic measures are required) each spring.

Upper branches on low growing junipers tend to block off light and air from weaker ones below. To prevent this, cut back and thin out some of top growth in late spring or early summer. Take entire branches where possible, always making cuts to enhance beauty of shrubs. Good time to cut back junipers that have outgrown their allotted space is just before Christmas holidays, when you can use the greenery for decorations.

Tree forms generally require less pruning than the lower growing junipers. Sometimes it's better to replace junipers that have outgrown their space than to prune them way back.

The preceding general advice applies to all junipers. Following are several forms for which some specific pruning or training information will be useful.

J. chinensis 'Pfitzeriana Aurea'. Golden pfitzer juniper. Has interestingly irregular outline that can be emphasized with selective pruning. Fast growing, needs to be pruned regularly.

(Continued on next page)

BY CUTTING BACK outward-facing branches, you make Juniperus horizontalis grow flat and wavelike against wall. Plants don't need supports when trained this way.

OCCASIONAL TRIMMING of Juniperus scopulorum maintains columnar symmetry.

J. c. 'Torulosa'. Hollywood juniper, twisted juniper. One of easiest conifers to train. Prune or shape in any direction. Looks awkward when young because of flexible branches; needs support for several years and can then be left to go its own way. To control shape, thin out selected branches in spring or fall. Never shear it. Pruning to encourage greater density tends to increase plant's susceptibility to twig blight.

J. horizontalis. Prostrata juniper. Can take espalier form against wall if supported and trained. Thin, do not chop back.

J. scopulorum. Silver king juniper, Rocky Mountain juniper, Western red cedar. Withstands heavy pruning, needs occasional trimming for symmetrical form. Prune moderately from the start for dense, compact shrub.

J. virginiana. Red cedar juniper, Eastern red cedar. Tree. Sometimes sheared, but best to train and prune as tree. Seldom requires much pruning, but size and form can be controlled by cutting back new growth in late spring or early summer.

JUPITER'S BEARD.
See Centranthus ruber.

KADSURA japonica. Scarlet kadsura. Twining evergreen vine. Fast growing. With support can be trained against wall or fence or on trellis; without support it sprawls over ground. Thin and shape in early spring.

KAFFIR LILY.
See Clivia miniata.

KAFFIR PLUM.
See Harpephyllum caffrum.

KALMIA latifolia. Mountain laurel, calico bush. Evergreen shrub. Like rhododendrons, kalmia will respond well to heavy pruning but seldom needs it. Some gardeners feel that faded flower heads weaken plant and should be removed. If you think they look untidy and want to remove them, shear off, being especially careful not to cut into growth buds at the base of leaves. If you injure them, you may not get flowers next year. Generally prune plant after flowering. Cut some oldest stems to ground to encourage new growth.

KATSURA TREE.
See Cercidiphyllum japonicum.

KEI APPLE.
See Dovyalis caffra.

KENTUCKY COFFEE TREE.
See Gymnocladus dioica.

KERRIA japonica. Deciduous shrub. Responds well to heavy pruning. Cut back to ground old growth that has flowered, along with dead or weak wood. For loose, open shrub, remove as many as half of old canes at ground level as soon as flowers fade. This will encourage new shoots.

KHAT.
See Catha edulis.

KINNIKINNICK.
See Arctostaphylos uva-ursi.

KIWI.
See Actinidia.

KLEINIA. Succulents. Keep unattractive flowers cut off to preserve foliage quality.

KNIPHOFIA uvaria (*Tritoma uvaria*). Red-hot poker, torch-lily, poker plant. Perennial. Remove flower spikes after bloom and cut old leaves off at base in fall. New leaves will replace them.

KOELREUTERIA. Chinese flame tree, goldenrain tree. Deciduous trees. Normal staking and training for shape while young (see *Training Young Trees,* page 15). Very little annual pruning afterward. You may want to cut off fat, papery capsules after they turn brown and unsightly; at the same time, selectively remove extra growth to maintain open, graceful forms.

KOLKWITZIA amabilis. Beauty bush. Deciduous shrub. Given enough room to grow in, plant shouldn't require heavy pruning. However, like deutzia, it can be pruned heavily right after bloom. Still, some gardeners enjoy silver brown, bristly fruits for winter interest and do not prune at that time, letting fruits develop and then removing them in spring. To control size and to renew, cut some oldest canes to ground each spring.

KOREAN SPICE VIBURNUM.
See Viburnum carlesii.

KOREAN YEW.
See Cephalotaxus harringtonia.

LABURNUM. Goldenchain tree. Deciduous tree or large shrub. Plants must be pruned regularly to keep them tidy. Prune right after bloom. To train as tree, take off side shoots along trunk. To train into bushy, low-branching shrub, head back to trunk to force new growth low on plant. To renew vigor of this fast-growing, comparatively short-lived tree, some gardeners prune drastically by cutting back to basic skeleton of branches. Remove seed pods because they are poisonous, untidy, and also because heavy crop of pods drains strength from plants.

LAGERSTROEMIA indica. Crape myrtle. Deciduous shrub or tree. Needs overall, heavy pruning after leaves drop to encourage new wood that will produce next season's flowers. Flower production will tend to be disappointing if it is left unpruned, though it has beautiful natural form that is especially attractive in winter.

To prune large shrub or tree, cut back new growth 12-18 in. from tip, removing whole branches where necessary for shape and symmetry. Cut out sucker growth and flower clusters, too. With dwarf shrub form, remove spent flower clusters and prune out small twiggy growth. You can train it as a small, vase-shaped tree to display attractive trunk and branch pattern.

LAGUNARIA patersonii. Primrose tree, cow itch tree. Evergreen tree. Needs no pruning aside from removal of dead or damaged wood. If injured when young, tree has tendency to sucker. Remove the suckers. If frost damaged, wait until new growth begins before taking out frozen wood. *Caution:* avoid contact with juice from cut stems and branches; this causes skin reaction, itching.

LAMB'S EARS.
See Stachys olympica.

LANTANA. Evergreen and deciduous vining shrubs. Tend to build up high, leafless underbrush, a potential fire hazard. To avoid this, prune hard each year in spring to remove deadwood. New growth breaks readily from old wood and from stumps. Remove leggy growth at any time during growing season to encourage compact habit. If damaged by frost, wait until spring to cut plants back. They will recover rapidly after weather warms.

LAPAGERIA rosea. Chilean bellflower. Evergreen vine. Slender stems need training to desired shape. Very little pruning required beyond that. Cut out weak, straggly growth in early spring to encourage strong, healthy wood. Blooms spring through fall.

LARCH.
See Chrysolarix.

LARIX.
See Chrysolarix.

LATHYRUS. Sweet pea. Annual vines or bushlike, perennial vines. Pinch back tips when 4-5 in. tall to make vines bushier. For longer bloom, do not allow to go to seed. Cut flowers often and

remove all seed pods. If neglected, will eventually make tangled mound of stems, tendrils, leaves, and flowers. When they reach this stage, simply cut off at ground level stems you wish to discourage.

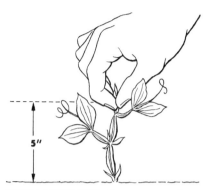

PINCH BACK TIPS of young sweet pea vines like this to make them grow bushy.

LAUREL, CALIFORNIA.
See Umbellularia californica.

LAUREL, EVERGREEN.
See Prunus.

LAUREL, MOUNTAIN.
See Kalmia latifolia.

LAUREL, NEW ZEALAND.
See Corynocarpus laevigatus.

LAUREL, SIERRA.
See Leucothoe davisiae.

LAURUS nobilis. Sweet Bay, Grecian Laurel. Evergreen tree or shrub. Responds well to heavy pruning and may be clipped into formal shapes — globes, cones, topiary shapes, standards, or hedges. Prune as necessary to shape.

LAURUSTINUS.
See Viburnum.

LAVANDULA. Lavender. Evergreen shrubs or subshrubs. All forms, even dwarf, require pruning to keep them bushy and in good health. After bloom, cut off all flowering stems at base. (If you intend to dry the flowers, pick them as they begin to open. At that time, concentration of fragrance is highest.) If there is danger of frost and plants were not pruned immediately after flowering, wait until spring. Fall pruning induces tender growth that will freeze, disfiguring the plants. If neglected, lavenders develop gnarled, silver gray trunks from which top-heavy head of silvery foliage tumbles toward ground. Bushes neglected for any length of time can never be restored to former appearance. In this case, it is best to take cuttings and replace old woody plants with young ones.

LAVENDER.
See Lavandula.

LAVENDER COTTON.
See Santolina chamaecyparissus.

LAVENDER STARFLOWER.
See Grewia caffra.

LEIOPHYLLUM buxifolium. Box sand myrtle. Evergreen shrub. Neat, compact, slow growth to 2 ft. Prune it lightly as you would an evergreen azalea (see page 81).

LEMON.
See Citrus.

LEMON VERBENA.
See Aloysia triphylla.

LEONOTIS leonurus. Lion's tail. Perennial. Cut back to ground each year after it flowers in mild winter climates, or as new spring growth begins in colder areas. Plant produces many stems from base and will grow 5-6 ft. high, even when trimmed back. Tends to be shrubby but striking if kept well-groomed.

LEOPARDS BANE.
See Doronicum.

LEPTOSPERMUM. Tea tree. Evergreen shrubs or small trees. Though they require little pruning, all types can take some surface shearing. When you do prune, cut back only to side branches, leaving some foliage. Best time to do this is early spring. Never cut into bare wood. Thin occasionally to maintain foliage on inner parts of plants. Instead of cutting branches to conform to set pattern, let them show you the way they want to grow. Some develop very irregular and interesting shapes. Trees have same potential for multi-stem use as described for *Feijoa sellowiana* (see page 53).

L. laevigatum. Australian tea tree. Large shrub or small tree. To grow as small tree, select and train main branches early. Some specimens need

TO RETAIN THIS GOOD PLANT SHAPE...

REMOVE A FEW OLD STEMS INSTEAD OF A BRANCH THAT IS TOO MATURE TO BE REPLACED

PRUNE LAVENDER selectively to keep its good shape; cut stems, not branches.

some thinning and heading back, especially when young. Others don't. Several planted close together will make thick natural screen or clipped hedge, not developing visible branching character as they do when grown as trees.

LEUCADENDRON argenteum. Silver tree. Evergreen tree or large shrub. Pinch back young plant as new growth develops to achieve bushier growing habit. For more open habit, do not pinch; instead, place more emphasis on thinning to shape as desired.

LEUCOPHYLLUM frutescens (*L. texanum*). Texas ranger. Evergreen shrub. Thin and shape in winter. If it becomes straggly, cut back to within few inches of ground and it will come back to form attractive, compact shrub.

LEUCOTHOE. Evergreen shrubs.

L. davisiae. Sierra laurel. Prune by removing old flower heads. If blossoms are removed before they can set seed, shrubs will bloom again in fall. If growth becomes too rank, cut to ground to give them fresh start.

L. fontanesiana (*L. catesbaei*). Drooping leucothoe. Left to their natural growth habit, they are likely to develop wild look by producing long sprays. Cut these sprays back to a good side branch or promising bud and use them for winter arrangements. This will strengthen and renew shrubs, force new growth, and keep them tidy. Easy to control by pinching. If they become too rank, cut to ground for fresh start.

LIGUSTRUM. Privet. Deciduous or evergreen shrubs or small trees. Can take heavy pruning in late winter or early spring and shearing during the growing season. Most widely used in hedges. Clip into formal shapes or train as trees.

L. japonicum. (Often sold as *L. texanum*.) Japanese privet, waxleaf privet. Evergreen shrub. Keep low by pruning or allow to grow informally to its natural height. Clip young privet hedge 3 or 4 times during growing season to make thick and bushy at base. Good choice for tall hedge or screen, both informal or clipped. Remember to clip hedge so it is narrower at top than at base.

L. lucidum. Glossy privet. Evergreen tree. Takes kindly to pruning. Train to almost any shape and keep at any height. Hold plant low and full for informal effects or train as small shade tree.

L. ovalifolium. California privet. Semi-deciduous shrub; evergreen only in mildest areas. Clip early and frequently to encourage low dense branching. Thin and head back for distinctive pot plant that can be dwarfed in container for years.

L. o. 'Aureum' (*L. o.* 'Variegatum'). Golden privet. To get larger leaves and best color, cut back overgrown shrub severely before growth starts in spring.

L. 'Suwannee River'. Evergreen shrub. Keep clipped as small hedge or shape into formal container plant by thinning and heading back.

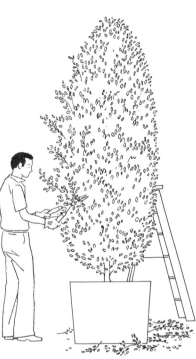

CLIPPING during growing season is necessary to maintain formal shape.

LILAC.
See Syringa.

LILAC, GATE.
See Centranthus ruber.

LILAC, WILD.
See Ceanothus.

LILIUM. Lily. Bulb. Cut off faded flower heads before they form seed; otherwise, the plant's energy goes into seed formation and not into bulb growth.

LILLY-PILLY TREE.
See Acmena smithii.

LILY.
See Lilium.

LILY, FORTNIGHT.
See Moraea iridioides.

LILY, GINGER.
See Hedychium.

LILY-OF-THE-VALLEY SHRUB.
See Pieris.

LILY-OF-THE-VALLEY TREE.
See Crinodendron patagua, arborea.

LILY, PLANTAIN.
See Hosta.

LILY TURF.
See Liriope and Ophiopogon.

LIME.
See Citrus.

LINDEN.
See Tilia.

LINGONBERRY.
See Vaccinium vitis-idaea.

LINOSPADIX monostachya.
See Palm.

LION'S TAIL.
See Leonotis leonurus.

LIQUIDAMBAR. Sweet gum. Deciduous trees. Trees branch from ground up and look most natural that way, but you can train them to form higher heads for easiest foot traffic. You'll need to do some training when trees are young in order to develop strong central trunks. Don't remove any side growth during the first 3 or 4 years. Pinch these side branches back during dormant season to divert growth to tops. After fourth year, remove lower branches to form heads of trees at desired height. (Don't try to force young liquidambar into bushier plants by pinching out tips. They just don't grow that way and will continue skyward by sending up more leaders.) If necessary, thin crown of trees during dormant season to encourage well-spaced framework of branches.

Mature trees have beautiful natural forms and need no pruning except to remove stubs of broken branches.

LIRIOPE and OPHIOPOGON. Lily turf. Evergreen grasslike perennials. They become ragged and brown with neglect. Cut back shaggy old foliage after new leaves appear.

LITCHI chinensis. Litchi nut. Evergreen tree. Like citrus, litchi fruits are borne terminally on current season's growth and do not require much wood renewal. One good method of pruning is to gather fruit in traditional manner— cutting off 10-12 in. long branches with fruit attached.

LITHOCARPUS densiflora. Tanbark oak. Evergreen tree. Needs early training for shape. Grows with multiple trunks but can be trained to single trunk by removing poorest trunks and keeping the best one. Corrective, preventive pruning is all that's required after it's established.

LIVISTONA.
See Palm.

LOCUST.
See Robinia.

LONICERA. Honeysuckle. Evergreen or deciduous shrubs or vines. All types respond well to heavy pruning, but bush forms are sufficiently self-contained to stay neat without severe pruning. How heavily you prune depends on whether or not you want the bushes to have definite shapes. Thin out some older branches during winter months to encourage fresh new growth. Cut out all branches you don't want, head others back slightly.

L. ciliosa. Deciduous vine. Becomes weedy if not controlled. Thin and head back, cutting out all wood that has borne blossoms.

L. 'Clavey's Dwarf'. Deciduous shrub. Slow growing, compact. Cut back to stems in winter if it becomes woody. New growth will emerge in spring.

L. fragrantissima. Winter honeysuckle. Deciduous shrub. Partially evergreen in milder areas. Willowy, requires considerable pruning, cutting back to keep within bounds. Good hedge plant but needs constant clipping, detracting from show of bloom.

L. heckrottii. Gold flame honeysuckle, coral honeysuckle. Deciduous, semi-deciduous vine or small shrub. Train on low fence, on wire along eaves, or as espalier.

L. hildebrandiana. Giant Burmese honeysuckle. Evergreen vine. Thin out older stems occasionally, removing some growth that has bloomed. Take out overlong shoots. Frequently head back terminals to keep vine from becoming stemmy at base.

L. involucrata. Twinberry. Deciduous shrub. Densely foliaged, needs heavy thinning and heading back in winter to keep it looking attractive.

L. japonica. Japanese honeysuckle. Evergreen vine, partly or wholly deciduous in coldest regions. Very vigorous. Needs regular pruning to keep it from spreading like a weed and becoming tangled, shapeless mass. To prevent undergrowth from building up and becoming a fire hazard, cut the vine back almost to the basic framework once a year any time after the peak of bloom or in winter. If you don't control this plant, it will climb trees and its roots may invade sewer and drain lines.

L. maacki. Bush honeysuckle. Will grow up to 15 ft. high and as wide unless severely pruned each year.

L. nitida. Box honeysuckle. Evergreen shrub. Untidy if left alone but easily pruned as hedge or single-stem plant.

L. tatarica. Tatarian honeysuckle. Deciduous shrub. You can let it reach its full 10 ft. or cut it back to any height.

LOQUAT.
See Eriobotrya japonica.

LOROPETALUM chinense. Evergreen shrub. Neat, compact habit, grows naturally into an attractive plant. Train while young as pot plant, a plant to drape over a wall, or grow it against a wall or fence. Little further pruning will be necessary.

LOTUS berthelotii. Trailing perennial. Vigorous plant. Prune heavily in spring and cut or pinch back stems occasionally to induce bushiness. Cut straggly branches off at base.

LUPINE.
See Lupinus.

LUPINUS. Lupine. Annuals, perennials, shrubs. Cut to ground after bloom, may flower again same year. Remove spent flowers from plants all during blooming period.

LYONOTHAMNUS floribundus. Catalina ironwood. Evergreen tree. Prune in winter to shape and control growth. It stump sprouts readily when cut or burned, so severe pruning will not hurt it. (In the country, hungry deer will do some pruning for you.) Trim off dead, brown flower clusters; they tend to hang on tree for a long time and may be unsightly. Can be clipped as hedge to any height you want.

LYSILOMA thornberi. Feather bush. Shrub or small tree. Evergreen in frostless areas, deciduous elsewhere. Train as dense shrub or as single-trunk tree. If frost damaged, cut out dead wood after danger of frost is past; plant should come back.

MAACKIA amurensis. Deciduous tree. Stake and train when young to develop clear trunk. Untrained tree is shrubby looking.

MACADAMIA NUT.
See Macadamia ternifolia.

MACADAMIA ternifolia. Macadamia nut, Queensland nut. Evergreen tree. Stake and shape young tree to central leader. When training, space side branches about 6 inches apart along trunks.

MACLURA pomifera. Osage orange. Deciduous tree. Responds well to pruning, can be kept to any size from 6 ft. up. With lower branches removed, makes good desert shade tree. Fast growing, it can spread into thicket. Do major pruning during dormant season.

MADRONE.
See Arbutus menziesii.

MAGIC FLOWER.
See Cantua buxifolia.

MAGNOLIA. Deciduous or evergreen trees and shrubs. Magnolias do not usually require much pruning. The type of pruning you do to train young plants depends upon what your objective is: if you want trees, prune to main frames; if you want shrubs, promote and protect new shoots from bases (however, shrubby forms, such as *M. kobus stellata*—star magnolia—do not make good trees).

Magnolias should be pruned only lightly to maintain their desired shapes. Remove interfering branches and sucker growth, thin inside for light and air. Cut winter-damaged wood back to healthy tissue. You can prune at almost any time. Some gardeners like to prune during bloom period for cut flowers. Always cut magnolias all the way back to another branch. Do not leave stubs, for they are particularly susceptible to disease. Deciduous magnolias sucker freely in their early years. However, especially on young vigorous trees, shoots that originate above the graft may well be worth keeping (cut off those from below). Since each shoot that appears is successively more vigorous, better wait until there are 2 or 3. Then choose the best shoot and cut out completely the weaker ones. The single remaining vigorous shoots will form the eventual trees. For bigger, better quality blooms, thin out excess flower buds.

MAHALA MAT.
See Ceanothus prostratus.

MAHERNIA verticillata. Honey bell. Evergreen perennial or subshrub. May be short lived. For longer life, cut off dead flowers. Cut back after bloom.

MAHOBERBERIS miethkeana. Evergreen shrub. Dense, upright growth. Gets leggy, but can be pruned back after spring bloom.

MAHONIA. Evergreen shrubs.

M. aquifolium. Oregon grape. Requires minimum of pruning when young. As plant matures, it tends to send out unbranched shoots 6 or more ft. long with foliage only near and at tip if left unpruned. To keep plant compact, cut these long shoots right to the ground in spring before new growth begins. Cut oldest, woody stems to ground at same time to keep fresh new growth coming. As rank new shoots emerge, pinch their tips part-way back so they will branch.

M. lomariifolia. Young plant tends to have a single vertical, unbranched stem; with age the plant produces more nearly vertical branches from near base. Cut stems at varying heights to induce branching. After that the plant needs little or no pruning, except for removal of old berry clusters in mid-year.

M. nevinii. Nevin mahonia. Normally loose, many-branched shrub, can be trained as hedge with regular pruning. Plant responds well to over-all pruning.

M. repens. Creeping mahonia. Spreading habit. Little pruning necessary except to keep it from spreading.

MAIDENHAIR TREE.
See Ginkgo biloba.

MALUS. Crabapple. Deciduous trees, rarely shrubs. Require regular annual pruning. Neglected, they tend to produce complicated tangle of branches. Too heavy pruning, on the other hand, stimulates growth of numerous unwanted shoots and dearth of flower buds for following spring.

Pruning can be done at any time during dormant season, up to just before growth starts in early spring. Although you can prune after flowering, it's best to wait until branches are bare and you can easily see what you're doing. This will lead to a better, more balanced pruning job. During this same period, branches are lighter and somewhat easier to handle.

AT TOP, tangled, twiggy growth on flowering crabapple. Below, plant after pruning.

If you like to use flowering branches in indoor arrangements, leave a few that you'd normally remove during dormant pruning, cutting them later when flower buds are beginning to show color. In addition to dormant pruning, some light thinning should be done throughout growing season. Instead of allowing unwanted growth to continue, literally "nip it in the bud" to allow time within same growing season for trees to direct their energy where growth is needed. The first step—as in pruning most trees—is to eliminate weak growth, conflicting and

tangled branches, and any wood that detracts from handsome shapes. Leave some stubby lateral branches, giving extra leaf surface to help thicken main branching and prevent sunburn.

Prune the crabapple you grow for jelly as you prune an apple (see Apple).

MANDEVILLA laxa (*M. suaveolens*). Chilean jasmine. Deciduous vine. Becomes top-heavy, tangled mass of intertwining stems, often with its base quite bare of foliage. Thin heavily after leaves fall to keep tangle to minimum. This will produce a neater looking plant during winter, encourage abundant fresh spring foliage.

MANZANITA.
See Arctostaphylos.

MANZANOTE.
See Olmediella betschleriana.

MAPLE.
See Acer.

MAPLE, FLOWERING.
See Abutilon.

MARANTA leuconeura. Prayer plant, rabbit tracks. Perennial house plant. In winter when the leaves become small and dry at tips, cut back to base. Will later begin sending up vigorous new growth.

MARGUERITE.
See Chrysanthemum frutescens.

MARGUERITE, BLUE.
See Felicia amelloides.

MATILIJA POPPY.
See Romneya coulteri.

MAYTEN TREE.
See Maytenus boaria.

MAYTENUS boaria. Mayten tree. Evergreen tree. Has much side growth and tendency to sucker. Train it to single trunk by removing unwanted side growth. For multiple trunk effect, preserve and encourage some side branches and suckers. Responds well to heavy pruning in fall or spring. Thin center to keep tree open. Every 2 or 3 years, you may have to remove some low hanging branches for foot and lawn-care traffic under tree.

MEADOW SWEET.
See Astilbe.

MELALEUCA. Evergreen trees and shrubs. Most are vigorous and fast-growing, need pinching back regularly. Control at any time by cutting back unwanted branches to well-placed side branches. Avoid shearing; it makes plants dense and lumpish. Smaller melaleucas are good screening materials; some large ones are useful as flowering or shade trees.

M. armillaris. Drooping melaleuca. Shrub or small tree. Clip as hedge or leave unclipped for informal screen. Can grow to 30 ft., but with training you can make it sprawling shrub or small tree.

M. decussata. Lilac melaleuca. Large shrub, small tree. Thin when necessary to show off trunk, branch character.

M. hypericifolia. Dotted melaleuca. Shrub. Clip into hedge, if you wish. Will bloom more profusely if left as informal, unclipped screen.

M. linariifolia. Flaxleaf paperbark. Tree. Young willowy plant needs staking, training. Thin out lower branches to shape.

M. nesophila. Pink melaleuca. Tree or large shrub. Versatile, can be pruned anytime. Use it as big informal screen, train as vase-shaped tree, or shear as hedge. Can also be trained as multi-stemmed specimen using same method as described for *Feijoa sellowiana* (see page 53). End result is rangy, open tree-shrub with interesting shape.

MELIA. China-berry, Texas umbrella tree. Deciduous tree. Does not require much pruning beyond cutting out suckers or weak and damaged wood when dormant.

MELIANTHUS major. Honey bush. Evergreen shrub. If you want a sprawling mass rather than a tall-stemmed plant, prune to bring on new surges of foliage. As soon as canes start vertical growth, make cuts 12 in. from base of each cane. Do this at practically any time in mild winter climates. (It is not necessary to remove the terminal flower spikes after bloom.)

If you want a tall plant, select 2 or 3 canes, staking and tying them to keep them erect; don't pinch them back. Keep dry, messy-looking leaves picked or cut off lower stems. Don't be afraid to take pruning shears to this plant, for it can get out of hand unless you tame it regularly by cutting back heavily. Prune it at any time, but most gardeners wait until after plant flowers. If plant looks shabby in fall, cut back severely to within 1 or 2 ft. of ground. This brings surge of new leaves that will look handsome during winter months.

MESCAL BEAN.
See Sophora secundiflora.

METASEQUOIA.
See Chrysolarix amabilis.

METROSIDEROS. Evergreen trees or large shrubs. If you prune them annually in late spring, can be kept to 6-10-ft. shrubs or windbreaks. (Can also be trained as hedge, but other choices are better.) To bring into tree forms will require careful staking and shaping. These trees have same potential for sculptured multi-stem use as *Feijoa sellowiana* and can be trained by same method (see page 53). Remove lower side branches to about 6 ft. to encourage top growth. Leave about 3 stems for multiple trunk effect. Do major pruning in late spring after new growth begins.

MEXICAN ORANGE.
See Choisya ternata.

MEXICAN PALO VERDE.
See Parkinsonia aculeata.

MICHAELMAS DAISY.
See Aster novae-angliae.

MICHELIA figo (*M. fuscata*). Banana shrub. Evergreen shrub. Slow growing. You can shape it almost at will. Shear as large evergreen hedge or espalier it. Spring is a good time to prune. Left untrained, it may reach 15 ft. high and 8-10 ft. across.

MICROCOELUM.
See Palm.

MIRROR PLANT.
See Coprosma repens.

MOCK ORANGE.
See Philadelphus.

MONKEY FLOWER, SHRUBBY.
See Diplacus.

MONKEY HAND TREE.
See Chiranthodendron pentadactylon.

MONKEY PUZZLE TREE.
See Araucaria.

MONSTERA deliciosa. (Often sold as *Philodendron pertusum.*) This split-leaf philodendron tends to get rangy and lose bottom leaves. If this happens and you want lower plant, cut it off lower down where you want new shoots. Or you can plant an overgrown plant in larger container and add younger, lower plant to fill in. On all plants, remove old fruit and spent leaves.

MORAEA iridioides. Fortnight lily. African iris. Corms or rhizomes. Have perennial stalks, producing flowers for many years unless they are completely cut off. When you cut stalks for arrangements, be sure to leave at least one node on remaining section of each stalk to carry flowers next season.

MORNING GLORY.
See Ipomoea.

MORNING GLORY, BUSH.
See Convolvulus cneorum.

MORNING GLORY, GROUND.
See Convolvulus mauritanicus.

MORUS alba. White mulberry, silkworm mulberry. Deciduous tree. Train tree when young (see *Training Young Trees*, page 15) to form high head. Stake carefully because it develops large crown rather fast, and it may snap from slender young trunk in high winds. Branches may grow so long for first few years that they droop from their own weight. Shorten such branches by cutting back to well-placed, upward growing bud.

Thin out excess growth each winter, always cutting back to scaffold branches. This will encourage sturdy branches that resist wind damage. In parts of the

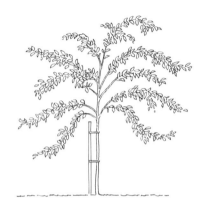

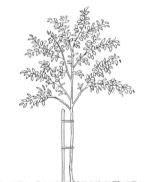

SHORTEN BRANCHES of young mulberry tree to encourage formation of sturdy, compact branching framework.

Southwest, for some reason it once became a fad to prune mulberry trees back to stubs. This practice is unwise. It develops dangerously weak growth because of rotten or hollow centers in larger branches. Such pruning also prevents tree from achieving its own natural beauty. A better approach is to thin out excessive growth to produce better-balanced shade tree.

MOUNTAIN LAUREL.
See Kalmia latifolia.

MOUNTAIN-MAHOGANY.
See Cercocarpus.

MUEHLENBECKIA. Wire vine.
M. axillaris. Creeping wire vine. Low carpeting ground cover. Shear back if it grows out of bounds.

M. complexa. Mattress vine. Naturally a tangled, filmy mass of wiry stems and tiny leaves. Let it scramble and ramble at will or shear it back to thicken it or mold it into topiary shapes.

MULBERRY, SILKWORM.
See Morus alba.

MULBERRY, WHITE.
See Morus alba.

MURRAYA paniculata (*M. exotica*). Giant orange jessamine. Evergreen shrub. Hedge; large, bushy, or small tree. Grows slowly into compact upright shrub. Adapts well to any type of pruning whenever necessary. Can be sheared, trained easily into tree form. Left on its own, it is a handsome shrub.

MUSA.
See Ensete ventricosum.

MYOPORUM laetum. Evergreen shrub or tree. Attractive multi-trunk tree if you stake and train it. Thin to prevent top-heaviness and wind damage. Cut back in spring to get lush, midsummer foliage. Heavily thin back old woody plant to rejuvenate it. If used as windbreak, prune side growth to keep heavy foliage at base coming.

MYRICA. Evergreen and deciduous shrubs. Respond well to heavy pruning, recovering rapidly.
M. californica. Pacific wax myrtle. Evergreen shrub or tree. Can also be used as screen, informal or clipped hedge. Grows most naturally as many-stemmed handsome and tidy shrub, 10-15 ft. high. A good time to prune is in late winter, early spring. (Waxy secretion may gum up pruning shears.)
M. pensylvanica (*M. caroliniensis*). Bayberry. Deciduous or partly evergreen shrub. Though it responds well to heavy pruning, little is required beyond thinning and corrective pruning. Prune when most dormant.

MYRSINE africana. African boxwood. Evergreen shrub. Floppy when young, stiffens up into dense, rounded bush that can easily be kept at 3-4 ft. with moderate pinching and clipping during growing season. Responds well to pruning whenever necessary. Good for low hedges, clipped formal shapes.

MYRTLE, OREGON.
See Umbellularia californica.

MYRTLE, TRUE.
See Myrtus communis.

MYRTUS communis. True myrtle. Evergreen shrub. Very tolerant of pruning whenever necessary, but can be left unpruned. Clip as formal hedge or thin to reveal attractive branches or leave untouched for informal shrub.

NANDINA domestica. Heavenly bamboo, sacred bamboo. Evergreen or semideciduous shrub. Some gardeners follow this rule of thumb: avoid pruning nandina until its foliage has turned from green to red, and then only if the plant is too tall for its location.

To encourage strong, airy growth habit, cut old stems to 6-12 in. above the ground. This forces strong new growth from stubs, making plant bushier. Mature plant gets 6-8 ft. tall; keep it lower by cutting tallest stems right back to the ground. If nandina gets too tall and straggly all over, prune it down in two stages. First, cut half the stems to 6-12 in. above the ground. After new foliage appears below, cut remaining stems for a much lower shrub.

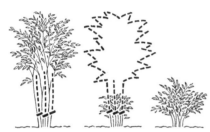

PRUNE too-tall nandina in two stages, cutting back half of the stems at a time.

N. 'Nana' ('Nana Compacta', 'Lemon Hill'). Small, compact. Will stay below 3 ft., so very little pruning required.

NATAL PLUM.
See Carissa grandiflora.

NECTARINE.
See Peach and Nectarine.

NECTARINE, FLOWERING.
See Prunus.

NEPETA. Perennials.
N. cataria. Catnip. Shear back after bloom.
N. mussinii. Catmint. Shear off unsightly faded flower spikes.

NEPHROLEPIS.
See Fern, Tender.

NERIUM oleander. Oleander. Evergreen shrub. Takes kindly to all types of pruning and can be grown as full, many-branched shrub. Also can be trained as handsome standard or multi-stem tree, growing as high as 20 ft. and sometimes spreading 15 ft. Looks neat as a hedge, but clipping with hedge shears also removes what would be flowering wood.

If required, prune in early spring to control size and form. Cut out old wood that has flowered. Cut some branches nearly to ground. To restrict height, pinch remaining tips or head back lightly. To prevent bushiness at base, pull (don't

cut) unwanted suckers. Caution children that all parts of plant are poisonous. Keep prunings, dead leaves, flowers away from hay or other animal feed; don't use wood for barbecue fires or skewers. Smoke can cause severe irritation, and skewers have poisonous sap.

NET BUSH.
See Calothamnus.

NEW ZEALAND CHRISTMAS TREE.
See Metrosideros.

NEW ZEALAND FLAX.
See Phormium tenax.

NEW ZEALAND LAUREL.
See Corynocarpus laevigatus.

NIEREMBERGIA. Cup flower. Perennials.
N. frutescens. Tall cup flower. Can be trimmed to low, rounded, shrublike shape. Trim to shape after flowering.
N. hippomanica caerulea. Dwarf cup flower. Plants usually form low mounds. If branches begin to get long and stringy after first long spell of bloom, cut them back with hedge shears to within 6 in. of the ground. New shoots will come out soon, and flowering will continue through fall.

NIGHT JESSAMINE.
See Cestrum nocturnum.

NINEBARK.
See Physocarpus capitatus.

NORFOLK ISLAND PINE.
See Araucaria.

NOTHOPANAX arboreum. Evergreen tree. Will grow moderately fast to 15-25 ft. tree if left unpruned, but can be trained as a multi-stemmed small tree only 6-8 ft. high. No other pruning required.

NUTMEG, CALIFORNIA.
See Torreya californica.

NYSSA sylvatica. Sour gum, tupelo, pepperidge. Deciduous tree. Part of charm is its crooked branches, twigs. Young tree has twiggy growth, with branches going in all directions. Remove crossing branches and any that might spoil shape. Very little pruning required once basic form is established. Prune while dormant.

OAK.
See Quercus.

OCEAN SPRAY.
See Holodiscus discolor.

OCHNA serrulata (*O. multiflora*). Mickey Mouse plant, bird's-eye bush. Evergreen shrub. Trim young plant to keep it shapely and compact, nipping back long, jutting branches. As plant gets older, prune less and permit plant

to spread. If too dense, thin branchlets (in spring, before new growth begins) to show off flowers and fruit.

OCTOPUS TREE.
See Brassaia actinophylla.

OLEA europaea. Olive. Evergreen tree. Tolerates heavy pruning or thinning and can be trained as a tree, shrub, or as large, dense hedge. For a tree, begin training early (see *Training Young Trees*, page 15). To develop single trunk, remove or shorten side branches below point where you want branching to begin, stake tree firmly, and cut off basal suckers when they appear.

To train with several trunks, stake lower branches or basal suckers to continue growth at desired angles. Thin each year to show off handsome branch and trunk forms and to let more light and air through. Though thinning can be done anytime, if you wait until after flowering it will decrease production of fruit (usually a nuisance). Fruit can stain paving and harm lawn if not removed. Beyond pruning, crop can be reduced by spraying with a plant hormone called naphthaleneacetic acid. Less efficient but easier is to knock off flowers with a good blast of water from the hose before they set fruit. If you want the crop, delay heavy pruning until after harvest.

OLEANDER.
See Nerium oleander.

OLEANDER, YELLOW.
See Thevetia peruviana.

OLEARIA haastii. Daisy bush. Evergreen shrub. Shear or tip when necessary to keep plants shapely. Cut off faded blooms, or they will persist right through winter.

OLIVE.
See Olea europaea.

OLIVE, BLACK.
See Bucida buceras.

OLIVER'S SNAPWEED.
See Impatiens oliveri.

OLIVE, RUSSIAN.
See Elaeagnus angustifolia.

OLIVE, SWEET.
See Osmanthus fragrans.

OLMEDIELLA betschleriana. Guatemalan holly, Costa Rican holly, manzanote. Evergreen shrub or small tree. Very adaptable to training and shaping whenever necessary. If you want several stems and bushier growth, pinch out leader; if you want a single-trunked tree, encourage the strongest stem and keep side growth pinched back. As a shrub, it remains thickly foliaged to the ground and can be clipped or left unclipped to provide a tall hedge or privacy screen.

ORANGE.
See Citrus.

ORANGE JESSAMINE.
See Murraya paniculata.

ORCHID TREE.
See Bauhinia.

ORCHID VINE.
See Stigmaphyllon ciliatum.

OREGON GRAPE.
See Mahonia aquifolium.

OSAGE ORANGE.
See Maclura pomifera.

OSMANTHUS. Evergreen shrubs or trees. Though relatively slow growing, these plants do need to be pruned and shaped. Pinch stem ends regularly during spring and summer to force side growth. Remove branches that are top-heavy or off balance when necessary.

O. armatus. Chinese osmanthus. Shrub. Once established, plant needs little pruning except to control height or remove straggly branches. Do this after flowers fade.

O. delavayi (*Siphonosmanthus delavayi*). Delavay osmanthus. Shrub. Easily controlled by light pruning if it has adequate growing room. Still blooms even when clipped as hedge, but natural habit is low and broad, with arching branches. Good espalier.

O. fortunei. Shrub. Good plant for large container. With occasional light pruning, you can keep it about 3 ft. high and about as wide.

O. fragrans. Sweet olive. Shrub. Can be trained as small tree, hedge, or espalier. Will grow to 10 ft. high (eventually much more) and almost as wide, but you can keep it lower by pinching out branch tips in spring and summer.

O. heterophyllus (*O. aquifolium, O. ilicifolius*). Holly-leaf osmanthus. Shrub. Cutting handsome foliage regularly for arrangements will keep shrub from growing too lanky.

O. h. 'Variegatus'. Grows slowly, filling out as it gets older. Pinch branch tips once a year to help it fill in sooner.

OSMARONIA cerasiformis. Oso berry, Indian plum. Deciduous shrub. As usually seen, it is a thicket that needs little pruning. Can be trained as single-stem tree by cutting out suckers. If pruning is required, do it during dormant season.

OSMUNDA.
See Fern, Hardy.

OSO BERRY.
See Osmaronia cerasiformis.

OSTEOMELES schweriniae. Evergreen shrub. Grows at least 10 ft. tall but can easily be kept down to 4 or 5 ft. with a little thinning and attention during year. Prune after plant flowers.

OSTEOSPERMUM. Evergreen subshrubs or perennials. Closely related to *Dimorphotheca* (Cape marigold) and often sold as such. Pinch tips of young plants to induce bushiness. Cutting back old, sprawling branches to young side branches will keep plants neat, often induce repeat bloom. Plants have tendency toward ranginess; can be minimized with regular pinching during the growing season and occasional pruning.

OXERA pulchella. Evergreen vine or viny shrub. Leaves grow densely on arching, twining stems, reaching 10-20 ft. if supported. Not supported, makes a mounding shrubby mass about 6 ft. high. Train as vine along eaves, over entryway, on arbors or trellises. Trim for unusual pattern quality against wall. Vine takes much guidance; tie stems in direction you want them to grow. Prune lightly as you train vine, trimming out dead and broken branches as soon as vines finish flowering.

OXYDENDRUM arboreum. Sourwood, sorrel tree. Deciduous tree. Needs only minimum of guidance and training while young, corrective and preventive pruning later. If needed, prune while dormant. Remove freeze-damaged wood only after danger of frost is past.

PACHISTIMA. Evergreen shrubs. Low hedges, edgings, ground covers. Prune whenever necessary to shape as desired.

P. canbyi. Ratstripper. Lends itself to use as a ground cover and as a low clipped hedge or edging plant.

P. myrsinites. Oregon boxwood. Takes shearing well so is suitable for clipped hedge.

PACHYSANDRA terminalis. Japanese spurge. Evergreen subshrub. Underground runners may become somewhat invasive, but plant is easy to keep in bounds with sharp shovel. Needs occasional light clipping or pinching in early spring to keep it compact. Do not cut all the way to the ground.

PACIFIC WAX MYRTLE.
See Myrica californica.

PAEONIA. Peony. Herbaceous perennials and deciduous shrubs.

Herbaceous peonies. Perennials. Pick flowers as they fade but leave as much foliage as possible to nourish the plants. When foliage turns completely brown in the fall, cut it just below the soil surface. (Be careful not to damage next year's new buds or eyes 2 in. or so below ground level.)

Tree peonies. Deciduous shrubs. As flowers begin to fade, cut them off just above the topmost leaf. Before spring growth starts, cut back all stems to the uppermost healthy live eye or bud. Some growers advocate cutting 3 or 4-year-old plants to ground. Do this in

fall, when it is too late for new top growth to start. This practice strengthens underground eyes, stimulates root growth, and induces growth of more stems the following spring.

Cut off winter-damaged stems as new spring growth begins. Subject to botrytis; remove afflicted flowers, buds, and stems, cutting back into healthy stems.

PAINTED DAISY.
See Chrysanthemum coccineum.

PALM. Pruning of palms is mostly restricted to manicuring to keep them neat. Because this process is continual rather than seasonal, you may have to remove dead leaves on some types about every 3 or 4 months. Also remove unsightly fronds damaged by disease, pests, storms, or freezing.

Feather-leafed palms require a split pruning operation. The yellow fronds should be cut off as close to the trunk as possible, leaving the leaf bases. Some palms shed these old leaf bases on their own; others, including *Arecastrums* and *Chamaedoreas*, may hold the old bases. The second stage is to remove the leaf bases, where necessary, by making shallow slices next to the trunk. Trunks of some palms wear a heavy overcoat of fiber. If you prefer the beauty of bare stems, the fibrous coat may be stripped off without injury to plant.

(Continued on next page)

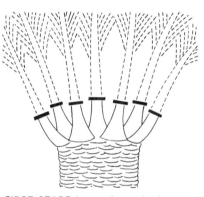

FIRST STAGE in pruning palm is to remove lowest tier of old fronds.

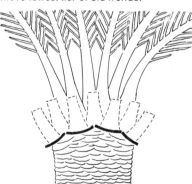

A YEAR LATER remove leaf bases by slicing off right at the trunk.

Be careful if you trim shag skirts of fan palms, for you'll leave ugly scars if you cut up into live growth. Some palm admirers say that the dead leaves of *Washingtonias* should remain on the tree, the thatch being part of the palm's character. The most convincing argument for removal of the dead fronds is that they are a fire hazard. An attractive way to handle them is to cut lower fronds in a uniform way close to the trunk, leaving the trimmed leaf bases to present a rather pleasant lattice surface.

PALM, DATE.
See Phoenix.

PALMETTO.
See Sabal.

PALM, WINDMILL.
See Trachycarpus.

PALO VERDE, MEXICAN.
See Parkinsonia aculeata.

PAMPAS GRASS.
See Cortaderia selloana.

PANDOREA jasminoides (*Bignonia jasminoides, Tecoma jasminoides*). Bower vine. Prune to direct or thin growth. Cut back frost-damaged wood when new growth begins in spring.

P. pandorana (*Bignonia australis, Tecoma australis*). Wonga-wonga vine. Head back ends of branches after spring bloom.

PANSY.
See Viola.

PAPAYA.
See Carica papaya.

PAPER MULBERRY.
See Broussonetia papyrifera.

PAPYRUS.
See Cyperus.

PARIS DAISY.
See Chrysanthemum frutescens.

PARKINSONIA aculeata. Jerusalem thorn, Mexican palo verde. Deciduous tree. Young plants must be staked and trained to get a tree shape started (see *Training Young Trees,* page 15). Select strongest leader for central stem or trunk; train it for high or low branching as desired. Mature trees require very little pruning, although dead inside branches may sometimes need to be removed.

PARROT-BEAK.
See Clianthus puniceus.

PARROTIA persica. Persian parrotia. Deciduous tree or large shrub. Densely foliaged branches spread wide and tend to grow in horizontal planes. Because of this, give special attention to training the young plant if you want to grow it as a tree (see *Training Young Trees,* page 15). By shortening side branches during summer months, you can encourage it to grow taller and more treelike in form. When tree reaches desired height, remove lower shortened side branches cleanly.

PARTHENOCISSUS. (Sometimes sold as *Ampelopsis.*) Deciduous vines. Boston ivy, Virginia creeper. Can be trained as either dense or open vines. Trim out at any time any long branches that obstruct view or walkway. However, if vines have been pulled away from support, cut back to a firmly holding portion. Require annual dormant pruning once they reach desired size; whenever necessary, trim away from doors and windows, cut off wandering branches that invade areas where they don't belong.

PASSIFLORA. Passion vine. Evergreen, semi-evergreen, or deciduous vines. If not controlled, these vines will grow rampant and may become thickly tangled masses of foliage with few flowers. They climb or crawl by wiry tendrils that grab anything they can wrap around, including the vines themselves. Thin by cutting wayward growth back to main structure at least once during growing season and cutting vines back before they get to nearby plants. In colder areas die-back acts as a natural annual pruning. But even in these areas, remove stems that are crowding and heading in wrong directions during rapid growth period to keep vines neat. If plants get out of hand, cut back all the way to ground in spring after danger of frost is past.

PASSION VINE.
See Passiflora.

PAULOWNIA tomentosa (*P. imperialis*). Empress tree. Deciduous tree. If tree is cut back hard annually or every other year during dormant season, it will grow as billowy mass of foliage with giant-sized leaves up to 2 ft. This kind of pruning, though, is done at expense of flowers and shade. A better approach would be to thin out weak wood and shape for an interesting, open form. In colder areas, remove frost-damaged wood in spring.

PEACH AND NECTARINE (*Prunus persica* and *P. nectarina*). Trees. Peach and nectarine are the most vigorous growing fruit trees. The voluminous new growth of long, willowy shoots bears fruit the following summer. New growth bears only once. Prune hard during dormant season to encourage new growth; otherwise, fruit will be produced farther and farther out on the branches each year.

Cut off ⅔ of the previous year's growth by removing 2 of every 3 branches formed last year (cut right at base); or head back each branch to ⅓ its length. Actually you will probably prune ⅔ of last year's growth by heading back some branches and cutting out others. If picturesque shape is desired, wait until 2 or 3 years after planting (see *Fruit Tree Training,* page 17); then give scaffold branches some special shape by twisting and tying them or by selectively removing secondary branches and leaving others that take off in angles to give some interesting shape to lower, visible part of tree.

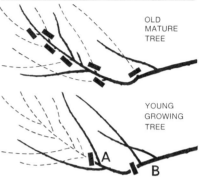

PEACH/NECTARINE TREES HORIZONTAL BRANCH

OLD MATURE TREE

YOUNG GROWING TREE

CUTS as marked for mature trees would remove ⅔ of last year's growth. On young tree, cuts at A or B would do same thing.

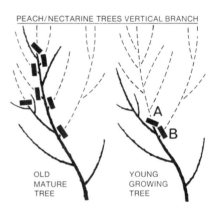

PEACH/NECTARINE TREES VERTICAL BRANCH

OLD MATURE TREE

YOUNG GROWING TREE

CUTS on mature tree would also remove 2/3 growth. On young tree, cut A would widen it, cut B would extend it upward.

PEACH, FLOWERING.
See Prunus.

PEAR. Pear trees, like apples, produce fruit mostly from the ends of long-lived spurs. Pears are also similar to apples in their pruning requirements, and pruning of mature trees consists primarily of cutting out the dead, twiggy, and misplaced branches and encouraging new branches. Do this in the dormant period. Heavy pruning of pears will stimulate vegetative growth and may increase the danger of fireblight. Blighted branches should be removed below the deadwood; wash the pruning tools with disinfectant after each cut. After trees have been trained early to a good framework of main branches (see *Fruit Tree Training,* page 17), prune them lightly to keep good form.

PEAR, EVERGREEN.
See Pyrus kawakamii.

PEARL BUSH.
See Exochorda.

PEA VINE, AUSTRALIAN.
See Dolichos lignosus.

PECAN.
See Carya illinoinensis.

PELARGONIUM. Geranium. Shrubby perennials. All the really common plants called geraniums are pelargoniums. All kinds require grooming and shaping, but timing and severity of pruning depend on the kind of plant and where it is grown. All but ivy geraniums grow as bushes but can be grown as single standards or trees by staking a single stem and rubbing out side buds until plant reaches desired height.

P. domesticum. Pelargonium, Lady Washington pelargonium, Martha Washington geranium, regal geranium. Pinch the growing tips of young plants to keep them full and bushy and to increase flower production. Snap off uppermost tip just above node or joint. This will send growth out at sides of plant. When side branches develop, pinch them so that they will develop their own side branches. Each tip left to grow will develop a flower truss. (If you are growing plants indoors or in a sheltered place outdoors, stop pinching after late December or early January to get maximum spring bloom.) Remove faded flowers regularly to encourage new bloom.

When peak bloom period is over in early fall, cut back plants to ½ of size. Then, as new growth develops, resume shaping plants by pinching out tip growth. If plants are leggy with woody stems and are holding green leaves only at tips, renew them in one of the following ways: 1) Cut back plants gradually, starting right after heavy spring bloom. Prune each stem back to the lowest pair of leaves. When some new growth breaks out below these leaves, cut back to the new leaves. Continue cutting back as new leaves develop until plant is compact and well shaped. 2) Cut plants down to within a few inches of the ground in spring after danger of frost is past to make them branch from the base. (You will lose bloom for one season this way, also may lose old woody plants if you cut them right to ground.) Some people like to replace old plants with new ones they grow from cuttings taken from old plant.

P. hortorum. Common geranium, garden geranium (including fancy-leaf geraniums). Pinch young, newly set plants to force side growth and bushiness (see *P. domesticum* left). Exception: don't pinch Carefree or other strains grown from seed; they are self-branching. Remove faded flowers regularly and occasionally cut back straggly branches to the lowest pair of leaves to force out lower growth. Cut back old, overgrown plants to reshape them. You can cut back in fall and root new plants from the wood you cut off, or cut back in spring after heavy frosts are past and plants are starting to grow. Cut back a little at a time so you can see what you are doing; don't prune all the way back to old wood. Retain some leaves on stems you prune. If possible, cut back just above a leaf bud. If no buds are visible, cut to lowest leaf and wait until buds break lower down, then cut back stub just above new bud break.

P. peltatum. Ivy geranium. Trailing, climbing, or hanging plant. Pinch growing tips to produce more stems. Not all varieties branch freely; some make long, trailing growth. Select compact ones for hanging baskets; longer, looser kinds as ground cover. Groom by cutting off faded flowers. Cut back stems that grow out of bounds.

Scented leaf geraniums. Many species of Pelargonium are grown for their scented foliage. They vary widely in appearance and habit but all take the same pruning: tip-pinch new growth to keep plants compact and bushy, and shape to desired size and form by cutting out unwanted growth and shortening stems to lowest healthy leaf. Many are effective as standards.

PENNISETUM setaceum (*P. ruppelii*). Fountain grass. Perennial grass. You can cut the plant back to the ground at almost any time during its active growing season and see a fresh crop of leaves within a few weeks. If you let flowers set seed, you'll have seedlings popping up all over the garden. In colder areas, cut back dead and frost-damaged leaves in winter. New growth will emerge in spring.

PENSTEMON. Beard tongue. Perennials, evergreen shrubs and shrublets. Keep seed heads removed. Plants will then produce new growth, another set of buds and flowers throughout summer. Cut perennials back to base after final bloom period is over.

PEONY.
See Paeonia.

PINCHING — first the uppermost tip, then the resulting side branches (center drawing) — produces a full, bushy pelargonium with increased flower production.

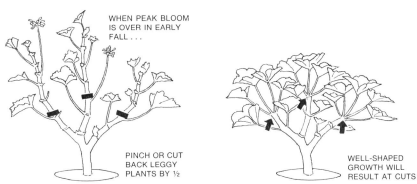

WHEN PEAK BLOOM IS OVER IN EARLY FALL . . .

PINCH OR CUT BACK LEGGY PLANTS BY ½

WELL-SHAPED GROWTH WILL RESULT AT CUTS

MORE PINCHING is necessary when peak bloom is over to prevent legginess and to restore pelargonium plants to their shapely selves.

PEPPERBUSH, SWEET.
See Clethra alnifolia.

PEPPERIDGE.
See Nyssa sylvatica.

PEPPERMINT TREE.
See Agonis.

PEPPER TREE.
See Schinus.

PEPPERWOOD.
See Umbellularia californica.

PERIWINKLE, DWARF.
See Vinca minor.

PERNETTYA mucronata. Evergreen shrub. Plantings spread by underground runners and can be invasive. Contain by root pruning or by putting plants in containers. Can be pruned heavily in late spring to keep bushy and well-rounded. Cut back straggling branches when necessary to keep neat and compact. Tends to grow many stems; cut back unwanted stems halfway to encourage branching.

PERSEA. Evergreen trees.
    P. americana. See Avocado.
    P. indica. Needs very little pruning. Dense and rather stiff growth may require thinning of branches to get proper shape.

PERSIAN PARROTIA.
See Parrotia persica.

PERSIMMON (*Diospyros*). Deciduous trees. Very little pruning is required except that necessary to remove dead-wood and to shape. If you start consistent training program when trees are young, you can fashion them into very interesting informal espaliers (see *Espalier*, page 21). Watch branching patterns when young trees are developing and select laterals with strong-angled crotches so that brittle wood won't split under a heavy load of fruit. They split easily at a crotch, and important crotches should be safeguarded by lightening branches and cross-cabling.

Persimmons tend to get dense in interior, causing fruit to be borne toward end of branches, so you must thin branches enough to allow sunlight to reach center. Thin before growth begins in spring to stimulate new wood which bears the fruit. Cut branches back to laterals, removing watersprouts (except when needed to fill in spaces). Do not prune heavily or stub back branches, for this will encourage vegetative growth at expense of fruits. Heavy pruning is recommended for old, neglected trees in order to force branching and new fruiting wood.

PHAEDRANTHUS buccinatorius (*Bignonia cherere*). Blood-red trumpet vine.

Evergreen vine. Rampant growth once established; must be pruned annually to be kept under control. Do major pruning in late fall after bloom in mild winter areas; in early spring after danger of frost is past elsewhere. First remove all weak, damaged wood and then thin out crowded stems inside plant to provide good air circulation and light. Train vine on a wall, a high trellis, an arbor, or a chain link fence.

PHELLODENDRON amurense. Amur cork tree. Deciduous tree. Moderate growing. Requires minimum training when young and little pruning later. If young tree grows multiple leaders, remove all but one to make single-trunk tree, retaining lower branches at desired height.

PHILADELPHUS. Mock orange. Deciduous shrubs. All mock oranges need annual pruning as soon as possible after flowers fade. To keep shrubs airy and open, cut all spent flowering branches back to first bloom-free shoot or to a bud on stem being pruned. Unless you intend to grow a trimmed hedge, don't shear shrubs. On some more vigorous kinds, you can remove fair percentage of old flowering canes at ground level each summer when they begin to crowd center of bushes.

PHILODENDRON. Evergreen vines and shrubs. One big problem with vining philodendrons and their near relative *Monstera deliciosa* (the so-called split-leaf philodendron) is that they become rangy, lose bottom leaves, and outgrow their place indoors or in garden. Here are possible courses of action: 1) Train plant to grow downward; 2) Cut back to make a fresh start.

The simplest way to keep a plant from getting too tall is to weight top growth down gradually until it makes a U-turn. Do by degrees so you don't break the stem. If plant has become very straggly and sparsely foliaged, cut back to within 1 or 2 joints (leaf buds) from ground. New growth will develop from there. Prune in spring or summer.

PHLOMIS fruticosa. Jerusalem sage. Shrubby perennial. Cut back ⅓ each year in fall to keep it in shape.

PHOENIX. Date palms. For all species except the two below, see *Palm*.
    P. dactylifera. Date palm. Suckers from base; remove these to keep tree single trunked.
    P. reclinata. Senegal date palm. Old leaves should be removed as they dry. After you have picturesque clump of 4 or 5 trunks, keep excessive suckers removed. You can direct growth to single trunk if you remove stem offshoots, but its clumping nature is part of its charm.

PHORMIUM tenax. New Zealand flax. Evergreen perennials. At least once each year, cut off dead or sunburned leaves close to ground and seal large cuts with asphalt emulsion. After a few years, clumps get quite thick. Thin out by cutting off some outside leaves at ground level. When it gets too large, divide in spring, using sharp spade or shovel to make cuts.

PHOTINIA. Evergreen or deciduous shrubs or small trees. Fast-growing, photinias should be pinched and shaped to encourage spreading, dense growth and the colorful new foliage that comes every time new growth breaks. Light pruning at least 4 or 5 times a year will keep plants neat and full. For continuous supply of bright scarlet new growth, cut branch tips back once a month in late spring, early summer. Thin and head back to shape when required; never allow new growth to get away and make long, bare switches.

PHYGELIUS capensis. Cape fuchsia. Perennial shrubs. In mild winter areas where plants remain evergreen, trim off dead flower stalks in fall to keep plants neat. Pinch out new growth while plants are young to encourage sturdy upright stems. Root pruning may be necessary to control invasive roots.

PHYSOCARPUS capitatus. Ninebark. Deciduous shrub. Pinch frequently when young to get bushy plant. Remove old and heavy wood after bloom to encourage new growth from base, unless you want to retain attractive pods that develop after bloom. In that case, prune in dormant season. Can be renewed gradually by cutting a few of the oldest stems to ground each year.

PHYSOSTEGIA virginiana. False dragon-head. Perennial. Cut to ground after bloom. Divide every second year to control sprawling habit, keep in bounds.

PICEA. Spruce. Evergreen trees and shrubs. Prune to shape only. If two main trunks develop, cut one out. If a branch grows too long, cut back to well-placed side branch. Promote new side growth and make more dense by cutting new growth back about halfway in spring. Cut out dead branches.

PIERIS. Evergreen shrubs. Respond well to heavy pruning, but this is seldom required. To keep plants looking neat, remove dead flower clusters and developing seed pods after blooming.

PIMELEA. Evergreen shrubs and shrublets. Light trimming after flowering is all that is normally required. Do not remove more foliage than necessary when doing this.

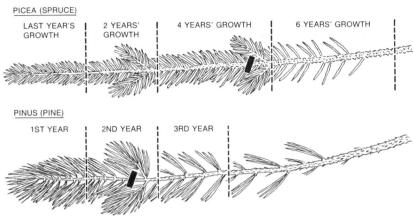

PICEA (SPRUCE)

LAST YEAR'S GROWTH | 2 YEARS' GROWTH | 4 YEARS' GROWTH | 6 YEARS' GROWTH

PINUS (PINE)

1ST YEAR | 2ND YEAR | 3RD YEAR

PRUNE FARTHER BACK ON SPRUCE—LESS ON PINE

NEEDLES of picea hold for six to seven years; pinus needles average three years before dropping. Picea withstands more extensive pruning.

PINCUSHION FLOWER.
See Scabiosa.

PINE.
See Pinus.

PINEAPPLE GUAVA.
See Feijoa sellowiana.

PINE, FERN.
See Podocarpus gracilior.

PINE, YEW.
See Podocarpus macrophyllus.

PINK.
See Dianthus.

PINK POWDER PUFF.
See Calliandra inaequilatera.

PINUS. Pine. Conifers, evergreen trees, rarely shrubs. (See *Conifers,* page 20.) All pines can be shaped and usually improved by some pruning. To slow a pine's growth or to fatten up a rangy one, cut back the candles (new growth) when new needles begin to emerge. Cut them back halfway or even more. Leave a few clusters of needles if you want growth to continue along the branch. To shape a pine in the oriental manner is trickier, but not really difficult; it's just a matter of cutting out any branches that interfere with the effect, shortening other branches, and creating an upswept look by removing all twigs that grow downward. Cutting the vertical main trunk back to a well-placed side branch will induce side growth, and wiring or weighting branches will produce a cascade effect.

P. mugo mughus. Mugho pine. Shrublike, dwarf mugho pine isn't always as full and compact as you would like. Grows slowly, tends to be broader than tall at maturity. You can maintain or increase compactness by pinching the candles back halfway as they begin to unfold in spring. To encourage taller growth and give the plant a more tree-like character, remove most branches that lie close to the ground and, if necessary, cut out a few others to accentuate the interesting branch structure. If you prune carefully, the resulting miniature tree often resembles a true bonsai.

P. pinea. Italian stone pine. If you want an Italian stone pine to grow more dense, remove straggling, down-hanging lower branches. At the top of the tree, remove candles annually in spring to force more growth inside the tree top. If you want to make an Italian stone pine look more open, remove several interior branches, cutting each one off where it joins the trunk or a main branch.

PISTACIA. Pistache. Deciduous or semi-evergreen trees.

P. chinensis. Chinese pistache. Deciduous tree. Mature, well-trained tree requires little more than corrective pruning. Young tree must be staked, then trained for several years to develop head high enough to walk under (see *Training Young Trees,* page 15). Sometimes, branches tend to grow downward; cut these off at trunk. Train to a single trunk and avoid crowding limbs in any one area on trunk during its youth. Avoid equal narrow crotches that may split later. This way, tree will require less bracing and limbs will not be so likely to split in its mature stages. If tree is budded or grafted, remove buds and suckers forming below graft. Where pendulous branches need stiffening, tie a piece of lath or similar material parallel and close to branch. It will serve as a splint.

P. vera. Pistachio, pistachio nut. Deciduous tree. Stake and train to form a head at desired height. Cut out branches that grow downward. When structure is

CANDLES (clusters of infant needles) on mugho pine. Candles on other kinds of pines are generally smaller. As a pruner, you remove these candles to keep a pine plant at about the same size; leave them intact to let the pine extend its growth.

formed, prune as little as possible, cutting out (as necessary) only weak or damaged wood and suckers below graft (if tree is grafted or budded).

PITTOSPORUM. Evergreen shrubs and trees.

Pittosporum, tree forms (*P. eugenioides, P. tenuifolium, P. undulatum*). Will take all forms of pruning. By clipping and heading back, you can grow them as a hedge and keep them at any level over 5 or 6 ft. almost indefinitely. To force bushiness, shear off 2-6 in. of plant tops several times each year between March and November. Begin shearing sides when necessary. Continue to do this 2 or 3 times a year until plants reach desired size. Then shear the surface whenever necessary—typically, once in spring, again in midsummer, and again in October or early November. If you prefer a softer, more natural-looking surface, prune overlong branches back to laterals or buds inside the body of the hedge. Leave those branches which terminate in approximately the plane where you want the soft and uneven surface.

If plants get woody at the base, cut back heavily in spring to encourage new growth. You can also train pittosporum as either a single or multi-trunked tree.

Pittosporum, shrub forms (*P. tobira, P. t.* 'Variegata'). Will also respond well to pruning whenever necessary, although excessive cutting can ruin the natural shape. Has same potential for handsome, multi-stemmed tree as *Feijoa sellowiana* (see page 53). Easily trained to any desired form, they can be grown as trees, used in clipped or informal hedges, kept in containers, or grown as single plants.

PITTOSPORUM TOBIRA clipped into tiers in narrow space alongside driveway.

If a wayward shoot grows above the desired height, pinch it back or cut it off at the base at any time. Pinching will encourage bushier plants.

P. crassifolium. Grows neatly enough so that you don't have to prune it often. Though it can grow to 25 ft. high in 8-10 years, it can be kept to 8 or 10 ft. and as narrow as 6-8 ft. with a yearly pruning in spring after new growth begins. If hedge effect is not desired, selective removal of branches will produce handsome, vertical tree.

P. phillyraeoides. Willow pittosporum. Has weeping, trailing habit. Needs little pruning. Stake against winter storm winds; open up form by thinning out branches to permit winds to blow through.

P. rhombifolium. Queensland pittosporum. Needs little pruning. Grow either as large shrub with foliage to ground, or as single or multi-trunked tree.

PLANE TREE.
See Platanus.

PLANTAIN LILY.
See Hosta.

PLATANUS. Plane tree, sycamore. Deciduous tree.

P. acerifolia. (Often sold as *P. orientalis.*) London plane tree. Can be pollarded yearly, after leaf fall, to create dense, low canopy (see *Pollarding,* page 23); can also be allowed to grow naturally. Full grown trees require no pruning except to repair damage. Benefit from thinning of smaller branches to open form and expose interesting bark.

P. occidentalis. American sycamore, buttonwood. Has beautiful, natural form in winter without leaves and needs little or no pruning. Thin out smaller branches to open up form.

P. racemosa. California sycamore. Stands heavy pruning in winter. Easily trained to any trunk and branch form you wish if you start when tree is young. Makes a picturesque multi-trunked clump if given careful early training. Remove dead twigs and erratic, reverse growth resulting from blight.

PLATYCLADUS.
See Thuja.

PLATYCODON grandiflorum. Balloon flower. Perennial. Keep pinching off old flowers to prolong bloom but don't cut back stems until leaves have withered.

PLUM AND PRUNE. The two kinds of plums are Japanese (*Prunus salicina*) and European (*P. domestica*). Both should be pruned while dormant. Pruning methods are different for each, however, as discussed below:

Japanese plums. Belonging to this group are these varieties: 'Beauty', 'Becky Smith', 'Burbank', 'Burmosa', 'Duarte', 'Eldorado', 'Elephant Heart', 'Formosa', 'Howard Miracle', 'Inca', 'Kelsey', 'Laroda', 'Late Santa Rosa', 'Mariposa', 'Nubiana', 'Peach Plum', 'Queen Ann', 'Santa Rosa', 'Satsuma', 'Shiro', and 'Wickson'.

Trees make tremendous shoot growth, requiring severe pruning at all ages. Train young trees to vase shape. Cut back to lateral branches. If tree tends to grow upright, cut to outside branches; if it is spreading, cut to inside or vertical branches. Heavy bearing results in quantities of small fruit and possible damage to tree. Thin green fruit drastically as soon as it is big enough to be seen. Leave the remaining fruits 4-6 in. apart.

European plums (including Prune). The following are some of the most popular varieties: 'Damson', 'French Prune', 'Green Gage', 'Imperial', 'Italian Prune', 'President', 'Stanley', 'Sugar', 'Tragedy', and 'Yellow Egg'.

Prune European plums to avoid formation of V crotches. Mature trees require little pruning—mainly thinning out of annual shoot growth.

PLUMBAGO auriculata (*P. capensis*). Cape plumbago. Semi-evergreen shrub or vine. Can be trained either as a shrub or a climbing vine. Heavy frosts will kill growth back, but recovery is good. Cut out damaged growth (or cut to ground if badly damaged) after frost danger is past. To train as a shrub, cut back to encourage side branching. Shrub can be renewed by cutting oldest stems to ground each year after blooming. To train as a vine, encourage long growth by pinching back side branches and providing climbing support for the main branches.

PLUMBAGO, DWARF.
See Ceratostigma plumbaginoides.

PLUME CEDAR.
See Cryptomeria japonica 'Elegans'.

PLUME CRYPTOMERIA.
See Cryptomeria japonica 'Elegans'.

PLUME FLOWER, BRAZILIAN.
See Jacobinia carnea.

PLUM, FLOWERING.
See Prunus.

PLUM, JAPANESE FLOWERING.
See Prunus.

PLUM, NATAL.
See Carissa grandiflora.

PODOCARPUS. Evergreen trees, shrubs.
P. andinus. Shrub or shrubby tree. Can be clipped like yew (*Taxus*) into hedge or screen.

P. falcatus. Tree. Prune it the same as *P. gracilior.*

P. gracilior. (Often sold as *P. elongatus.*) Fern pine. Tree, often grown as an espaliered vine. Generally do not require much pruning, though they respond well (will stump sprout if cut to ground) and can be trained to take various forms: small trees or shrubs, green walls, espaliers, vines, ground covers, or container and house plants.

Fairly slow growing, so pinching new tip growth is usually sufficient to keep them to desired size. If you plan heavier pruning, do it in spring or fall. To grow compact shrubs or hedges, cut leggy branches to ground. When growing as espaliers, keep stems securely tied and remove unwanted growth as it develops.

More than most trees, it needs staking when young until strong trunk develops. Slow to develop, but eventually gets big. Some espaliers have reached 40 ft., towering above walls they were trained against. For ground cover, peg down pliable stems and cut off vertical growth. Trees should be thinned out at regular intervals to show up the handsome gray branch structure.

If not especially trained, fern pine becomes 25-30-ft. tree with graceful growth habit. If a plant becomes tall and spindly, cut it back to ground and let it start over. Tree is excellent for multi-stemmed development or low-branching form. This requires selection of desired leaders in first 2-3 years and the removal of competitive growth. An old, freely-grown tree can be shaped in same way if studied carefully before cutting.

P. macrophyllus. Yew pine. Shrub or tree. Let it go its way as a narrow, dense, upright tree, or train as hedge, screen, or topiary plant. Can take shearing or severe thinning as a sort of giant bonsai.

P. m. maki. Shrubby yew pine. Shrub. Slower to grow, smaller, shrubbier.

P. nagi. Tree. To preserve weeping look, prune only to remove dead and damaged wood or extra leaders.

P. totara. Totara. Tree. Can be clipped like yew (*Taxus*) into hedge or screen.

POINSETTIA.
See Euphorbia pulcherrima.

POKER PLANT.
See Kniphofia uvaria.

POLYGALA. Evergreen shrubs, shrublets. Respond well to heavy pruning, though a light trimming after bloom is all that is normally required. Head rangy plants back to bring down to size.

POLYGONUM. Knotweed. Evergreen and deciduous perennials and vines.

P. aubertii. Silver lace vine. Freezes to ground in winter in most regions and can be cut to ground at that time each

year if desired (this will delay bloom until late summer). Where it doesn't freeze to ground, wait until spring to prune; thin out side shoots and cut all main and secondary stems back to third or fourth bud of last year's growth. Fast growing; cut back and pinch tips as necessary in summer to keep in bounds.

P. capitatum. Evergreen perennial. This tough ground cover will invade other beds unless confined by edging boards or curbs. It also spreads by seeding. Whenever it mounds up too much, you should whack it back. If burned by frost, don't prune. It will come back nicely.

P. cuspidatum. Japanese knotweed. Perennial. Extremely invasive. Cut to ground in late fall or winter. Underground roots must be controlled to keep plant in bounds.

POLYSTICHUM munitum.
See Fern, Hardy.

POMEGRANATE.
See Punica granatum.

POMPON TREE.
See Dais cotinifolia.

POPLAR.
See Populus.

POPPY, MATILIJA.
See Romneya coulteri.

POPPY, YELLOW HORNED.
See Glaucium flavum.

POPULUS. Poplar, cottonwood, aspen. Deciduous trees. Roots extremely invasive; some have reputation for invading and breaking sewer lines. Most produce suckers freely, especially if roots are cut. Nevertheless, greedy roots have to be cut back to stop them from getting out of bounds. Rapid growing, with easily-broken limbs. Give usual training while young, maintenance pruning later. Responds well to heavy pruning when required. Some gardeners prefer to let it grow naturally.

PORCELAIN GINGER.
See Alpinia speciosa.

PORTUGAL LAUREL.
See Prunus lusitanica.

PORTULACARIA afra. Elephant's food, purslane tree, spekboom. Succulent. Pruning not necessary, though it can be shaped into an informal screen, unclipped hedge, or high-growing ground cover. Responds well to opening up and is willing subject for almost any form. Prune to shape at any time.

In containers, terminal growth will take on weeping character if placed in shade for 2 or 3 months and then returned to sun. Some pruning may be necessary to prevent plant from becoming top-heavy or to bring symmetry to lopsided plant.

POTATO VINE.
See Solanum jasminoides.

POTENTILLA. Cinquefoil. Evergreen and deciduous perennials and shrubs. Shrubby types respond well to heavy pruning, although they require almost none beyond removal of any damaged wood in early spring.

PRAYER PLANT.
See Maranta leuconeura.

PRIDE OF MADEIRA.
See Echium fastuosum.

PRIMROSE TREE.
See Lagunaria patersonii.

PPINCESS FLOWER.
See Tibouchina semidecandra.

PRIVET.
See Ligustrum.

PRUNE.
See Plum, European.

PRUNUS. Deciduous and evergreen trees and shrubs. The edible-fruit trees that belong to *Prunus* are better known as the "stone fruits" and are listed elsewhere in this encyclopedia under their common names (see Almond, Apricot, Cherry, Peach and Nectarine, Plum and Prune).

Take away the fruit trees and you have left two classes of ornamentals: evergreens, and deciduous flowering fruit trees and shrubs.

EVERGREEN FORMS

P. caroliniana. Carolina laurel cherry. Evergreen shrub or tree. Slow growing, needs little pruning if grown as upright shrub. Pinch back wayward shoots whenever they develop above main body of the plant. It can be well branched from ground up and useful as a formal, clipped hedge or tall screen. Can be sheared into formal shapes. Trained as a single-trunk tree, it will become broad topped and reach 35-40 ft. Requires some thinning to shape; heading back causes it to spread.

P. ilicifolia. Hollyleaf cherry. Evergreen shrub or small tree. Use as small tree, tall screen, or formal clipped hedge of any height (for hedge training procedures, see *Pittosporum*). Responds well to pruning at any time.

P. laurocerasus. English laurel. Evergreen large shrub or small tree. Stands heavy shearing, but this will cause considerable mutilation of leaves and loss of flowers and fruit. Unless grown as formal, sheared hedge, needs some thinning to open dense canopy of foliage. For low hedges or screens, plant dwarf varieties. Best pruned not by shearing but one cut at a time, just above a leaf on overlong twigs. Untrimmed plant will grow 18-30 ft. tall, occasionally more. If too large, reduce size by selective pruning in spring over a season or two. To transform overgrown shrub into tree, see *Viburnum plicatum*.

P. l. 'Zabeliana' Zabel laurel. Evergreen shrub. With branches pegged down it makes effective bank cover. Can be espaliered or grown flat against an entrance wall; clip twice yearly. Moderately fast growing—to 4 ft. high and usually wider—but can be held lower by removing vertical branches. Then branches fan out, reaching no more than 2 ft. high, much wider.

P. lusitanica. Portugal laurel. Evergreen shrub or tree. If left to grow naturally, becomes densely branched large shrub 10-20 ft. high or many-trunked spreading tree to 30 ft. However, can be kept to 6 ft. or under without difficulty. Sometimes used as formal hedge, but clipping mutilates its 5-in. leaves, destroys grace, and eliminates flowers and fruit. Cut branches for indoor arrangements at any time since it stands heavy pruning. Makes an unusually neat and controllable tub plant and can be trained into formal tree or espalier while kept in container.

P. l. azorica. Left unpruned, it grows into gigantic columnar bush 20 ft. high and half as wide. Responds to pruning at any time.

P. lyonii (*P. integrifolia, P. ilicifolia integrifolia*). Catalina cherry. Evergreen shrub or tree. Can be held to any height desired by pruning whenever necessary and can be trimmed to any shape or can be left to grow normally with a minimum of maintenance pruning.

FLOWERING FRUITS

Flowering Cherry. Fast growing deciduous tree 20-25 ft. high and as wide. Tends to branch close to ground; remove lowest branches if you want a canopy shape. Requires only a minimum of pruning. Remove sucker growth — any buds or branches that appear below the graft. Cut branches while tree is in bloom for use in arrangements. Remove awkward or crossing branches. Pinch back an occasional overly ambitious shoot to force new growth. If diseased branch dies back, prune out affected area. To be on safe side, disinfect pruning tools between cuts. Training in early years to force multiple branching can correct its rather open and sparse growth habit.

Flowering Nectarine. Pruning procedures are the same as for Flowering Peach (see below).

Flowering Peach. Training and growth habits are same as for fruiting peach (see Peach and Nectarine). Heavy pruning is required for good show of flowers. Cut branches back to 6-in. stubs at, or immediately after, flowering time. With lighter pruning you avoid sheared-back look but reduce next year's flower display. Entire top growth flowers on 1-year wood. Thin out old wood, dense or crossing branches, and dead growth. Remove suckers from understock.

Flowering Plum. Train young tree to establish a head at height you can walk under. Remove suckers that appear below graft. As tree develops, take out crossing and inward-growing branches. Remove vigorous vertical branches that shoot up from inner parts of tree (watersprouts) unless one is needed to replace a broken or damaged branch. Densely branched, so must be pruned to prevent twigginess. Do heavy pruning when trees are dormant. Prunings can be taken inside for forcing into bloom. Light trimming after flowering controls shape. To put in container, prune roots heavily and thin top branches to an open frame.

P. glandulosa. Dwarf flowering almond. (See also *P. triloba.*) Deciduous multi-stem shrub. Flowers carried on year-old wood, so prune back hard either just after blooming or when in bloom to get long whips for next year's wands of bloom.

P. mume. Japanese flowering apricot, Japanese flowering plum. Deciduous tree. Prune heavily after flowering. Cutting back long, one-year, whiplike growth forces laterals which produce heaviest crop of flowers. Let grow for a year, then prune back all shoots to 6-in. stubs. The following year cut back half of young growth to 6-in. stubs; cut back the other half the following year, and continue this routine in succeeding years.

P. triloba. Flowering almond. Small tree or treelike large shrub. Usually grows slowly to about 15 ft. high, with equal spread. Cut branches as soon as flowers fade in spring. At the same time, remove any old wood and dead growth. If grafted and trained as small standard tree, remove suckers below graft and rub off buds along trunk.

PSEUDOTSUGA menziesii (*P. taxifolia*). Douglas fir. Conifer. As a garden tree, its height is difficult to control; you can't keep it down without butchering it. To slow the growth, pinch young growth as described on page 20. Trees need guidance when young. Be sure a good, strong single leader is formed. If young leader is damaged, select best upper horizontal branch, brace and train it upright to become new leader (see page 20). Roots are greedy and invasive, need occasional cutting back. You can plant young trees close together, top them, and trim into a 10-12-ft. hedge.

PSIDIUM cattleianum. Strawberry guava. Evergreen shrub or small tree. If it gets tall and unmanageable, it can be shaped by removing whole branches to form into small tree or cut back to make bushy shrub. Thin small branches to make an informal pattern. Makes a good informal hedge or screen, fine bonsai subject. Can also be trained into interesting multi-stemmed form (see *Feijoa sellowiana*, page 53). Prune in spring.

ARTISTIC PRUNING EMPHASIZES the open and sparse growth habit that is typical of these flowering cherry trees. Cut flowering cherry branches while they are either in bud or in bloom for use in indoor arrangements.

PTEROSTYRAX hispida. Epaulette tree. Deciduous tree. Will grow up to 40 ft. but can be held to shrub height of 15-20 ft. and width of 10 ft. Needs normal guidance to shape while young (see *Training Young Trees,* page 15). Cut out winter-damaged wood in spring.

**PTYCHOSPERMA macarthuri.
See Palm.**

PUNICA granatum. Pomegranate. Deciduous tree or shrub. If you buy a bare-root pomegranate, cut it back hard before planting to restore balance between large, bushy top and roots which have been severely cut back in digging. Whether it becomes a thicket, shrub, or tree depends upon how you train it. If not pruned each year by removing suckers at the base, it can become a formless thicket. You can select the number of stems you want and hold it to those as a shrub, or you can force it to become treelike by cutting away all but its strongest single stem when you plant it, cutting out any new growth from the base each year.

To train as an espalier, select a few strong shoots and fasten fanwise to a support. Suppress suckers and shorten side branches to hold plant in bounds. Dormant pruning consists of thinning out oldest, weakest wood. Old, neglected plants are good subjects for pruning into interesting shapes.

P. g. 'Chico'. Dwarf carnation-flowered pomegranate. Compact bush, can be kept to 18 in. tall if headed back occasionally.

P. g. 'Nana'. Dwarf pomegranate Rounded, dense, and twiggy, will grow to 3 ft. tall but can easily be kept at 2 ft. by cutting back upright growth.

**PURPLE CONEFLOWER.
See Echinacea purpurea.**

**PURPLE HEART.
See Setcreasea purpurea.**

**PURSLANE TREE.
See Portulacaria afra.**

**PUSSY WILLOW.
See Salix discolor.**

PYRACANTHA. Firethorn. Evergreen shrubs. Blossoms and fruits are produced on short spurlike branches growing from 2-year-old wood. Withstands severe pruning. If it is not pruned regularly, berries will form farther and farther out on branches. Degree and timing depend somewhat on gardener's objectives.

Normally grown as bushes or espaliered (formally or informally) against walls and fences. Can also be trained as standards, clipped into hedges or topiary, though many gardeners feel clipping spoils plant's rugged informality (it will probably also curtail the colorful berry crop).

Low growing varieties are good ground covers; on these, shorten any runaway vertical shoots. Size and form can be controlled from the start by pinching new young growth in spring and shortening overly long branches that tend to develop during the years. During bloom period, pinch out flowering branches just above first flower cluster. This will produce neat little packages of berries to form in following fall and winter and will keep plant in check. Cut branches that have borne berries back to a well-placed side shoot (don't leave stubs to die back and cause rot). For maximum fruit crop, remove all bearing wood as soon as berries have dropped.

To keep plant vigorous and renewed, cut oldest wood to ground in most dormant period (between berry drop and the beginning of new growth). In areas where temperatures occasionally drop below 24°, prune after March 1. When cutting berried branches for decoration, let cutting serve as constructive pruning. Thin out crowded centers and try not to alter basic shape of shrub. Don't try to grow pyracantha in small area or you'll be continually butchering it to keep in bounds. Susceptible to fireblight; remedial pruning is same as for *Cotoneaster.*

**PYRETHRUM.
See Chrysanthemum coccineum.**

PYROSTEGIA venusta (*P. ignea, Bignonia venusta*). Flame vine. Evergreen vine. Fast grower; prune before new growth begins in spring to keep it under control.

PYRUS kawakamii. Evergreen pear. Evergreen shrub or tree. The way it accommodates pruning makes it a most versatile plant. You can make it take almost whatever form you wish: limber-limbed sprawling shrub; formal or informal espalier; neat, middle-sized spreading street or lawn tree as tall as 30 ft.; screen; or container plant. The first year or so it grows rather bushy and needs staking. Without support, evergreen pear becomes a broad, sprawling shrub, or in time, a multi-trunked small tree. With willowy young branches fastened to fence or frame, it makes a good-looking espalier.

Evergreen pears trained as trees take a couple of years to outgrow young gawky stage but in 10 years can be 20 ft. wide and reach as high. To make a tree of it, stake one or several trunks, remove side growth, and keep staked until trunk is self supporting. Beef up framework branches by shortening (when young) to upward facing buds or branchlets. For a thick screen, space plants 10 ft. apart. For espaliers, just bend long limber branches where you want them to go, thin out growth that will not become part of structure, and shorten long stems. Continuous pruning can keep a plant small enough for a trellis or in a formal candelabra shape but may curtail or prevent flowering.

You can train a plant to grow flat against a wall by supporting it with a wire framework and cutting off branches that head out. Vigorous plants trained like this can sometimes cover the side of a two-story house in 7 or 8 years. Spring

STYLIZED SHAPE of this pyracantha demonstrates its versatility. Original trunk and side shoots are tied in place to make pattern; cutting back side shoots regularly holds pattern. Pyracantha withstands severe pruning, trains well as an espalier.

pruning can encourage more flowers. After bloom, cut ⅔ of previous year's growth off each branch. Plants are susceptible to fireblight; remedial pruning is the same as for *Cotoneaster*.

QUEENSLAND KAURI.
See Agathis robusta.

QUEENSLAND NUT.
See Macadamia ternifolia.

QUEENSLAND POPLAR.
See Homalanthus populifolius.

QUEENSLAND UMBRELLA TREE.
See Brassaia actinophylla.

QUERCUS. Oak. Deciduous or evergreen trees. Young oaks tend to grow twiggy. Growth is divided among so many twigs that none elongate fast. To promote fast vertical growth, pinch off tips of unwanted small branches, retaining all leaf surface possible in order to sustain maximum growth. A young healthy oak that is heavily thinned will often grow at a much faster rate than one that is left alone. If the young oak has been shaped and trained properly, annual pruning will be primarily corrective and preventive: removing dead branches, spurs of broken branches, suckering growth, or diseased and weak wood, and thinning out to avoid wind and storm damage.

Oaks can be pruned at just about any time. Where mildew is a problem on evergreen oaks, prune in winter to reduce mildew-susceptible new growth. Some tree experts feel you can do a better job on deciduous types when they are in full foliage. Large cuts on oaks and other trees should be treated with sealing compound (repeat yearly for cuts over 4 in. until they have healed over).

Q. palustris. Pin oak. Deciduous. May require more attention than other oaks. As a young tree, it may need help to develop natural leader. Lower branches tend to support each other. Best planted where you don't need to walk under it. Removal of down-sweeping lower branches is only temporary solution because lowest branch left on tree will then assume down-sweeping aspect of the ones you removed.

QUILLAJA saponaria. Soapbark tree. Evergreen tree. Tends toward multiple trunks and excessive bushiness but responds quickly to pruning. Prune to shape whenever necessary. Can be pruned as tall hedge if desired.

QUINCE, FLOWERING.
See Chaenomeles.

QUINCE, FRUITING. Deciduous shrub or small tree. Prune only to form a trunk and shape the frame. Keep the center open for air and light, and thin out and cut back only enough to stimulate new growth. Heading back will re-

duce the crop since fruit is borne on new wood at the tips. It's desirable to have many small shoots on the tree.

RABBIT TRACKS.
See Maranta leuconeura.

RAPHIOLEPIS. Evergreen shrubs. Require little pruning or training, but for bushier, more compact plants prune them from start. Pinch back tips of branches at least once each year, after flowering. For more open structure, let grow naturally, sometimes thinning out branches. Encourage spreading by shortening vertical branches. Pinch side branches to encourage upright growth. Occasional pinching of stem ends will control their shape.

Some raphiolepis have been budded on quince rootstock; you may have to cut off quince shoots occasionally. They will appear from below the graft with light green, soft leaves. As plant grows and base becomes shaded by foliage, suckering is less frequent. Encourage rather flat growth by removing the central or crown branches. Or encourage erect growth, leaving vertical branches intact and removing some side branches.

RASPBERRY. Most popular and heaviest bearers are red raspberries that have erect canes and do not branch readily. They can be grown as free standing shrubs, staked, or tied to wires or trellises. At planting time, cut the 1-2-ft. cane back to about 8 in. This young cane serves mainly as a marker; new shoots arise from its base. Let shoots grow undisturbed through one growing season. Next spring, just before growth starts, cut out small and weak canes and cut back remaining canes to 5 ft. (They will probably be tied to a stake or trellis to keep them from whipping in the wind.) Beginning the second year, prune plants as follows: remove all canes that have fruited immediately after harvesting. This pruning makes room for new canes to develop freely. Leave about 7 canes on an average mature plant, more on an especially vigorous one, fewer on a weak one. Tie selected canes in a bunch in fall to protect over winter.

Do major pruning in spring before buds begin to swell. (In areas with strong winter winds, head back in fall.) In the spring, head back canes to 4½-5 ft., shorten side branches to 2 in. Retie individual canes for support. As soon as red raspberries begin active growth, they start sending up suckers. Leave canes that come up where you first planted them; pull others up by roots to prevent too rampant growth.

Fall-bearing varieties differ slightly in pruning needs. Fruit laterals form and bear fruit near top of the current year's cane. Cut off upper portion that has

borne fruit instead of taking out entire cane. Lower parts will then fruit next spring. Cut out cane only after it has fruited along its entire length.

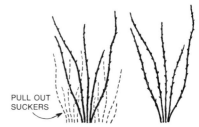

RED RASPBERRY sends up suckers. Leave canes; pull up suckers by their roots.

Black raspberry (Blackcap). These have a branching growth habit. New plants form when arching cane tips root in the soil. Red raspberries, in contrast, come up from roots. This is why growers tip pinch black raspberries during growing season to encourage branching. Tip pinching red raspberries, on the other hand, tends to encourage more sucker growth instead of more branching. Post-harvest care of black raspberries is similar to that of red raspberries: cut out portions that have borne berries. Dormant pruning and training are quite different, though. With black raspberries, encourage branching by heading back or pinching new shoots when they reach 2-2½ ft. Completely remove any new canes that appear during or after harvest. Dormant season pruning consists of shortening side branches on headed canes to from 5-8 buds.

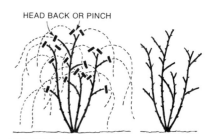

TIP-PINCH black raspberry to encourage branching, discourage new plants.

RATSTRIPPER.
See Pachistima canbyi.

RAUWOLFIA samarensis. (Often sold as *Alstonia scholaris*.) India devil tree. Semi-deciduous tree. Prune in spring. Cut off any limbs that tend to grow toward the center of the tree in a way that would be incongruous with the natural skeleton. Remove lower branches that have died from overhead shading. It is normal for rauwolfia to become high-headed. Under no circumstances permit shearing, for the charm of this plant is an open structure that displays pale gray areas between layers of elegant foliage.

REDBERRY.
See Rhamnus crocea.

REDBUD.
See Cercis.

RED CEDAR, WESTERN.
See Thuja plicata.

RED CHOKEBERRY.
See Aronia arbutifolia.

RED-HOT POKER.
See Kniphofia uvaria.

RED VALERIAN.
See Centranthus ruber.

REDWOOD.
See Sequoia sempervirens.

RHAMNUS. Evergreen or deciduous shrubs or trees.

R. alaternus. Italian buckthorn. Evergreen shrub. Can be kept in bounds with minimum of training. Easily shaped or sheared as screen or tall clipped hedge. Can also be trained as single-stem small tree.

R. a. 'Variegata' (*R. a.* 'Argenteo-variegata'). Has leaves edged in creamy white. To retain striking appearance, cut out plain green branches that occasionally appear.

R. californica. Coffeeberry. Evergreen shrub. Doesn't require much pruning. To keep dwarf varieties low and compact, pinch or cut out upright growth whenever it occurs.

R. crocea. Redberry. Evergreen shrub. Will stand a lot of shearing. Untrimmed, it may reach 3 ft. Prune when necessary.

R. c. ilicifolia. Holly-leaf redberry. Evergreen shrub to 15 ft. Prune to shape and to increase density of foliage whenever necessary.

R. frangula. Alder buckthorn. Deciduous shrub or small tree. Requires a minimum of pruning. Do necessary pruning to shape while dormant, maintenance pruning at any time. Set 2½ ft. apart for tight, narrow hedge that needs minimum of trimming and can be kept as low as 4 ft. by cutting back vertical growth as necessary.

RHAPIDOPHYLLUM.
See Palm.

RHAPIS.
See Palm.

RHODODENDRON (including azalea). Evergreen or deciduous shrubs, rarely trees. If plants have been pinched and trained for proper branching and shape from an early stage, later major pruning chores will be corrective and limited to the removal of damaged or deadwood.

To keep mature plants healthy and productive, continue a regular program of pinching shoots and cutting the flowers. The major difference between azaleas and rhododendrons is that azaleas have growth buds all along their stems, just under bark surface. As a result, new growth will originate close to any cut you make. (Some growers therefore give azaleas a "butch haircut" by clipping with hedge shears.)

Cuts on rhododendrons, on the other hand, should always be made just above leaf rosettes since new growth emerges from dormant eyes there. If you have to cut into the stem below any leaf rosettes, look for faint rings on bark that mark where there once were leaves at the ends of previous growth periods. Small bumps under the bark there are growth buds; cuts should be made just above these.

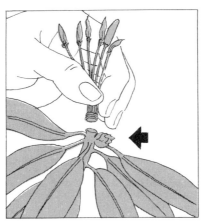

REMOVE spent flowers carefully. Bend back old flower cluster and pull. Don't harm growth buds below flowers.

NEW GROWTH shown here sprouted from bud under removed flower truss as illustrated in top drawing.

Winter or spring is the preferred pruning season in mild climates; spring, after frost no longer threatens, is preferable where winters are severe. Best pruning time for maximum bloom is just after flowering (or during bloom if cut flowers are to be used). Winter and prebloom pruning is likely to remove some of bloom unless pruning is very light and selective, allowing many flower buds to remain.

One good pruning technique when plants are in bloom is to cut out crossing, awkward branches that destroy the symmetry of the plants, using them as cut flowers. To conserve plants' energy, remove faded flower trusses on rhododendrons before seed pods form. Be careful not to damage the buds just starting growth at the base of the flower stem. (These will form next year's flowers and leaves.)

After azaleas' main blooming period, you can (if the plants need pruning) pinch out tips of new growth or shear the surface with hedge shears. This produces bushy, uniformly branched plants with a crop of flower buds uniformly distributed over the surface. Both azaleas and rhododendrons respond well to restorative pruning. Stems of deciduous azaleas often become woody and unproductive as they grow older. They will remain vigorous and give you lots of flowers if you systematically remove old, declining wood each year. At any indication of reduced vigor, cut weakening stem to ground; new growth will soon replace it.

(Continued on next page)

PINCH OUT tips of new growth to make an azalea bushy. First, pinch as at upper left; then upper right. Result, bottom.

You may also rejuvenate overgrown evergreen azaleas and rhododendrons in the same way. Cut back oldest, heaviest limbs to a foot or less (but always above growth rings on rhododendrons); from these, strong new shoots will grow to fill in plants. By doing this progressively over 3 seasons, removing about ⅓ of old growth each year, you can transform rangy, open, overgrown shrubs into compact and colorful ones. The entire plant can be cut back in one operation (sometimes it is necessary to treat a damaged plant this way). However, you will lose all flowers for a year or two and run a greater risk of losing the plant. Be sure to cut out old weak stems entirely. These will not improve under better care.

RHODOTYPOS. Jetbead. Deciduous shrub. Will withstand heavy pruning, preferably after flowers and berries are gone. Prune to shape whenever required, cutting out some oldest canes to ground every few years to renew.

RHOICISSUS capensis (*Cissus capensis*). Evergreen grape. Evergreen vine. Needs to be controlled to keep in bounds. Do this with constant pinching back of tips during growing season rather than pruning severely at one time; heavy pruning may cause dieback.

RHOPALOSTYLIS.
See Palm.

RHUBARB. Perennial. It's best to harvest stalks by grasping near base and pulling sideways and outward. Cutting with a knife is supposed to leave stubs that will decay (it doesn't always happen). Cut out flower stalks as soon as they appear, or plant's energy will go toward producing them at the expense of foliage.

RHUS. Sumac. Evergreen or deciduous shrubs or trees. Pruning and training varies with type and function.
R. aromatica. Fragrant sumac. Deciduous shrub. Should be pruned each year in early spring. Because fast-spreading stems root and sprout readily, some root pruning may be necessary to keep in bounds.
R. glabra. Smooth sumac. Deciduous large shrub or small tree. Treated best as shrub. Can be invasive; root prune and pull or dig out suckers if plant spreads too far. Cut back hard in early spring to control form.
R. lancea. African sumac. Evergreen tree. Can be trained in several different ways: with foliage to the ground, with a single trunk, or in an interesting multiple-stemmed effect (its natural way to grow). Prune to shape in spring.
R. laurina. Laurel sumac. Evergreen shrub. Tends to become rangy unless pinched or headed back frequently. If it freezes, it will recover quickly and grow back from stump. Can also be trained as espalier or trimmed as hedge.
R. ovata. Sugar bush. Evergreen shrub. Can be trained as small tree. Slow to fill in if heavily pruned or after limb breakage. If required, prune in spring.
R. typhina. Staghorn sumac. Deciduous shrub or small tree. Best trained as small tree. One attractive feature is bare-branched winter form, so prune lightly in early spring and remove only weak, crossing, or unattractive limbs.

RIBES. Currant, gooseberry. (See these entries for fruiting kinds.) Deciduous and evergreen shrubs.
R. alpinum. Alpine currant. Deciduous shrub. Usually sheared as hedge. Best pruned in late spring after new growth is established.
R. aureum. Golden currant. Deciduous shrub. Shape by pruning after bloom. Can be rejuvenated in fall by cutting back to the ground the oldest, weakest stems. Do not head back branches in the fall or you'll remove next spring's flowers.
R. sanguineum. Pink winter currant, red flowering currant. Deciduous shrub. Responds well to pruning after blooming period.
R. s. 'glutinosum'. Pink flowering currant. Can take any amount of pruning after flowering.
R. viburnifolium. Catalina perfume, evergreen currant. Spreading evergreen shrub. Will take a moderate amount of pruning as necessary. Can be used as a ground cover, trailer, or low-spreading border shrub. To keep lower, cut out upright growing stems. It can also be trained against a wall, but its slender stems must be supported.

RICE PAPER PLANT.
See Tetrapanax papyriferus.

RICINUS communis. Castor bean. Annual in colder areas, perennial in mild climates. Can be pruned severely to keep it bushy and under control. New growth shoots out readily along the cut-back stems. In areas of light frosts, where plant is fairly well established, it will break out new growth from lower portions of stems in the spring. After new growth has progressed, cut frost-killed leaves and stems back to green wood. In frost-free areas, you may want to renew plant's vigor by cutting it back to 4 or 5 ft. each spring. The beans are highly toxic, so it is best to cut them off. If it gets too woody, dig it up and start a new one.

ROBINIA. Locust. Deciduous trees or shrubs. Fast growing, brittle wood. Need training for structure and shape in early years. Roots are aggressive, and plants will spread by suckers if not contained. Prune while dormant.
R. hispida. Rose acacia. Deciduous shrub. Has spreading, suckering habit. Root prune to keep in bounds. If grafted on black locust to produce umbrella-shaped tree, it will need careful staking to prevent breakage, blowover. Prune while dormant.
R. pseudoacacia. Black locust. Deciduous tree. Attractive bare-leafed form in winter can be considerably improved by selective branch removal after bloom. Wood is brittle; corrective pruning is sometimes required for broken, damaged limbs.

ROCKCRESS.
See Arabis.

ROCKROSE.
See Cistus.

ROMNEYA coulteri. Matilija poppy. Perennial. Flowers, cut in bud, will open in water and last a few days. Plant dies back each winter and should be cut nearly to the ground in early fall. New shoots will emerge, and next spring you'll have a much more vigorous plant with better blossoms than if you had left plant to its own devices. Vigorous, spreading roots may need curbing.

RONDELETIA. Evergreen shrubs. Cut back as soon as flowering season is over, especially when young. Remove old leaves that tend to hang on, as well as faded flower clusters, to keep plants neat and encourage longer blooming.

ROSA. Rose. Deciduous, bushy or climbing shrubs (a few evergreen in warm climates). Rose plants require pruning to make them produce good flowers and to keep them from growing into hopeless thorny tangles. Some gardeners favor only a light annual pruning, others advocate cutting roses back heavily each year.

Pruning requirements for the different types of roses vary. Some climatic factors also influence pruning methods. Generally, however, most rose growers have come to favor a light to moderate pruning instead of the hard cutting back which was once the accepted practice.

Timing. The best time for pruning roses is toward the end of the dormant season when growth buds along the canes begin to swell. In general, you should do the pruning in winter or early spring but not so early that the tender new growth which follows will be damaged by late frosts.

Basic objectives are to develop an attractive framework and to encourage growth of new, flowering wood. Here are a few basic guidelines for pruning the various types of roses.

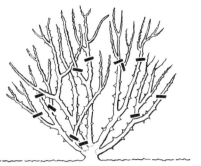

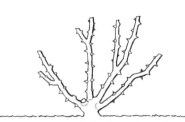

BASIC GUIDELINES for pruning dormant bush roses: remove all deadwood, weak and twiggy branches, and crossing branches, opening up center.

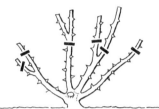

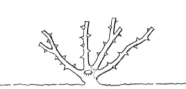

ADDITIONAL PRUNING is necessary in cold-winter climates. Remove all damaged wood, reducing the bush to ½ to ⅓ the size it was in the fall.

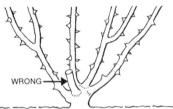

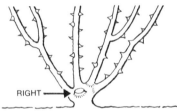

DON'T LEAVE A STUB when cutting off a cane at the bud union. Cuts should be flush with bud union and leave no stub to die back, allowing entry for disease.

Bush roses: Hybrid Teas, Grandifloras, Floribundas. Remove all deadwood and all weak, twiggy branches. If an older cane produced nothing but weak growth, remove it right at its base —at the bud union.

Open up the center of the bush by removing all branches that cross through the center. This gives you a "vase shaped" plant. It's a slender or a fat vase, depending on how upright or spreading the variety grows. The vase should be free of twigs and leaves in the middle where insects could hide.

Remove up to ⅓ of the length of all growth that was new during the previous year. A convenient rule-of-thumb: don't cut into growth of the past season that is bigger around than a pencil.

If you live where winter protection is necessary and you use a method that requires reducing the bush size to fit the protector, you will probably have to remove more than ⅓ of the past year's growth. Cut out *all* damaged wood regardless of how low this leaves your bushes. Prune all stems and canes back to wood that is light green to cream white in the center. Even though a cane

may be green on the outside, if the center is brown it is damaged.

Make all cuts ¼ in. above a leaf bud and at a 45° angle, with the lowest point on the side of the stem opposite the bud (see page 15).

Paint all cuts larger than pencil size with a sealing compound. This is especially important for cuts to the bud union.

Secondary Pruning. Any removal of flowers or spent blooms can be considered pruning, with a few guidelines of its own. Remember that, since leaves help provide nutrients for the plants, you must leave a good supply on the bush. When you want a few long-stemmed beauties for inside, cut each stem so that you leave *at least* two sets of leaves on the branch from which you cut the flower. Otherwise, when you remove faded blooms from the bushes, cut down only as far as the first five-leaflet leaf that points away from the bush's center.

New rose bushes and weak or small plants that you're trying to build up need all possible leaves to manufacture nutrients. With these plants, just snap off the faded flowers and cut no blossoms with stems for the house.

Climbing Hybrid Teas, Grandifloras and Floribundas. Several distinct growth and flowering habits are grouped in the category of "climbing rose." What they all have in common are long, flexible canes which produce flowers along their length. For their first 2 or 3 years in your garden, just tie new canes into position, remove dead canes, weak growth, and spent flowers. Then, after growth patterns are established and some wood has matured, you can begin to prune plants.

In several years' time, the plant will consist solely of long canes produced after you planted it in your garden. From these canes will come side branches (laterals) which will bear the flowers. Beginning then, prune to encourage growth of more flowering laterals and to stimulate production of new canes to gradually replace the oldest and less productive ones. Varieties differ in this respect; some will always throw out new canes from the base each year while others get woodier and produce long new cane growth from higher on the plant. Don't cut back the long canes at all unless any of them are growing too long for the allotted space. Whenever any long canes or branches grow in a direction you don't want, train them into place. If you can't train them, remove them. But remember—the long growths produce the flowering laterals.

For the annual pruning, remove only old, unproductive wood. Then cut back to 2 or 3 buds all laterals that bore flowers during the last year. Best blooms grow on laterals from 2 or 3-year-old wood.

During the flowering season remove all spent blooms. Cut them back to a strong bud 2 or 3 leaves away from the flowering shoot's point of origin.

Pillar Rose. Two sorts of climbing roses are grown as flowering pillars up to about 10 ft. tall. One is the Hybrid Tea or Floribunda climber which grows short climbing canes (about 8-10 ft. long); the other is a natural pillar type which grows 6-10-ft. upright canes that will flower along their length. Pruning objectives and methods are the same as for climbing Hybrid Teas; the principal difference is that you will want to train all long new growth vertically.

Large-Flowered Climbers. Some of these bloom only once a year (examples: 'Dr. W. van Fleet' and 'Paul's Scarlet Climber'). After they finish flowering, cut out the least productive old wood and any weak or entangling branches. New growth will come from the base, and other strong new growth will come from older canes that you leave. From this strong new growth come most of the lateral branches that will carry next year's flowers.

(Continued on next page)

Large-flowered climbers that repeat their bloom throughout the growing year include such favorites as 'Don Juan', 'Golden Showers', 'Kassel', and 'New Dawn'. They produce flowers from new canes and laterals as well as from wood more than a year old. Prune them like climbing Hybrid Teas (see previous page).

Ramblers. Each year after spring bloom Rambler roses produce many long, vigorous, and limber canes from the base of the plant. Next spring's flowers come from this new growth. Typically, flowers are small but in large clusters or trusses and come only once annually. However, this spring flower display can be overwhelming.

Wait to prune Ramblers until flowering has finished and new growth is underway. Then, cut out all canes that just flowered and show no sign of producing any long, vigorous new growth. As the new canes mature, train them into correct position.

These are perhaps the highest-maintenance plants among roses because they renew themselves almost completely each year and require annual training to look their best.

Training Climbing Roses. The most profuse bloom comes from Climbers whose canes are trained horizontally or are trained upward and arched over. A long climbing cane left alone will continue to build new tissue to increase only its upward growth. This is a situation known as *apical dominance*: the topmost growth continues at the expense of any lateral growth. However, when a long, upright cane is arched over or bent down to a horizontal position, many eyes along the cane will begin to grow—each one growing upward. These laterals off main canes and long branches make flowers.

If you have a high fence, wall, or side of a house to cover, let the vertical canes grow to about 10 ft. long. Then spread them out at an angle from the plant's base, spacing them evenly, and arch each one and tie it in place with the end pointing downward. Flowering shoots will come from the arched sections of the canes.

Climbers trained horizontally along a low fence or wall will tend to produce flowering shoots from most buds in the horizontal portions of the canes.

Pruning Shrub and Old Roses. These durable and venerable species and varieties represent so many types and growth habits that it is difficult to make many generalizations. Most, however, are vigorous growers which may need some thinning and shaping each year but very little actual cutting back. As most of these roses are used for showy shrubs or in hedges, the main pruning should be to trim and shape them to fit their place. Cut back any shoots which mar the general pattern and remove any old, unproductive canes. Removal of weak or damaged wood completes the job.

Pruning Standard Roses. Objective in pruning tree roses is to keep crowns symmetrical and branches evenly spaced. First remove all leaves, rose fruits (hips), and dead, weak, and damaged branches. Next, cut out small twiggy growth and crossing branches. Then, cut back branches in the crown to a promising, outward facing bud. (Make slanting cuts, just above the bud.) If you remove an entire branch, cut it flush to the trunk or stem. Be careful not to remove branches that are essential for a balanced crown. Finally, remove any suckers that have formed below bud union. Retie plant to its stake if necessary.

ROSE.
See Rosa.

ROSE ACACIA.
See Robinia hispida.

ROSE APPLE.
See Syzygium jambos.

ROSEMARY.
See Rosmarinus officinalis.

ROSE OF SHARON.
See Hibiscus syriacus.

ROSMARINUS officinalis. Rosemary. Evergreen shrub, herb. Under good growing conditions, growth can get rather leggy without adequate pruning. Control growth by frequent tip pinching when plant is small. Prune older plant lightly, making all cuts to side branches. Some varieties can be clipped as hedges. Head back after bloom to encourage new growth. Leave bushy to ground or cut off lower branches to expose one or more gnarly trunks. Gnarly old branches need no pruning.

R. o. 'Prostratus'. Dwarf rosemary. Low growing, needs little pruning. Thin out old wood after bloom to keep new growth coming. Can be pinched or sheared to keep as flat cover.

ROYAL TRUMPET VINE.
See Distictis 'Rivers'.

RUBBER PLANT.
See Ficus elastica.

RUDBECKIA hirta. Gloriosa daisy, black-eyed susan. Biennial or short-lived perennial. Cut plant back down to ground after it finishes blooming in fall and before it goes to seed; or remove spent flowers before seeding.

R. laciniata 'Hortensia' Golden glow. Perennial. Spreads aggressively by underground stems. Root prune to keep in bounds.

RUSSIAN OLIVE.
See Elaeagnus angustifolia.

SABAL. Palmetto. Fan palms. On some types, dead leaves are shed; on others, they fold and hang down. Only pruning required is removal of dead leaves for appearance.

SACRED FLOWER OF THE INCAS.
See Cantua buxifolia.

SAGE.
See Salvia.

ST. JOHN'S BREAD.
See Ceratonia siliqua.

ST. JOHNSWORT.
See Hypericum.

SAINTPAULIA ionantha. African violet. Evergreen perennial. As plant sheds its lower leaves it may develop an awkward trunklike stem. You can shorten the stem and restore plant to more pleasing appearance by taking off the lower row of leaves and cutting off rosette with an inch of stem. Plant that piece to make it root again. If bare part of stem is not long enough for this procedure, take plant out of pot and cut off bottom of the root mass. Scrape bare stem slightly above remaining roots (dust with rooting hormone) and repot to about ¼ in. below bottom row of leaves. As new roots develop quickly, you'll have greatly improved plant.

Separate multiple-crown plants into single crowns and repot. Carefully trim off side growths (suckers) and root them for new plants.

SALAD BURNET.
See Sanguisorba minor.

SALAL.
See Gaultheria shallon.

SALIX. Willow. Deciduous trees or shrubs. All forms have invasive roots and may need to be root pruned occasionally to keep them in bounds. On any willow, at any time, cut out branches that are dead, diseased, or infested with borers. Prune to shape during dormant season.

S. alba 'Tristis' (*S. babylonica aurea*, *S.* 'Niobe'). Golden weeping willow. Tree. Left to its own way, it will head too low to furnish usable shade. Stake up a main stem and keep it staked right up to 15-18 ft. Shorten lower side branches and remove them as they lose their vigor; keep growth directed into a tall main stem and high-branching scaffold limbs. This treatment will give you a tree you can walk under.

S. babylonica. Weeping willow. Tree. Train to full-fledged weeper as described under *S. alba* 'Tristis'.

S. caprea. French pussy willow, pink pussy willow. Shrub or small tree. Can be kept at shrub size by cutting to ground every few years during dormant season. Forces easily indoors and can be cut for winter arrangements.

S. discolor. Pussy willow. Shrub or small tree. Large and spreading shrub, grows 6-8 ft. a season if cut to ground after flowering. If not pruned back each year, will grow to 20 ft. Heavy pruning encourages a large crop of catkins on long new shoots for use in winter arrangements.

S. gracilistyla. Rose-gold pussy willow. Shrub. Cut stems for indoor decoration in the winter to help curb size. Or cut it back every few years to keep it lower and less wide spreading. It's best to cut back the whole plant to short stubs every 3 or 4 years during dormant season. You'll be rewarded by vigorous shoots with large catkins.

S. matsudana 'Tortuosa'. Twisted Hankow willow, corkscrew willow. Prune to give a head of branches you can walk under as described for *S. alba 'Tristis'*. Thin and shape by cutting picturesque, bare branches in winter for indoor arrangements.

S. purpurea. Purple osier, Alaska blue willow. Shrub. Usually grown as a clipped hedge and kept 1-3 ft. high and equally wide.

SALTBUSH.
See Atriplex.

SALVIA. Sage. Annuals, perennials, shrubs.

S. azurea grandiflora (*S. pitcheri*). Perennial. Should be pinched back when young to promote bushy growth. Can also be cut back in late spring or early summer to make plants bushier. Plants grow to 4 ft. high.

S. clevelandii. Shrub. In summer, after the plant finishes blooming, prune back about half of the most recent growth to shape plant and to encourage new flowering wood when growth starts again. You may also correct plant's shape in spring after danger of frost is past, but you will sacrifice some bloom.

S. gracilistyla. (Often sold as *S. rutilans.*) Pineapple sage. Perennial herb. Cut back after bloom in fall. Use leaves (fresh or dried) as seasoning.

S. leucantha. Mexican bush sage. Shrub. Cut old stems to ground as flowers fade; new ones bloom continuously.

S. officinalis. Garden sage. Perennial herb. Cut back after bloom. Use leaves (fresh or dried) as seasoning.

SAMBUCUS. Elderberry. Deciduous shrubs or trees. Rampant, fast-growing, wild looking but can be tamed to a degree. To keep dense and shrubby, prune

hard every dormant season. New growth sprouts readily from stumps.

S. caerulea (*S. glauca*). Blue elderberry. Shrub or tree. If thinned to single or multiple trunk, becomes a graceful rounded tree with slightly weeping branches. If cut back to within a few feet of the ground, tree will stump sprout readily. To keep it from becoming dense and cluttered, thin out excess twiggy growth in fall. To grow it as shrub, prune drastically every year.

S. canadensis. American elder, sweet elder. Deciduous shrub. Makes a number of shoots from the base each year. Tip pinch these during following winter to force heavy branching for bloom and fruit. Cut out unproductive 2-3-year-old shoots at soil level in fall or winter.

S. racemosa. Red elderberry. Bushy shrub. Grows as a 2-6-ft. spreading shrub. If cut back to within few feet of ground, will stump sprout readily. To keep it from becoming dense and cluttered, thin out excess twiggy growth in fall. To grow as shrub, prune drastically every year when dormant.

SANDHILL SAGE.
See Artemisia pycnocephala.

SANGUISORBA minor (*Poterium sanguisorba*). Small burnet, salad burnet. Perennial herb. Keep blossoms cut as they develop, or it will self-seed too freely. Don't cut plant back more than half, though.

SANTOLINA. Herbs, evergreen subshrubs. Good as ground covers, bank covers, or low, clipped hedges. Look best if kept low by pruning. Clip off spent flowers. Cut back in early spring. May die to ground in coldest areas but roots will live and resume growth.

S. chamaecyparissus. Lavender cotton. Brittle, woody stems. Can reach 2 ft., but makes a better hedge if kept trimmed to 1 ft. As a clipped hedge, it probably won't develop flowers, but it may be just as attractive without them. If you want blooms, prune plant in early spring and again in late summer after it flowers.

S. virens. Compact little evergreen 2 ft. high and wide. Most often seen as a clipped dwarf hedge. Needs at least a yearly trimming in early spring to keep it from becoming woody.

SAPIUM sebiferum. Chinese tallow tree. Deciduous tree. Prune only to correct shape. Tends toward shrubbiness, multiple trunks, suckering, but easily trained to single trunk. Winter freezes usually deaden a few twig ends; cut them off in spring or let new growth cover them.

SAPPHIRE BERRY.
See Symplocos.

SARCOCOCCA. Evergreen shrubs. Slow and orderly growing, generally need no more than shaping to stay neat and compact; but it may be desirable to remove old stems to encourage younger growth. Do this at any time. If corrective methods are needed, don't be afraid to cut to ground. Will sprout from roots.

S. ruscifolia. Will form a natural espalier against a wall, sheared boxwoodlike hedge, or a trained single shrub.

SASSAFRAS albidum. Sassafras. Deciduous tree. Normal training while young, prune only when required for shape when mature. Suckers tend to pop up if roots are cut in cultivating, should be removed when they appear.

SATUREJA montana. Winter savory. Perennial or subshrub. Keep clipped. Clip at start of flowering season for drying. In fall shoots can be cut down to near ground level to produce new growth next season.

SAWLEAF ZELKOVA.
See Zelkova.

SAXIFRAGA. Saxifrage. Perennials. Shear off faded blooms to keep plants looking neat.

SAXIFRAGE.
See Saxifraga.

SCABIOSA. Pincushion flower. Annuals, perennials. Bloom begins in midsummer and continues until winter if flowers are cut.

SCARLET KADSURA.
See Kadsura japonica.

SCARLET WISTERIA TREE.
See Daubentonia tripetii.

SCHINUS. Pepper tree. Evergreen and semi-deciduous trees.

S. molle. California pepper tree. Evergreen tree. Young tree needs training: remove lower branches if you wish to walk under it. Prune to shape in early spring. Once a California pepper grows branches as thick as your arm, don't saw them at all except in case of real emergency. (Tree is very susceptible to troubles.) If you have to saw, keep large cuts sealed with pruning compound. Greedy and invasive roots have been known to get into sewer lines and crack pavement. Plant where it has room to spread. Young pepper trees can be planted 2 ft. apart and trained into graceful, billowy hedge. Even a 20-30-year-old hedge can be kept trimmed to 4-ft. height. It will be graceful and well behaved, easily controlled by clipping.

S. polygamus (*S. dependens*). Peruvian pepper tree. Evergreen or semideciduous tree. Occasional thinning of excess twiggy growth and thinning inner branches of tree in early spring will make branch pattern and structure more interesting. Be careful pruning and handling branches—small hidden spines can hurt.

S. terebinthifolius. Brazilian pepper. Evergreen tree. Better behaved than *S. molle.* Bushier, stiffer looking in its youth. Tends to get top-heavy if not kept thinned out but with little training makes a broad, umbrella-shaped crown. Stake young trees well and train to make a fairly high crown. To reduce possibility of storm breakage, shorten overlong limbs and do some late summer thinning so wind can pass through. Young tree may be killed back to main trunk in a heavy freeze. Prune to shape after danger of frost is past.

SCIADOPITYS verticillata. Umbrella pine. Evergreen tree. Versatile, lends itself to bonsai, container use, and special training and pruning at any time. Can be thinned to create oriental effect.

SCIMITAR SHRUB.
See Brachysema lanceolatum.

SEA PINK.
See Armeria.

SEDUM. Stonecrop. Succulent perennials or subshrubs.

S. amecamecanum. Mexican sedum. Looks brown for about 6 weeks after flowers fade, but it should not be cut back. The dried flowers drop down through foliage and make good moisture-holding mulch.

S. spectabile. Dies back in winter. Divide clumps after bloom in fall or early spring. Plant them and remove old stems. New growth will soon appear.

S. spurium 'Dragon's blood'. Keep neat by cutting off dead flower stalks at base.

SEMELE androgyna. Climbing butcher's broom. Evergreen vine. Thin as necessary to keep it from getting too dense and to retain inherent graceful and emphatic foliage pattern. Remove deadwood.

SENECIO. Perennials, shrubs, vines.

S. cineraria. Dusty miller. Shrubby perennial. Old growth tends to become leggy and brittle, so best procedure is to cut back plant in spring and encourage new shoots from close to ground level. New foliage will be fresher gray green and usually more deeply cut than the old.

S. greyii. Evergreen shrub. Keep it compact and stimulate new wood by removing oldest or damaged growth in early spring. Use pruned-off branches for indoor arrangements.

S. leucostachys. (Often sold as *S. cineraria* 'Candidissimus'.) Pinch tips of young plant to keep it compact; whenever necessary, continue to head back

branches that grow out of bounds as plant matures.

S. petasitis. Velvet groundsel, California geranium. Perennial or shrubby perennial. Prune hard after bloom to limit height and sprawl. Can be kept 2-4 ft. tall in big pots or tubs.

SENNA.
See Cassia.

SEQUOIADENDRON giganteum (*Sequoia gigantea*). Big tree, giant sequoia. Evergreen tree. Tree tends to grow so precisely that little pruning is necessary, aside from occasional obvious training while young.

SEQUOIA sempervirens. Coast redwood. Evergreen tree. Mature trees normally require little more than corrective pruning. If you want to walk under the tree, remove lower branches high enough to give head room. To make a beautiful hedge, plant trees 3-4 ft. apart, top them at least once a year after new growth begins in spring.

SERVICE BERRY.
See Amelanchier.

SETCREASEA purpurea. Purple heart. Perennial. If tops killed back by frost, growth will resume in warm weather. Remove dead portions to base.

SHADBLOW.
See Amelanchier.

SHADBUSH.
See Amelanchier.

SHASTA DAISY.
See Chrysanthemum maximum.

SHELL FLOWER.
See Alpinia speciosa.

SHEPHERDIA. Buffalo berry. Prune lightly after it blooms if required for shaping.

SHRIMP PLANT.
See Beloperone guttata.

SHRUB ALTHAEA.
See Hibiscus syriacus.

SIBERIAN PEASHRUB.
See Caragana arborescens.

SIERRA LAUREL.
See Leucothoe davisiae.

SILK OAK.
See Grevillea robusta.

SILKTASSEL.
See Garrya.

SILK TREE.
See Albizia julibrissin.

SILKWORM MULBERRY.
See Morus alba.

SILVER BELL.
See Halesia carolina.

SILVERBERRY.
See Elaeagnus pungens.

SILVER LACE VINE.
See Polygonum aubertii.

SILVER TREE.
See Leucadendron argenteum.

SIMMONDSIA chinensis. Jojoba, goatnut. Evergreen shrub. Slow compact growth, requires little or no training. Many branched stems from base form compact, rounded mound 4-6 (even 10) ft. high. Like boxwood, can be kept at height you want by shearing back. Plant is not damaged by frequent shearing and trimming. If you are patient, it will also make a handsome 4-6-ft.-high clipped hedge or compact unclipped screen.

SKIMMIA japonica. Evergreen shrubs. Don't have lanky tendency of many shrubs and need to be pruned only to shape, and remove deadwood. Make rounded, spreading shrubs to 5-6 ft. high.

S. reevesiana (*S. fortunei*). Dwarf form, won't go over 30 in. and can easily be kept under 16 in. without looking overtrimmed.

SKY FLOWER.
See Thunbergia grandiflora.

SMALL BURNET.
See Sanguisorba minor.

SMOKE TREE.
See Cotinus coggygria.

SNEEZEWEED.
See Helenium autumnale.

SNOWBALL, COMMON.
See Viburnum opulus 'Roseum'.

SNOWBALL, JAPANESE.
See Viburnum plicatum.

SNOWBERRY, COMMON.
See Symphoricarpos.

SNOWDROP TREE.
See Halesia carolina.

SNOWDROP TREE, JAPANESE.
See Styrax japonica.

SNOWFLAKE TREE.
See Trevesia.

SNOW-IN-SUMMER.
See Cerastium tomentosum.

SOAPBARK TREE.
See Quillaja saponaria.

SOLANDRA hartwegii. (Usually sold as *S. guttata.*) Cup-of-gold vine. Evergreen vine. Pinch and head back to induce laterals and more flowers. Can be cut back to make rough hedge, or pegged down as coarse bank cover.

SOLANUM. Evergreen and deciduous shrubs and vines.

S. jasminoides. Potato vine. Evergreen or deciduous vine. If allowed to grow free, many stems will interlace and twine to 30-ft. tangle. Cut back severely in fall or early winter to prevent tangling, promote vigorous new growth, and keep new flowering wood coming. Remove rampant runners that grow along ground.

S. rantonnetii. Evergreen or deciduous shrub or vine. Can also be staked and trained as tree form, or left to sprawl as ground cover. Bushy and straggly, it needs a severe cutting back every year in early spring to keep it a neat shrub. Support if you want a vine. Can be cut back to the ground in early spring to encourage better blooms, new stem growth.

SOLLYA fusiformis (*S. heterophylla*). Australian bluebell creeper. Evergreen shrub, vine, or ground cover. Unless trained, its stems will spill out over ground, twining about each other or any object within reach. To make the most of its growing habit, use it as a ground cover. To grow as a shrub, keep pinching back vinelike shoots that grow out of bounds. As a vine, encourage strongest shoots and cut out all others that develop at the base of the plant. Prune after danger of frost is past in spring.

SOPHORA. Deciduous or evergreen trees or shrubs.

S. japonica. Japanese pagoda tree, Chinese scholar tree. Deciduous tree. Usually trained for form while young (see *Training Young Trees,* page 15). Little or no pruning later. You may want to remove seed pods to prevent staining of a patio and tidy up tree after flowering in fall.

S. secundiflora. Mescal bean, Texas mountain laurel. Evergreen shrub or tree. Tends to grow shrublike but with training it will eventually grow 25 ft. high with narrow head, slender trunk, and upright branches. Untrained, makes good large screen or bank cover. Scarlet seeds in gray pods are attractive but poisonous; remove before they mature.

SORBUS aucuparia. European mountain ash. Deciduous tree. If necessary, train young trees (see *Training Young Trees,* page 15) to help them achieve mature form—erect with drooping outer branches.

SORREL TREE.
See Oxydendrum arboreum.

SOUR GUM.
See Nyssa sylvatica.

SOURWOOD.
See Oxydendrum arboreum.

SPARMANNIA africana. African linden. Evergreen shrub, tree. This vigorous grower will stand heavy pruning at almost any time. Having rangy habit, it needs to be thinned out and headed back regularly to promote bushiness. Prune heavily every few years to give desired height and to control legginess. Tends to grow many trunks from base if frosted back or pruned back for size control.

SPEKBOOM.
See Portulacaria afra.

SPICE BUSH.
See Calycanthus occidentalis.

SPIDER PLANT.
See Chlorophytum comosum.

SPIRAEA. Deciduous shrubs. For the many different spiraeas, the rule is to prune according to form and time of bloom. Most spiraeas will take severe pruning, even cutting back to near ground level. Those with loose, graceful look need annual renewal of new growth. Thin some branches, head others back to young laterals. Remove some of the oldest wood that has produced flowers, cutting back to ground. Most shrubby types require less severe pruning.

Prune spring-flowering kinds when they finish blooming. Prune summer-flowering species in late winter or very early spring. If in doubt, wait for plant to bloom; then prune at proper season. Missing one pruning won't hurt. Some forms will produce second set of blooms if pruned immediately after flowering.

SPIRAEA, FALSE.
See Astilbe.

SPRUCE.
See Picea.

SPURGE.
See Euphorbia.

SPURGE, JAPANESE.
See Pachysandra terminalis.

SQUAW CARPET.
See Ceanothus prostratus.

STACHYS olympica (*S. lanata*). Lamb's ears. Perennial. Cut back in spring.

STACHYURUS praecox. Deciduous shrub. Slow growing, shrub needs little pruning.

STAR BUSH.
See Turraea.

STAR JASMINE.
See Trachelospermum.

STAUNTONIA hexaphylla. Evergreen vine. Can become a tangled mess if not pruned occasionally after spring flowering. Train on trellis or grow on pillars.

STENOCARPUS sinuatus. Firewheel tree. Evergreen tree. Needs only pruning to shape in early years.

STENOLOBIUM stans (*Tecoma stans*). Yellow bells, yellow trumpet flower, yellow-elder. Evergreen shrub or small tree. Cut faded flowers to prolong bloom, remove deadwood and bushy growth, prune to control size and form whenever necessary.

STEPHANANDRA. Deciduous shrub. After frost danger is past, take out freeze-damaged wood. Cut some oldest wood to ground, head other branches back to strongest laterals.

STEWARTIA. Deciduous shrubs or trees. Slow growing; need some training while young, practically no pruning thereafter.

STIGMAPHYLLON ciliatum. Orchid vine. Evergreen vine. Moderate to fast grower. Prune whenever required to keep in bounds. Cut out any dead or weak wood.

STOKES ASTER.
See Stokesia laevis.

STOKESIA laevis. Stokes aster. Perennial. Will continue to bloom if old flowers are cut off as they fade. Or cut it back after main bloom for second crop in fall.

STONECRESS.
See Aethionema.

STONECROP.
See Sedum.

STRANVAESIA davidiana undulata (*S. undulata*). Evergreen shrub. Irregularly shaped plant about 5 ft. tall and 6-8 ft. wide. You can keep it to 3 ft. by cutting back taller and wider growing stems to lower and close-to-center laterals whenever necessary. Prune at Christmas if you want to use berried branches for holiday foliage.

STRAWBERRY. Most are reproduced by offset plants at ends of runners. Pinching off all runners results in large plants and small yields of large berries; allowing offset plants to take root and grow gives heavy yields of smaller berries. (Pinch off further runners when plants have made enough offsets.)

STRAWBERRY GUAVA.
See Psidium cattleianum.

STRAWBERRY TREE.
See Arbutus unedo.

STRELITZIA. Bird of paradise. Evergreen perennials.

S. nicolai. Giant bird of paradise. Keep dead leaves cut off and thin out surplus growth. If it gets too tall, remove main stem and allow lower growing suckers to take its place. As large trunklike stems mature, you can remove old leaves and leaf stalks, cutting close to trunk as you would on palms.

S. reginae. Bird of paradise. Needs a yearly clean up of old, torn, sun-burned leaves. At end of growing season, cut off old spent flowers and stalks to within 1 in. of clasping leaf sheath.

STREPTOSOLEN jamesonii. Evergreen viny shrub. Responds well to heavy pruning, but normally you only need to remove deadwood after last frost in spring, thinning and pruning to shape. (Don't wait too long because it blooms on new wood formed in spring.) Cut back leggy, spindly plants to promote thicker growth below.

STYRAX. Deciduous trees.

S. japonica. Japanese snowdrop tree, Japanese snowbell. Prune after flowering to control shape; tends to be shrubby, but by early pinching lower side branches can be suppressed so that it will form single-trunked tree with wide spreading, horizontal canopy (sometimes twice as wide as tree is high).

S. obassia. Fragrant snowbell. Prune after flowering. Branching pattern is more upright than that of *S. japonica*, does not require as much pruning to keep it a well-formed tree. Because branches tend to be brittle, it may require thinning to protect it against strong winds.

SUMAC.
See Rhus.

SUMMER FORGET-ME-NOT.
See Anchusa capensis.

SUMMER HOLLY.
See Comarostaphylis diversifolia.

SUMMERSWEET.
See Clethra alnifolia.

SUNROSE.
See Helianthemum nummularium.

SWAN RIVER PEA SHRUB.
See Brachysema lanceolatum.

SWEET GUM.
See Liquidambar.

SWEETLEAF.
See Symplocos paniculata.

SWEET OLIVE.
See Osmanthus fragrans.

SWEET PEA.
See Lathyrus.

SWEET PEPPERBUSH.
See Clethra alnifolia.

SWEETSHADE.
See Hymenosporum flavum.

SWEET SHRUB.
See Calycanthus.

SWORD FERN.
See Fern, Hardy.

SYCAMORE.
See Platanus.

SYMPHORICARPOS. Common snowberry, coral berry, Indian currant. Deciduous shrubs. All send out vigorous underground shoots from which suckers grow. Control suckers and shoots by pulling (or digging) them up. Remove fruited branches in early spring when berries lose their attractiveness. Cut older growth to ground, leaving younger shoots. You can also cut the entire plant back to ground in early spring to prevent legginess. Do such cutting back annually or every 2 or 3 years.

SYMPLOCOS paniculata. Sweetleaf, sapphire berry. Deciduous shrub, small tree. May need occasional thinning of branches to prevent brushy look.

SYRINGA. Lilac. Deciduous shrubs. Control growth during early years by pinching and shaping. Flower buds for next year form in pairs where leaves join stems. After bloom, remove spent flower clusters just above points where buds are forming. Heavier pruning will

REMOVE THESE DRIED FLOWER HEADS RIGHT AFTER BLOOMING

THESE WILL PRODUCE NEXT YEAR'S FLOWERS

CUT OFF spent syringa flower clusters just above point where a pair of next year's flower buds are developing.

result in loss of much of next year's bloom. Lilacs require only minimum amount of pruning. When you cut flowers in spring and remove faded flower clusters, you have given the young plants all the pruning they need. Keep suckers cut off at ground level around grafted plants. If plants are on their own roots and you want to increase your lilac planting, let suckers remain until they strike roots. Then plant them. Early spring is best time to prune to promote bush growth, but some bloom will then be sacrificed.

To rejuvenate old plants, remove a third of the old wood each spring. When you do this, the shrub is never without some flowers during bloom period, and

after 3 years all wood has been replaced. Old plants grown on their own roots can also be cut back hard (to about 18 in.) in late winter. This gives them a growing season to recover and ripen new wood before next dormant season so they can subsequently produce blooms. Grafted plants should be rejuvenated over several seasons, for they may not have enough strength for this treatment and might send out shoots from the rootstock.

SYZYGIUM. Evergreen shrubs or trees.

S. jambos (*Eugenia jambos*). Rose apple. Slow growth means little or no pruning is necessary.

S. paniculatum (*Eugenia myrtifolia, E. paniculata*). Brush cherry, Australian brush cherry. Can take severe pruning and is frequently used as a clipped hedge, column, topiary plant or espalier. But it also makes a beautiful moderately large tree if guided during its early years: stake main stem to a sturdy support and allow all side branches to stay on. If the terminal stem divides, allowing 2 or more upright stems to form, cut out all but the strongest. When the plant reaches 8-10 ft. high, it will require no further training. Do heavy pruning after danger of frost is past.

TABEBUIA chrysotricha. (Sometimes sold as *T. pulcherrima*.) Golden trumpet tree. Briefly deciduous, sometimes evergreen tree. Growth habit is awkward. Stake while young and keep plant to single leading shoot until 6-8 ft. tall. Prune annually after spring blooming period to shape. Cut back any branches that get out of line and give tree lopsided look.

TALLOW TREE, CHINESE.
See Sapium sebiferum.

TAMARISK.
See Tamarix.

TAMARIX. Tamarisk. Deciduous and evergreen-appearing shrubs and trees. Time of pruning varies, depending upon whether they are spring flowering or summer flowering, as noted below. All have greedy roots and need to be root-pruned occasionally for control. Spring flowering varieties—*T. africana, T. juniperina, T. parviflora,* and *T. tetrandra*—should be pruned after blooming in spring to control shape and size and to maintain graceful effect. This pruning will limit height and produce new flowering wood. Cut oldest stems to ground to promote growth of new wood. Summer flowering varieties are *T. chinensis, T. gallica, T. hispida, T. pentandra,* and *T. odessana.* These spreading feathery shrubs grow to 6 to 12 ft. if pruned to ground in early spring. Flowers are borne on wood of current season, so this type of pruning will not only keep plants down but will also produce mass of flower plumes from July to fall.

TANBARK OAK.
See Lithocarpus densiflora.

TARO.
See Colocasia esculenta.

TAXODIUM distichum. Bald cypress. Deciduous tree. Requires only such corrective pruning as removal of deadwood and unwanted branches whenever necessary.

TAXUS. Yew. Evergreen shrubs or trees. Slow growing, long lived, tolerant of much shearing and pruning, though they don't normally require much. These are the plants commonly used for topiary work—fashioned into birds, baskets, or free form sculptures. Trim anytime, doing most drastic cutting in late winter before new growth starts. (That is best time to shape them if they look straggly or lopsided.) Keep plants looking neat by making cuts so that they're well concealed by surrounding foliage.

If you let them grow to the desired height, you can trim them into the neatest of formal hedges.

Young yew hedges should be sheared in midsummer, removing about half the new growth. As the hedge begins to reach full size, prune 2 or 3 times a year—once in late winter before growth starts, then in late May or early June when new growth has reached full length, and then again (if needed) in late summer.

Columnar Irish yews tend to spread outward with age; slow the tendency by heading back any branches that fall outward to a sturdy vertical side branch. Tie together branches of very large plants with wire. Join branches on opposite sides of the plants, so that wires run through the center of the plants.

TEA TREE.
See Leptospermum.

TECOMARIA capensis (*Tecoma capensis*). Cape honeysuckle. Evergreen vine or shrub. Can be trained as vine, espalier, or large shrub. Fast growing, it can scramble to 15-25 ft. if supported. Its natural sprawling form makes it adaptable as large-scale bank planting. Can be held to 6-8-ft. upright shrub with frequent cutting back as necessary to restrain it.

TERNSTROEMIA gymnanthera (*T. japonica*). Evergreen shrub. Pinch out all the young tip growth to promote branching and compact form. Can be used as a big landscape shrub, informal hedge, or tub plant. Prune to shape when necessary.

TETRAPANAX papyriferus. Rice paper plant. Evergreen shrub. Tends to have ungainly stems. In general, reduce the number of stems by thinning some out for more interesting structural effects. Extra suckers should be removed to keep plant from taking over a bed. Cut off flowers after blooming to keep foliage lush for more effective display and to prevent tall branches from falling over. However, if you allow flowers to stay and set seed, there is less tendency for the plant to form suckers. Cut back at any height to force it to branch. New buds break readily, forming new leaf clusters. Pull off yellow leaves. Can sometimes prove hard to eliminate because of deep root system that sometimes sprouts long after tops have been cut off. Digging around roots stimulates suckering.

TETRASTIGMA voinierianum (*Cissus voinieriana, Vitis voikeriana*). Evergreen vine. Travels by strong, steely tendrils and sends out long, trailing, pendulous branches. Cut these long branches back whenever necessary to keep under control.

TEUCRIUM. Germander. Evergreen shrubs or subshrubs. Respond well to pruning and shearing.

T. chamaedrys. To keep neat, shear back once or twice a year, forcing growth at sides. This will make a dense mass of foliage right down to ground. If trained as a hedge, shear twice in midsummer when plants are well established. Pruning at this time keeps plants from blooming and keeps them in shape. If you aren't growing it as a hedge, you can enjoy its loose spikes of rose or purple red bloom in summer and then shear it to shape after it flowers.

T. fruticans. Bush germander. Makes a neat, easy to trim hedge. Thin and cut back in late winter, early spring. Its slender branches seldom get woody and hard to cut. An electric hedge clipper does a fast, efficient job of shearing it. Plant normally grows as a rather loose shrub about 4-6 ft. high and wide.

TEXAS MOUNTAIN LAUREL.
See Sophora secundiflora.

TEXAS RANGER.
See Leucophyllum frutescens.

TEXAS UMBRELLA TREE.
See Melia.

THERMOPSIS caroliniana. Perennial. Cut to ground after bloom.

THEVETIA. Evergreen shrubs, small trees. Fast-growing.

T. peruviana (*T. nereifolia*). Yellow oleander. Shallow-rooted; selectively remove branches to lessen wind resistance. Can be grown as tree or cut short into 6-8-ft. hedge or screen. Pruning is seldom necessary unless you want plants kept in hedge form or kept more compact. If top is frozen, hold off pruning until plant begins to put out new growth. New growth appears rapidly from uninjured basal wood, will bloom same year. Head back and thin to shape after bloom.

THREADLEAF FALSE ARALIA.
See Dizygotheca elegantissima.

THRIFT.
See Armeria.

SHEARING makes the difference between formal and informal appearance of the same plant. Teucrium chamaedrys in left photo is sheared regularly to maintain neat, dense hedge. Photo at right shows how infrequent shearings result in a soft, casual look.

THUJA, PLATYCLADUS (*T. occidentalis,* American arborvitae, and *Platycladus orientalis,* Oriental arborvitae). Evergreen shrubs or trees. Arborvitaes can stand heavy shearing. Shape in late winter or early spring before new growth starts if they look straggly or lopsided. Try to make cuts so that they're well concealed by surrounding foliage. Prune again if necessary in summer to control size and shape. Brown, dead foliage inside dense thuja is normal. Although it's not necessary to remove it, a good hosing will sometimes blow it out.

T. plicata. Western red cedar. Evergreen tree. Tall-growing giant, it can be held to compact, 6-ft. hedge. Has greedy roots that must occasionally be cut back to control. Prune to shape in late winter, early spring.

THUNBERGIA grandiflora. Sky flower. Perennial vine. Vigorous, needs guidance or training only to control growth. Retrain or shape when necessary. Will come back to bloom in a year if frozen back.

THYME.
See Thymus.

THYMUS. Thyme. Ground cover; erect shrubby perennial herb. Restrain plants as needed by clipping back growing tips.

T. serpyllum. Mother-of-thyme, creeping thyme. Ground cover. To restrain, clip around margins of clump.

T. vulgaris. Common thyme. Shrubby perennial herb. Prune after flowering.

TI.
See Cordyline terminalis.

TIBOUCHINA semidecandra (*Pleroma splendens*). Princess flower. Evergreen shrub or small tree. Minimize legginess by light pruning after each bloom cycle, heavier pruning in early spring. Pinch tips of young plant to encourage bushiness and continue pinching back new growth during summer for a more compact plant. Will sprout from stump if it dies back in winter. Wait until danger of frost is past and new growth has a good start before removing freeze-damaged wood.

TILIA. Linden. Deciduous trees. Young trees need staking and shaping. Older trees need only corrective pruning.

TIPUANA tipu. Tipu tree. Deciduous or semievergreen tree. Fast and awkward grower. Needs staking and training for attractive form when young. Can be lightly thinned to emphasize natural umbrella shape or headed back to make narrower, denser crown. Prune in late winter, early spring.

TIPU TREE.
See Tipuana tipu.

TORCH-LILY.
See Kniphofia uvaria.

TORREYA californica. California nutmeg. Evergreen tree. Train early and then it will require only occasional pruning. Withstands heavy pruning and will usually send up new growth from stumps. Full grown tree may reach 50 ft., can be kept smaller by pruning. Prune to shape whenever necessary.

TOYON.
See Heteromeles arbutifolia.

TRACHELOSPERMUM (*Rhynchospermum*). Star jasmine. Evergreen vines or sprawling shrubs. Used as ground covers, spillers, or climbers.

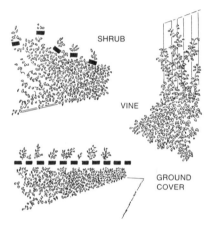

STAR JASMINE'S roles. As shrub or ground cover, needs pinching or pruning.

T. jasminoides. Can take a great deal of pruning but seldom needs it. Without support and with some tip pinching, it becomes a spreading shrub or ground cover, 1½-2 ft. tall and 4-5 ft. wide. To grow as a vine, do not tip pinch, and give stems some support. Older plant should be cut back about ⅓ each year in spring to prevent inner growth from becoming too woody and bare. You can also cut it back to main branch framework; in a year, new growth and flowers will replace it. To grow as ground cover, cut back upright shoots to keep it low.

TRACHYCARPUS fortunei. (Sometimes sold as *Chamaerops excelsa.*) Windmill palm. Confine pruning to cutting off occasional dead frond. Sometimes develops a skirt of dried foliage that should be removed to keep palm neat in appearance.

TRADESCANTIA. Trailing or clumping perennials.

T. fluminensis. Wandering Jew. Trailing evergreen for pots, baskets, window boxes. Pinch tips or head back to shorten stems whenever necessary. Cut pieces root easily in water. Can spread fast as ground cover in mild climates; hoe or pull out by shallow roots if it invades other plantings.

TRANSVAAL DAISY.
See Gerbera jamesonii.

TREE-OF-HEAVEN.
See Ailanthus altissima.

TREVESIA. Snowflake tree. Evergreen shrubs or small trees. Little pruning is required; trim to shape as necessary.

TRICHOSTEMA lanatum. Woolly blue curls. Evergreen shrub. Blooms in late spring; prune in bloom for arrangements. Pinch tips of new growth frequently when young to develop a fuller bush.

TRINIDAD FLAME BUSH.
See Calliandra tweedii.

TRISTANIA. Evergreen trees.

T. conferta. Brisbane box. Leaves tend to crowd toward ends of branches, so trees should be headed back or pinched occasionally to make them bush out more, give better leaf distribution. Shape to retain an attractive branch pattern.

T. laurina. Tree is easy to train and takes shearing. Young plant is densely shrubby and can be kept that way with a little pinching. To make a tree, stake plant and shorten side branches. Remove shortened side branches when treelike growth pattern is established; then only light shaping will be necessary.

TRITHRINAX.
See Palm.

TROCHODENDRON aralioides. Slow growing multi-stem shrub or small tree. Needs only corrective pruning.

TRUMPET CREEPER.
See Campsis.

TRUMPET TREE, GOLDEN.
See Tabebuia chrysotricha.

TRUMPET VINE.
See Campsis.

TRUMPET VINE, BLOOD-RED.
See Phaedranthus buccinatorius.

TRUMPET VINE, ROYAL.
See Distictis 'Rivers'.

TRUMPET VINE, VANILLA.
See Distictis laxiflora.

TRUMPET VINE, VIOLET.
See Clytostoma callistegioides.

TRUMPET VINE, YELLOW.
See Anemopaegma chamberlaynii. Doxantha unguis-cati.

CLIPPED about 6 months ago, this tall, wide hedge of Tsuga heterophylla requires pruning once a year to remain dense and to maintain desired shape.

TSUGA. Hemlock. Coniferous evergreen trees and shrubs. Mostly large trees but can be kept small by pruning new growth to shape desired. If you want a tree, keep a single leader and prune out competitors. Will tolerate hard pruning and shearing when necessary.

T. canadensis. Canadian hemlock. Normally a graceful tree for screen or background, but can be clipped into an outstandingly beautiful hedge 3-15 ft. tall. Give hedge main pruning in late winter or early spring before new growth begins. Shear again in midsummer if you want a dense (as opposed to a feathery) effect.

T. heterophylla. Western hemlock. Normally a fast growing, tall, pyramidal tree. Good for background use, or can be pruned as hedge or screen, following procedure for *T. canadensis.*

T. mertensiana. Mountain hemlock. Slow growing in home gardens. Adaptable to shaping into horizontal, twisted form. Use in rock gardens, containers, as bonsai subjects. Prune to shape when necessary.

TUCKEROO.
See Cupaniopsis anacardioides.

TUPELO.
See Nyssa sylvatica.

TUPIDANTHUS calyptratus. Evergreen shrub or small tree. Can be pruned into almost any form. Do it in spring outdoors, anytime indoors. Can be trained easily as a semivine or shrub. For multi-stemmed effect, cut plant back to its base to produce several stems. If you prefer shorter and more bushy plant, cut top and encourage lower branching. Can also be trained into interesting bonsai.

TURRAEA. Star bush. Evergreen shrub. Slow growing, adaptable. Responds well to pruning whenever necessary. Can be grown as a shrub, sheared as a hedge, or trained as a ground cover by removing vertical growth and encouraging horizontal spreading.

UGNI molinae (*Myrtus ugni*). Chilean guava. Evergreen shrub. Young plant may sprawl awkwardly, but usually fills out with age to make attractive shrub. To use as hedge or informal low screen, shorten overlong branches back into foliage mass. Prune to shape whenever necessary.

ULMUS. Elm. Deciduous or partially evergreen trees.

U. americana. American elm. Deciduous tree. This tall-growing tree and the similar English, Dutch, and Scotch elms respond well to pruning, but mature trees require little pruning if carefully trained to desired shape while young. Do major pruning in dormant season; groom, remove weak and damaged wood at any time. Because roots are fast spreading, you may have to root prune occasionally for control (they have been known to lift pavement). Remove suckers with spade or mattock. Remove and destroy diseased wood as soon as you can spot it.

U. parvifolia. (Often sold as *U. p.* 'Sempervirens'.) Chinese elm, Chinese evergreen elm. Evergreen or deciduous according to winter temperature and tree's heredity. Train when young to branch at desired height and to encourage graceful weeping habit. Branches tend to be brittle and form dense crown. Thin some of these crowded branches in winter to cut down wind resistance. Leading shoot should be staked and headed higher than in other shade trees to compensate for weeping tendency. Rub or cut out small branches along trunk for first few years. Shorten overlong branches or strongly weeping branches to strengthen tree scaffolding.

Older tree may need thinning to lessen chance of storm damage. Rapid growth can take it to 40 ft. or more, but you can prune almost at will to hold it back or to shape or thin it out. Often planted on slopes where it is cut back and forced to branch low for controlling weeds.

U. pumila. Siberian elm. Can be pruned and trained similarly to *U. parvifolia.* However, wood is more brittle, and tendency to develop weak crotches should be watched. Prune mature tree each winter to lighten weight on branches, prevent breakage. Root system can also be troublesome in gardens and requires root pruning to control. Tends to have much dead and diseased wood that should be removed. Tree responds well to pruning; can also be sheared as hedge and kept to 3-4 ft. height.

UMBELLULARIA californica. Pepperwood, California laurel, California bay, Oregon myrtle or myrtlewood. Evergreen tree. Though it responds well to heavy pruning and will readily stump sprout, mature tree usually needs no pruning at all. Under certain circumstances, it may need shaping, thinning, and removal of weak, diseased wood. Tends to cast very dense shade unless thinned. Good for screening or tall hedges. Often forms several trunks. Good patio or street tree when thinned to one or a few trunks.

UMBRELLA PINE.
See Sciadopitys verticillata.

UMBRELLA PLANT.
See Cyperus alternifolius.

VACCINIUM. Evergreen and deciduous shrubs.

V. ovatum. Evergreen huckleberry. Evergreen shrub. Can be trimmed into hedge or grown in container. Takes heavy pruning; cut branches are attractive in arrangements. Selectively thin and head back branches to maintain desired shape every year after new growth has lost its bronzy tints.

(Continued on next page)

V. parvifolium. Red huckleberry. Deciduous shrub. Slow growing. Little pruning needed; how you prune depends upon whether blossoms (for arrangements) or showy, delicious berries are more important. Prune in bloom to get branches for indoors (this will, of course, reduce berry crop). Remove some oldest wood, weak and crossing branches in dormant period.

V. vitis-idaea. Lingonberry, mountain cranberry. Evergreen shrub. Slow growing, needs very little pruning, but will have to be clipped back whenever necessary to contain it. Spreads by underground runners. Cut these if necessary with spade or hoe them to keep plants from spreading into other areas.

VANILLA TRUMPET VINE.
See Distictis laxiflora.

VELVET GROUNDSEL.
See Senecio petasitis.

VERBASCUM. Mullein. Perennials. Remove spent flowers as soon as you can, then cut spikes to ground after blooms are faded. Plants may flower again the same season.

VERBENA. Perennials, some grown as annuals.

V. hybrida (*V. hortensis*). Garden verbena. If used as perennial, cut back severely in winter or early spring.

V. peruviana (*V. chamaedryfolia*). Perennial, often grown as an annual. Ground cover. To keep it looking its best, cut back once a year (after frost danger) with shears or rotary mower. Occasional pinching during growing season will help to maintain compact growth.

VERBENA, LEMON.
See Aloysia triphylla.

VIBURNUM. Deciduous or evergreen shrubs, rarely small trees. All viburnums can be pruned heavily without injury, though some in this large and diverse group need more than others. Deciduous varieties are usually rapid and vigorous growers, benefit from having oldest wood removed every second or third year. May also be necessary to cut out any thin, weak wood in spring in order to maintain their form. Evergreen forms usually require little pruning, but shaping or pruning some plants that are awkward or rangy looking in youth will bring them to graceful maturity.

V. burkwoodii. Deciduous shrub in coldest areas, nearly evergreen elsewhere. Light, whippy wood makes it a good and easily trained espalier or wall plant. Early growth is straggly and rather weak, and plant can become a tangle if not trained when young. Flowering branches make fine display. Prune quite heavily during or after flowering for more compact shrub. Selectively head

back some branches to laterals or promising buds; thin out others.

V. carlesii. Korean spice viburnum. Deciduous shrub. Little pruning necessary. Remove weak branches and occasionally remove older wood to ground to renew. Not unattractive as bare plant in winter, can be shaped to make most interesting bare branch pattern of light brown wood.

V. dentatum. Arrow-wood. Deciduous shrub. Fast, vigorous grower, requires thinning out frequently. Prune during, after flowering; remove some of oldest stems to ground.

V. odoratissimum. Sweet viburnum. Evergreen shrub. Useful as thick screen or can be trimmed to form neat, lustrous hedge. Prune to shape as necessary.

V. opulus. Highbush cranberry, European cranberry bush. Deciduous shrub. Remove oldest wood to renew. Normally multi-stemmed, can easily be trained to small, single-trunked tree. Prune while dormant.

V. o. 'Nanum'. (Dwarf form of above.) Needs no trimming as low hedge.

V. o. 'Roseum' (*V. o.* 'Sterile'). Common snowball. Normally a large, upright, many-stemmed shrub, it can be easily trained to a small, single-trunked tree. If trained to tree form, pinch leader when it reaches proper height to encourage branching.

V. plicatum (*V. tomentosum* 'Sterile'). Japanese snowball. This and *V. p.* 'Sterile', doublefile viburnum, are deciduous shrubs. Instead of transplanting or discarding a shrub that has grown too large, transform it into tree instead. To do this, remove all but strongest upright stem and all side growth to the height desired, bracing with strong stake. Or keep it lower by trimming back to one of the side (unflowered) branches after flowering. (Don't prune shrub lower than 4 ft. or it will lose its natural shape and become bushy.) Do major pruning during dormant period.

V. rhytidophyllum. Leatherleaf viburnum. Evergreen shrub. Instead of pruning at or right after flowering as with other viburnums, wait until new growth is stronger in late spring, early summer.

V. suspensum. Sandankwa viburnum. Evergreen shrub. This rapid growing, vigorous shrub benefits from pruning. Cut out old wood every second or third year during winter months. Cut out any thin or weak wood in spring to maintain desired form.

V. tinus. Laurustinus. Evergreen shrub or small narrow tree. Usually grown as screens, clipped or unclipped hedges, densely foliaged shrubs, or shrubbery borders. Will take heavy pruning at any time. Cut flowering branches freely for indoor decoration and delicate fragrance. If grown as a hedge, clip frequently to maintain desired shape. Having dense

foliage right to ground makes it good plant for clipped topiary shapes. In wet climates, clipping and shearing may increase the mildew susceptibility of the plant, so it's best to let it grow more naturally.

VINCA. Periwinkle, myrtle. Evergreen perennials.

V. major. Fast growing, long trailing stems root as they spread. To restrain, cut when necessary. When used as ground cover, shear close to ground occasionally to bring on fresh new growth.

V. minor. Dwarf periwinkle. Becomes more compact when sheared back annually in spring. It keeps the plants dense, compact, and free blooming.

VIOLA. Violet, pansy. Perennials, some treated as annuals. Keep picking flowers and faded blossoms of pansies and violas to keep them blooming.

V. cornuta. Viola, tufted pansy. Cut back after spring bloom, feed and water heavily, and they will produce a second crop of flowers lasting well into summer. Pinch violas if leggy. Keep blooms picked off until plants are established. If plants are bushy and making plenty of sideshoots, let them have their head. Once in full bloom, pick flowers as often as you can.

V. odorata. Sweet violet. Easy to keep under control by cutting off runners you don't want. Shear rank growth in late fall for better spring flower display.

V. tricolor. Johnny-jump-up. **V. t. hortensis.** Pansy. Cut blooms freely for house, taking long stems with foliage. Will then spread and bloom much better. Regularly remove faded flowers before they set seed.

VIOLET.
See Viola.

VIOLET TRUMPET VINE.
See Clytostoma callistegioides.

VIRGINIA CREEPER.
See Parthenocissus.

VITEX. Chaste tree. Deciduous and evergreen shrubs or trees.

V. agnus-castus. Chaste tree. Deciduous shrub or small tree. Summer and fall blooming. Heavy pruning in midwinter assures good show of flowers following summer (wait until spring in colder areas to minimize chances of frost damage). Dies back in severe winters but new growth will spring from roots. Prune out deadwood.

V. lucens. New Zealand chaste tree. Evergreen tree. Requires little pruning. Groom when necessary, cutting out weak, damaged wood.

WALNUT (*Juglans*). Deciduous trees. Mature walnut trees require very little pruning. You may need to prune to maintain shape, also removing water-sprouts, suckers, dead, weak and diseased wood. Thin out crowded and crossing branches as necessary.

Young walnut trees require careful training. Following procedure is generally accepted for a central leader tree: *At planting,* head the whip back severely to 3-5 buds and 2-4 ft. in height (even lower where summer sunburn is a problem). As young tree develops, select a single shoot for leader and subdue all others by pinching back. As young tree grows, keep some shoots along trunk and branches to protect against sunburn. These can be pinched back and eventually removed when tree top has grown enough to shade and protect trunk. *In first dormant season,* the selected leader should be headed back (preferably to a bud facing toward prevailing summer winds) to stimulate growth of laterals below. *In second dormant season* and later, select the primary scaffold branch from 5-6 ft. off the ground to fix clearance as high as you want. Scaffold branches above should then be selected to form spiral pattern around trunk with vertical separation of 18-24 in. (If closer, they will crowd and shade branches below.) As tree grows, continue to head back leader (always to a bud facing toward prevailing summer winds) until tree structure and height are where you want them. At that point, you may allow the leader to bend down and assume the position of topmost scaffold branch.

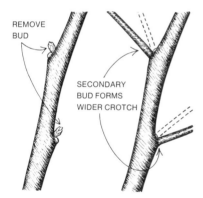

REMOVE BUD

SECONDARY BUD FORMS WIDER CROTCH

ELIMINATE "necked" buds on young walnut. Secondary buds make better branches.

Laterals that develop on walnuts the same season as the parent branch tend to form narrow angles and weak crotches. These new buds are soft and have a definite "neck;" they should be pinched off and permanent laterals chosen from those which form the following year. A good rule to follow in training a young walnut: remove all laterals developing the same year as the parent branch.

WASHINGTONIA.
See Palm.

WEEPING CHINESE BANYAN.
See Ficus benjamina.

WEEPING WILLOW.
See Salix babylonica.

WEIGELA. Deciduous shrubs. Vigorous growers, require considerable pruning. After flowering, prune branches that have bloomed back to unflowered side branches. Leave only 1 or 2 of these laterals to each stem. Cut most wood older than 2 years back to ground to keep plant renewed and vigorous. Save only strongest and healthiest new shoots that develop, removing others at base. Prune any time to remove weak, injured or deadwood. In colder climates remove injured wood in spring after danger of frost is past. It may also be necessary to lightly prune tips in midsummer to keep these rangy growers under control. Older specimens can be renewed by cutting to ground and then selecting sturdiest canes that appear.

WESTRINGIA rosmariniformis. Evergreen shrub. Prune lightly to shape after main blooming period in spring. Blooms most of year in mild areas.

WHITE FORSYTHIA.
See Abeliophyllum distichum.

WHITE SAPOTE.
See Casimiroa edulis.

WIGANDIA caracasana. Treelike, woody perennial. As plant gets older, it becomes smaller leaved and ungainly. You can keep fresh new growth coming

if you cut old canes off at base each spring. Even when plant is frozen down, new growth usually springs up from crown in early spring. Wigandia is rank grower, but it can be kept small by cutting to ground occasionally.

WILD BUCKWHEAT.
See Eriogonum.

WILD LILAC.
See Ceanothus.

WILGA.
See Geijera parviflora.

WILLOW.
See Salix.

WILLOW, AUSTRALIAN.
See Geijera parviflora.

WILLOW MYRTLE, AUSTRALIAN.
See Agonis.

WINDMILL PALM.
See Trachycarpus fortunei.

WINTER HAZEL.
See Corylopsis.

WINTER SAVORY.
See Satureja montana.

WINTER'S BARK.
See Drimys winteri.

WINTERSWEET.
See Chimonanthus praecox.

WISTERIA. Deciduous vines. Can also be trained as trees and shrubs. Pruning and training are important for bloom production and control of plant's size, shape. Let newly set plants grow to establish framework, and remove stems

WISTERIA TRAINED as a single-trunked tree. You can purchase a tree-form wisteria or train your own, following the text and illustrations on page 94.

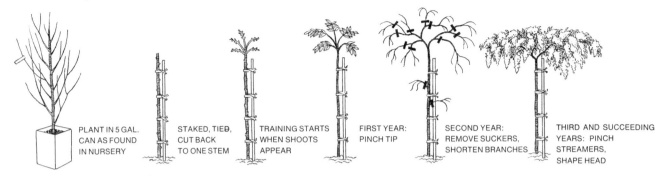

PLANT IN 5 GAL. CAN AS FOUND IN NURSERY

STAKED, TIED, CUT BACK TO ONE STEM

TRAINING STARTS WHEN SHOOTS APPEAR

FIRST YEAR: PINCH TIP

SECOND YEAR: REMOVE SUCKERS, SHORTEN BRANCHES

THIRD AND SUCCEEDING YEARS: PINCH STREAMERS, SHAPE HEAD

FROM VINE TO TREE. How to convert a young wisteria plant into a tree.

that interfere with desired shape. Pinch back side stems and long streamers, rub off buds that develop on trunk. Wisterias can be trained as big shrubs or multi-stem, small, semi-weeping trees. Aim for well-spaced branches to form the framework. Shorten side branches and nip long streamers. Pinch or cut back all errant shoots to second or third leaf whenever you see them. If you leave them, they may grow more than 20 ft. in a season and form a tangled mass.

Even after your wisteria has developed a permanent structure, it will need additional attention. Prune regularly every winter by cutting back or thinning out as necessary the side shoots produced off the main or structural stems and by shortening to 2 or 3 buds the flower-bearing laterals off these side shoots. You won't have any trouble recognizing short, fat-budded spurs that will carry next spring's flowers. A meticulous pruner who wants a clean-looking vine also knocks or cuts off dry slender stems that carried last season's flowers (these hang on tenaciously for months). To be well-groomed, a wisteria also needs summer pruning. Cut off long green winding stems (gardeners often call them streamers or trailers) before they start getting tangled up in main body of vine. Best, and in the long run, easiest way to control these unruly growths is to keep a pair of pruning shears handy and snip these stems off whenever you see them.

The above procedure may be varied somewhat in warmest areas, such as Southern California. Here, many gardeners prune most heavily at the end of spring bloom. This allows another crop of shoots to form for bloom later in summer. In fall, following second bloom, head back these new shoots to control the plant and encourage more large clusters of flowers.

Tree wisterias can be bought ready made or you can train your own. Remove all but one main stem and stake this one securely. Tie stem to stake at frequent intervals. When plant has reached height at which you wish head to form, pinch or cut out tip to force

branching. Shorten branches to beef them up. Pinch back long streamers; rub off all buds that form below head. Container-grown wisterias thrive indefinitely but need faithful watering and hard pruning. If plants in open ground grow too vigorously and fail to bloom, prune roots by cutting around plant with spade.

WITCH HAZEL, CHINESE.
See Hamamelis mollis.

WONGA-WONGA VINE.
See Pandorea pandorana.

WOODWARDIA. Chain fern.
W. fimbriata. See Fern, Hardy.
W. orientalis. See Fern, Tender.
W. radicans. See Fern, Tender.

WOOLFLOWER, CHINESE.
See Celosia.

WOOLLY BLUE CURLS.
See Trichostema lanatum.

WORMWOOD, COMMON.
See Artemisia absinthium.

WORMWOOD, FRINGED.
See Artemisia frigida.

XANTHOCERAS sorbifolium. Hyacinth shrub. Deciduous. Cut flowered branches back to good lateral immediately after bloom. Thin by taking out some of oldest branches, heading back others to a good lateral to keep an attractive form. Weak and crossing branches can be removed in winter, but heavy pruning at this time will reduce bloom.

XANTHORHIZA. Yellowroot. Deciduous shrub, ground cover. Prune as needed to check spreading, cut back with scythe (or mow) to thicken.

XYLOSMA congestum (*X. senticosum*). Evergreen or partially deciduous shrub or small tree. Pruning requirements depend upon your objective. Easily trained as an espalier, or stake the shrub, removing side growth to shape into a 15-30-ft. spreading tree. Can be shaped into attractive, multi-stemmed, large arching

shrub or single-trunk tree; ground or bank cover (prune out erect growth); clipped or unclipped hedge (twine long branches together to fill in gaps faster). If left alone, plant develops angular main stem that takes its time zigzagging upward. Eventually it forms a loose, spreading, graceful shrub, 8-10 ft. high and about as wide, with long, graceful side branches, arching and drooping to the ground.

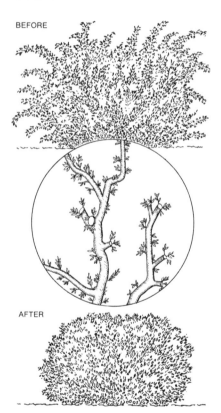

BEFORE

AFTER

XYLOSMA quickly sprouts new growth (see circle) after heavy pruning.

As indicated by its various uses, xylosma responds rapidly with new growth after heavy pruning. You can prune it (in February or after frost danger in

GIANT BONSAI EFFECT is created by pruning to show off the basic branch structure of these xylosma plants.

colder areas) back to skeleton of main framework branches, and in about 4 months, bare branches become almost completely concealed by fresh, vigorous new growth. With pruning shears and a discerning eye, you can transform ordinary looking plant into interesting one. Start by thinning out weak, crowded stems and twiggy growth; step back every now and then to survey what you've done and decide where to make the next cut. Little by little, you'll see basic branch structure you didn't know was there.

YARROW.
See Achillea.

YELLOW BELLS.
See Stenolobium stans.

YELLOW-ELDER.
See Stenolobium stans.

YELLOW HORNED POPPY.
See Glaucium flavum.

YELLOW OLEANDER.
See Thevetia peruviana.

YELLOWROOT.
See Xanthorhiza.

YELLOW TRUMPET FLOWER.
See Stenolobium stans.

YELLOW TRUMPET VINE.
See Anemopaegma chamberlaynii, Doxantha unguis-cati.

YELLOW WOOD.
See Cladrastis lutea.

YESTERDAY-TODAY-AND-TOMORROW.
See Brunfelsia calycina floribunda.

YEW.
See Taxus.

YEW, KOREAN.
See Cephalotaxus harringtonia.

YEW PINE.
See Podocarpus macrophyllus.

YUCCA filamentosa. Adam's needle. Evergreen perennial. After flowering, remove flower stalk. New plant will grow from side suckers. You may wish to thin plant, making it less bushy, by removing some of these suckers.
   Y. aloifolia, Y. gloriosa, and other yuccas with treelike growth should have dead flower stalks removed. Remove or tie back branches that might jab passersby with sharp leaves. *Y. recurvifolia* can be pruned to a single trunk.

ZANTEDESCHIA. Calla. Rhizome. Nearly evergreen in mild areas, deciduous where winters are cold. Cut off old droopy leaves and dead flower stalks to keep plant neat during growing season. Cut plant to ground after bloom (this is optional where mild winters favor all year growth). If you don't want plant to self-seed (it's prolific), remove old flowers before seed heads form.

ZANTHORHIZA.
See Xanthorhiza.

ZAUSCHNERIA. California fuchsia, hummingbird flower. Perennials or subshrubs. Need control, for they tend to be rangy, spread their invasive roots into other garden beds, and reseed themselves. Cut or shear back to about 5 in. from ground in fall to keep in bounds. Cut off dead or frozen growth in spring.

ZELKOVA serrata. Sawleaf zelkova. Deciduous tree. Young tree needs careful training to develop strong framework (see *Training Young Trees,* page 15). Head back excessively long, pendulous branches to force side growth; thin competing branches to permit full development of the strongest. Prune in spring before new growth begins.

ZIZYPHUS jujuba. Chinese jujube. Deciduous tree. Prune while dormant to shape, encourage weeping habit, reduce size. Remove suckers from base of tree.

Index

This index gives page numbers for general pruning information only. Requirements and directions for pruning specific plants are found under the plants' botanical names in the alphabetical Pruning Encyclopedia, pages 24-95.

Photographers

William Aplin: 34, 40, 76. **Glenn M. Christiansen:** 63. **Ells Marugg:** Cover, 42, 93. **Don Normark:** 30, 33, 39, 46, 52, 59, 64, 75, 79, 91. **John Robinson:** 89. **Darrow M. Watt:** 35, 54, 95. **Doug Wilson:** 78.